CW00419096

Don't Call Me Jupiter

Book Two – "Lightning Crashes"

Tom J. Bross

The events and conversations in this book have been set down to
the best of the author's ability, although some names and details
have been changed to protect the privacy of individuals. Memories
are not an exact science especially when copious drug use, abuse,
abandonment and general bad craziness are part of the equation.
I did my best. So, suck it.

Copyright © 2021 Tom J. Bross

rev. 2022.09

All rights reserved. No part of this book may be reproduced in any
form or by an electronic or mechanical means, including information storage and retrieval systems, without permission in writing
from the publisher, except by a reviewer who may quote brief
passages in a review.

ISBN: 9798499401965

This book is dedicated to Christina Marie Bross,
aka Chris Bross the Great.

CONTENTS

Acknowledgments

Writing a book series does not happen in a vacuum—or a toaster oven—although it does sometimes feel like it happens inside a blender. So many people helped move this project forward. I'm grateful to all of them, including the ones I don't personally know. These are the readers who left reviews or talked the first book up with their friends or took a picture of the book in their neck of the woods and posted it on social media. Thank you. I'd also like to thank my beta readers/ proofreaders/armchair psychologists who read and reread the manuscript; James D. Laughlin, Angie K. Love, Shane Rand and Debbie Gravenstien. Special thanks to my Aunt Mary in Pewaukee for her relentless support, to Roger and Tracy Becker for theirs, to Alan Chambless, Amy Powers and Bob Beyn for being virtual cheerleaders. (Bob is more of a song leader, but that's not the point.) And most of all, I'd like to thank my wife Tanya for everything she's done and continues to do to support this book series. She designed the covers, formatted the manuscript, created a website, managed promotions and will be editing the audiobook when I get around to it. This book is in your hands (or in your ears) because of her. May I be fortunate enough to continue our timeless flight.

Authors Note

∞

You need to read book one, "Tightrope" before reading this second part of the series. Seriously. What are you—nuts? Not only will this part make more sense, you'll get much more out of it knowing the characters and the stories that led to this point. Don't be like my mother and brother who read books in mini, out of order segments based on the page they open at random. Seriously? Each book in this series has a beginning, a middle and an end. Each book dove tails off the previous book. So, please don't be difficult and do the right thing. You'll be glad you did. Seriously.

∞

Prologue
July 3rd, 1996

I wake up starving every day. It's what motivates me to get out of bed. I open my eyes, stretch, and listen to my stomach growl. It's just another day. Wednesday. Hump day. No rain. Does that make it a dry hump day? Ha! I'm funny. But it's not just another day because tomorrow is the Fourth of July, which means I'm looking at a four-day weekend. Work will be a breeze. Some people will come in late; others will leave early and a few of them won't bother showing up at all. It's like the party has already started. I leap to the floor with excellent form and salute the imaginary judges. Once I'm up, I'm up. I'm guilty of being one of those joyfully annoying morning people. I look at my wild bed-head hair in the mirror. It's so bad—it almost looks good. People pay good money for this look.

"Who does your hair?" I ask my reflection, in the closet door mirror.

"Serta."

Cereal, ice coffee, onion bagel, cream cheese, sliced ham—I feel even better. Morning routine... shower, shave, dress, hair, keys, wallet, feed the fish, hair again, and out the door. I press the garage door button. It slowly opens. Sunlight gradually illuminates my beloved metallic-blue 1978 Datsun 280z. I don't hear the squeal of the door opening. Instead, the theme from *2001: A Space Odyssey* fills my head. Like the ape-man to the monolith in the movie, I extend my finger and touch the glossy surface of the hood. It's a private ritual performed daily. Yes, I'm a total geek who loves his car.

I'm a thirty-four year old late-bloomer who's finally taking on an 'adultish' appearance. I have a house and a decent job with a bitchin' title, Creative Director. I'm a single, sunburned, successful Sagittarius with hormones rising. Hot tub. Check. Left-handed. Check. Right brained. Check. Still do a standing backflip? Check. I have blond hair with a Hawaii 5-0 wave that would make Jack Lord proud. My brain is like a videocassette recorder. I can recite the best scenes, word for word, from several of my favorite Bill Murray movies. I've also been blessed with essentially the same vocal chords as Dana Carvey, from Saturday Night Live. So, Garth, The Church Lady, John Travolta, Johnny Carson and George Bush impressions are right up my alley. I live to laugh and everything in my shallow little world is just fine and dandy.

I slide my wrap-around Ray Bands into place, turn the key, and listen to the six-inline engine roar to life. I slice my way onto the freeway and patrol the heavy traffic on Highway 50 for 'chick cars'. Something happens to me in this car. I become like James Bond—albeit a dorkier version with highlighted hair. Blond. James Blond. I'm confident, charming, foolish, sophisticated, naughty, and licensed to thrill. I'm a composite of all the comedic sidekicks and misunderstood eccentrics who have always been the real movie stars to me. What's the harm in a little high-speed flirting to make the morning commute more interesting?

There's a babe in a plasma green Honda Civic del Sol that I'm able to slide next to without causing an accident. We pass each other back and forth in slow traffic for the next mile. For her, I'm Billy Crystal being Fernando. It's better to feel good than to look good. And you, my friend, you look marvelous! Although she can't hear me, she can see that I'm talking to her. I watch her putting on make-up and fixing her hair. We come to a stop in the same place. I start to do what she's doing and flip down my visor and smear pretend lipstick on my Mick Jagger-like pursed lips. She smiles. I smile back. The moment is over. The guy mowing through his breakfast burrito gives me a mean look. So what if I made a dangerous lane change that put several lives at risk? We smiled at each other. It was totally worth it.

Some of my radio commercials are in rotation so I keep hitting the presets hoping to land on one. I find a song I like by Live on 93 Rock. Something about an angel opening her eyes. I crank it up. My best options for the holiday parties are in the Bay Area and Tahoe. That's the thing about Sacramento, there's nothing special about it. Its greatest asset is its central location. Our city motto should be, Sacramento, a great place to *leave* on the weekend. The song ends as I'm getting off the freeway and it's followed by one of my spots. It's for Q58, a new TV station coming to town. It's a teaser campaign that uses various types of fortune-tellers who foresee something exciting happening in the near future. I wrote this spot with my mother in mind…

(Male Voice) 'I notice you don't have a name badge on.'

(Female Voice) 'We don't need those here. It's a psychic convention. My name is Rainbow. Rainbow on the Rocks. Two years ago… I mean yesterday, I had my lucky crystal recharged and it showed me a vision of cosmic proportions.'

The woman playing the part is perfect. She talks not so much to you, but to the universe surrounding you in a lofty, self-absorbed, ethereal tone inspired by my mother.

(Female Voice) 'Converging harmonic energies will channel us to The Q.'

There's some announcer copy, then Rainbow comes back for a stinger:

(Female Voice) 'I also read auras.'

Instead of laughing, I cringe. Then I become Dana Carvey doing John Travolta.

"That's just like so weird. You know… to hear dat shit—like dat here."

It will be fun to play it for my mother. She's either going to kill me or love it.

I think she'll love it.

I park under the largest blob of precious shade I can find. Sacramento is a Spanish word linguistically tied to sacrament, but I tell people it's an Indian word that means *surface of the sun*. I hate hot weather and have the sweat glands of a gladiator to prove it. The dash from the car to the building has to be fast enough not to get sunburned and slow enough to keep from sweating. Stepping through the back door of the agency and into the air-conditioned office is like entering another world through a decompression chamber. I'm already wondering what time I can leave as the door closes behind me.

Pam's office is the first door to the left and it's wide open.

"Good morning. I didn't see your car outside."

"Jake dropped me off. He's picking me up in a couple of hours and then I'm out of here. What are you doing for the Fourth?"

"I haven't decided for sure. I might visit Brad in the Bay Area or go see Sharon up in Tahoe. What are you guys doing?"

"We're taking the boat out to Folsom Lake."

I can't sing so I do it all the time. "Rock the boat. Don't rock the boat baby. Rock the boat—don't tip the boat over… So, rock or no rock? They need to make up their mind in that song."

She laughs. She has nice smile lines around her eyes. Pam is one of the agency's two media buyers. She's attractive despite her affinity for tweezers. A couple of months ago, I scanned her wedding picture into the computer and digitally corrected her eyebrows to perfection. But Pam insists they won't grow that way, nor will she allow me pencil them in for her every morning like I offered. Bob accused me of being a little too much in touch with my feminine side. I shrugged and told him I grew up with a lot of sisters. The eyebrow-wedding picture is displayed on her wall and we've been adding to it ever since. First, Bob drew a Manson-like, third eye-swastika on her forehead. Mike added stitches and Frankenstein pegs. Ernie drew a thin mustache and blacked out some teeth— then someone added devil horns. There's a lot of talent in this agency.

"I'm leaving early too," I say. "If I don't see you, have a great time."

"You too."

Mary, the other media buyer, is also in her office. She's a hugger and is already off her chair and coming in for one. It's all very pure and innocent, how hard we press our chests and thighs into each other; the way she breathes on my neck and sighs into my ear. We release. No harm, no foul, just a morning office hug between mutually consenting adult employees. I feign having a boner as I walk away. She's laughing. Good news. No lawsuit.

My office is always open. As I walk to my desk, the light on the phone starts blinking red. It's Bob, my boss.

"B-r-r-r-r-a-a-a-a-h-h-h-h-s-s-s-s!" he bellows into the phone, turning my last name into the wail of a hippo in heat.

"Did you come up with any ideas for Pete's Pizza, you incredibly worthless pile of pooh?"

For no particular reason, my reply comes wrapped in an English accent. "Indeed m'Lord. While enjoying some figgie pudding, I might add. Care to hear them?"

"Yes. Get your arse in here now!"

Advertising is the greatest career invention ever; for folks who detest repetitive work, as well as those who don't want to work at all. It allows you to regress and submerge yourself into a child-like state of existence. You get to play for a living. I'm not saying it doesn't get stressful, or that practically every client isn't a dick, because it does, and they are. But the fact that you can actually make a living thinking up silly ways to sell things is a beautiful concept indeed.

Bob is sitting in his office chair enjoying an imaginary blowjob, which was funny the first five-hundred times, but is starting to get old. He's a Great Dane of a man who towers out at a whopping six feet seven inches tall. He has an unreserved frank face, dark hair and a semi-managed beard. He looks like a missing member of the Monty Python ensemble. He's sarcastic as all hell. His delivery is dry and almost always directly on target. But his physical comedy leaves something to be desired. I quietly review my notes waiting for him to finish. He throws back his head and gurgles, chest heaving. Then his whole body shakes in a climatic, spastic orgasm before he passes out cold. Once his jeans are zipped back up, he's ready to talk business.

"So, what have you got?" He asks, drumming his alien-like, long fingers on the edge of the desk.

"My first idea is to play off a Beatles song: All we are saying, is give Pete's a chance… But that makes Pete's Pizza sound desperate for business, and it's not like our client has the budget to purchase the rights to that particular song." I'm talking myself out of this concept based on his vacant expression.

"Let's see," I say, deciphering my notes. "Oh, here's a campaignable idea: 'Original Pete's, the fine art of pizza.' It's a play on the word *original*, like one-of-a-kind masterpieces. The visuals are famous fine-art paintings and sculptures altered in Photoshop. Picture *Mona Lisa* holding up a slice. A simple headline: 'Of course she's smiling.' Or, put a slice on the pitchfork in *American Gothic*. We can show The Thinker contemplating great pizza, or…"

"Get in your VAN, GO to Pete's!" Bob says, interrupting me, quite pleased with his not-so-clever pun.

"You don't always want to blurt out the first thing that pops into your head because it often sucks," I say, exactly like he said to me on my first day of work.

"HA!" he shouts, slamming his hands on his knees. He gets me. We brainstorm for a while, flushing the concept out in more detail. Two minutes and a thousand tangents later, we're interrupted by the speakerphone. Bob takes the call, allowing my eyes to gaze in wonder at the fascinating wall behind him.

The wall behind Bob's desk houses an odd collection of toys and memorabilia that clutter the shelves from floor to ceiling. There are autographed baseballs, antique metal vehicles, and lunch boxes from the '60s and '70s, including The Monkees and The Six Million Dollar Man. There's an Elvis bust, two Slinkys, a stack of Mad magazines, wind-up tin toys, ray guns, Hot Wheels, board games and enough bits and pieces of pop culture to make you realize how much we forget. The Pee-wee Herman doll kind of creeps me out, which is strange, because I'm a big fan.

Bob hangs up the phone and tells me to continue with his body language.

"All the art is license-free, so it won't cost a dime. I can just download them off the Internet or scan them out of fine art books from the library."

"It's about time you had an idea that didn't suck this agency dry! It's good. Not as good as the religious masterpieces you'll be mutilating in the name of crust, but good… lots of possibilities. You have to think about how to make it work on radio, too. Now get started. Mock it up. Get mocking! And don't think about leaving any earlier than you know you can get away with. Is that clear? Now get back to work, B-r-r-r-r-a-a-a-a-h-h-h-s-s-s!"

Sunita, our receptionist, is laughing at Bob's disgusting rendition of my name at the front desk. I stop and lean on the counter above her desk. "Bob's pronunciation of my last name isn't that far off. 'Bross' is the folk-German word for 'throat phlegm.'" She's especially cute when she laughs. Her teeth are extra white against her dark skin. I try to focus on her smile but can't resist looking down at her incredible chest. She's wearing a tight, low-cut blouse that's begging for attention and my eyes drop into the deep, dark mysteries of her lovely cleavage. In my mind, I have gently placed my face between her bare breasts and am making romantic motorboat sounds. Suddenly the phone rings and the daydream vanishes. I wave goodbye. On the way back to my office I pass Scott in the hall; 'Mr. Mellow'. He's wearing his sunglasses. He's our one-client account executive who works very little and makes big bucks.

"Sup?"

"Nuch."

We talk in shorthand because he's that laid back. Scott has the Bill Graham account and access to the best tickets and backstage passes in town. There's no way I can ever repay him for putting me on various VIP lists. I'm surprised he even showed up today. He'll no doubt be the first to leave.

I turn on the radio in my office and boot up my Mac. I might as well do a little work as long as I'm here. I search the Internet for pictures and import them into a client folder. It takes a while to download each image, which gives me time to think about the long weekend ahead. When the right set of songs play on the radio, it's easy to lose track of time. About an hour later the phone rings.

"You have a call on line two," Sunita says.

"Thank you." I roll my chair away from the computer and pick up the phone.

"Hello, this is Tom," I say smoothly, my standard greeting, pretty sure it's one of my friends calling about weekend plans.

"Tom. It's Lisa Thomas—"

My stomach hurts. I get a lump in my throat. The only time Lisa calls is when something's wrong with my sister Chris.

"I have to talk to you. You better sit down."

"What happened this time?" I ask, standing up.

"Chris had to go to the hospital this morning."

No surprise. This has happened before. Three times in the last two years that I know about, though the real number must be higher. She gets beat up by her loser boyfriend and it happens way too often.

"How bad? Is she okay?" I say, hoping for the best. She doesn't answer. "Lisa? Lisa?"

"No, Tom. They couldn't revive her… She died. At the hospital. This morning… I'm sorry I have to be the one to break the news. I'm so sorry for your whole family…"

The sounds I hear are bullets passing right through me. I slip into a dream where this phone call never happened, and Chris is fine. There must be something closer to the truth that's not so final. *Chris isn't dead! She got beat up really bad again. Somehow, she'll be okay.* But the undeniable truth of Lisa's news knocks the wind out of me. I can't breathe. In a last-ditch effort to escape the words echoing in my head, I drop the phone and cover my ears. The weight becomes unbearable, pulling me down into an abyss of massive pain. I fall back into my chair but end up sliding to the floor and curling into a ball crying, "Chris is gone?… She's gone? …My sister is gone…"

At some point, I pull myself back into the chair and retrieve the phone. Lisa is still there. A clump of people, just shades of gray shapes, have gathered outside my door to see what's wrong. My mind searches one last time for a miraculous escape route.

This can't be happening. I just saw her. She can't be dead.

It fails.

"Where are Shane and Skyler?" I manage to ask.

"They're at Kelly's house. You need to write down this number." Kelly is one of my sister's newer friends. My hand is shaking. I find a pen and scratch down barely legible marks.

"Did Jeff, do it?"

"I don't know. He's being held for questioning though."

"Who else knows?"

"No one."

"What do I do now?"

"I guess you have to tell your family. And you need to pick up the kids."

"Oh my fucking god."

The rest of the conversation is meaningless. She's hurt and is genuinely sorry. She wants to help but feels helpless.

I have to get the kids.

I have to tell my family.

We hang up. I'm shaking. I can't think. Tears are gushing down my face. I don't want to face the blurred bodies lingering in the hall. The pain is unbearable; I'm no match for it. I want my mother. I'm about to fall back to the floor to escape and disappear. But someone is standing next to me, holding me up. It's Scott. I bawl into his shoulder. My voice is shattered glass.

"My sister is dead. Chris is dead... she's gone... she's a mother... Her kids...Oh my god, what about her kids?"

"I know... I know... I know..." he says, over and over and over.

Time stops. Nothing is the same. Everything's wrong. Nothing matters. I'm confronted with the incomprehensible.

I am nothing; a nobody, worthless...

First

July 3rd, 1996

Nothing is the same.

One phone call changes everything. Chris is gone. Is this real? Everything is wrong. I can't think. I'm lost. I give up. What's the point of dealing with a world that's this harsh? I don't want to be here anymore. I quit. I'm done.

My chest has been crushed flat. Shallow breaths. Stomach cramps. Nausea. Mouthfuls of spit. Neck pain. Jaw pain. Shoulder pain. Head pain—even eye pain. I need sleep. I need to wake up safe in bed and be done with this horrible nightmare. I can't undo what I know. I can't talk, negotiate, plead, buy, bluff or trick my way out of this unyielding disaster. Chris is gone.

Forever.

Emotional pain beyond the imaginable. I'm clueless drowning in unfathomable sorrow and guilt. *I could have done more to help her.* Shame. *I can't live with myself knowing it's true.* Panic. *What about Shane and Skyler?* Fear. *This is a devastating loss for her kids.* Anger, rage and fury also like never before. *I want to fucking kill Jeff for what he did to my sister!* Regret. Despair. *The boys have no mother.* Solitude. *I miss her so much. I need her. She's gone.*

Forever.

It feels like I've been abducted by the spiraling forces of an enormous whirlpool; a rag doll tumbling along in a sweeping deluge. As it gets stronger, I get weaker. I'm locked in its ice-cold grip and can no longer keep my head above water. I can't even tell which way is up anymore. Round and round I go, stuck in an endless orbit. *This is how it works? A loved one can just be ripped away from you?*

Forever.

How long have I been sitting in my car? Two minutes… ten, twenty? I turn the key, click the seatbelt, look over my shoulder and back up. The car is strangely heavy. The should-be-familiar world inside my car and beyond the windshield is different. The drive home is a blur of cut-paper shapes sliding by my teary eyes.

Wait a second. We live in a strange universe. Maybe there's a supernatural explanation. The magnetic poles just flopped, creating an anomaly in the space-time continuum. This is a warning, a cosmic wake-up call! Maybe there's a way back to our version of reality and there's still time to save Chris…

Denial is a strong mother fucker.

The magic is gone. Miracles don't exist. My sister is dead. Shane and Skyler saw their mother for the last time yesterday. I can't change this. I'm nothing. The simple joy of being is gone. Life is pointless. I want to withdraw—escape… disappear.

Forever.

I'm thirty-four years old. I just grew up and I hate it.

Suddenly, I'm home and parked in the garage and can't recall the last twenty minutes of driving at all. One thought keeps stinging my brain; *Call Mom.* Mare needs to know. The longer I wait, the harder it will be. I make myself open the car door. I make myself enter the house. I make myself splash cold water on my face. In the mirror's reflection, the vacant lost soul of a ghost stares back at me.

The phone has become an alien object in my hand. This is the tool I must use to give my mother the worst news of her life. What do I say? What words do I use? No matter how I tell her, it's going to crush her to the core. There's no point in practicing or procrastinating. Just dial the number. Don't think. Just talk. Get it out. Get it over with. She has to know. Their answering machine picks up. *Fuck!* Mare and Journey always screen their calls.

"Hey it's Tom. It's really important. Call me back as soon as you can."

There's no masking the frantic edge to my voice. A minute later the phone rings. My shaking hand lifts the receiver.

"Hi Honey, it's me and Journey. You're on speakerphone. What's wrong?"

I don't have private conversations with my mother anymore because her husband, Journey, is a control freak. This has been a family issue for years and right now it's beyond annoying.

"Oh Mom… I have the worst news in the world." I'm practically shouting so I won't lose my nerve and stop. "Chris is dead. She died at the hospital in Davis this morning. I just found out. Shane and Skyler have no mother." Each word is like a dagger I'm stabbing into her heart.

"No… No… No…" I hear her cry; her pain is killing me. She sounds far away, like she dropped the phone, but I can still hear her moaning. Some time passes before she speaks again. When she does, I can hardly hear her. "Tell me what h-h-hap…" She breaks down in the middle of her sentence like a mortally wounded animal trying to right itself after being shot. Her pain is unbearable. I'm worthless and can do nothing to help her. The news of death creates a smoke ring of poison that spreads in all directions. Soon, it will reach the rest of my family, Chris's friends, her stepchildren, the kids she cared for, their parents, the people she worked with—everyone she knows. The ring of fire comes with no warning and there's no escaping the toxic fumes. Getting the news was horrible; spreading the news is almost just as bad.

Eventually Mare finds some strength and is able to speak more clearly. "How did you find out?"

"Lisa Thomas called me at work."

"Journey and I will be at your house tomorrow. We'll pick up Shelley along the way. The rest of us will get there as soon as possible. What else do you know?"

"Nothing really. Jeff is being held for questioning. I'll have to get more info. Shane and Skyler are with Chris's friend, Kelly, for now. She might know more. We should call the hospital and maybe the police to get—"

"Get my grandchildren into your house and under your wing right away. You got that?"

"Yes."

"Good."

"Can you help me tell the rest of the family? I don't want to have to call everyone with this news. I can't…

"I'll call Shelley, and Alex. You can call your father and ask him to tell Molly."

"Okay. I got it. Thank you."

"I love you," she says, sad yet strong. I tell her that I love her too and the call ends.

I'm so full of emotion and so entirely empty at the same time. I've never needed my family more, but we've become so fractured. The only noise in the house is the hum of the aquarium, but it's as if I'm screaming inside my head. This is going to impact her children the most. There's no feeling sorry for myself when I think about their loss. I've got to keep it together for Shane and Skyler.

Within the last hour, I have both received and made the worst phone calls of my life, and yet, according to the object on the wall that displays time, the day's still young. Ten million thoughts rip through my head, and they are all interrupted by the cold, non-negotiable truth: *Chris is gone. She left her children motherless.* Death is unbending, unfair and so fucking permanent.

Forever.

I dig out the scrap of paper with Kelly's number and carefully push the correct buttons on the phone. This has to be done. I need to confront the details of my sister's death. I need to get my nephews. I don't know Kelly, but I've heard Chris talk about her and seen pictures of her at my sister's duplex. She picks up after just one ring as if waiting for my call. After telling her who I am, she begins crying softly and speaking rapidly—spilling her guts.

"My boyfriend, Scott and I partied with Chris and Jeff last Saturday night—only a little and we didn't stay late." Hearing this makes me uncomfortable. I don't like acknowledging my sister's addictions. "We smoked some rock and were having a good time, but then Jeff became super angry for no reason at all. He locked us out of their bedroom. We could hear him yelling. It sounded like Chris was getting pushed around. Then things calmed down and eventually they came out, so we stayed a little longer. But I wish we hadn't. We should have called the police again. That's what we did the last time he got violent. But we didn't. We just went home."

She's crying harder now. "If we had just called the police. Jeff would have been arrested and Chris would still be alive. I could have saved her. Don't you see? This is *my* fault. I knew this was going to happen sooner or later and I did nothing. Nothing!"

"Kelly, I feel the same way, so do a lot of other people. I could have done more—a lot more. I knew about my sister's addictions long before you ever met her. I allowed it to go on and on."

"We shouldn't have been smoking crack in the first place."

"Well, I have to agree with you on that and I know quitting isn't easy, but at this time, all I really care about is getting Shane and Skyler over to my house. I have a small car. They both won't fit in my car." There's a pause. She asks me to hang on and sets down the phone. Then she's back.

"I have a spare key to your sister's car. When my boyfriend gets off work, we could pick up her car. Hopefully Jeff's father won't be there. I'll drive the kids to your house. Scott can follow me in his truck."

"That works. What time?"

"I don't know. Between six-thirty and seven?"

"Perfect." I give her directions and ask her to read them back to me. We have a plan. This is good.

"By the way, Shane thinks his mom is still in the hospital."

Hearing this forces the air from my lungs. I know I'll have to tell Shane the truth when the time is right. I don't recall the end of our conversation or hanging up the phone or moving to the couch. The next thing I know I'm crouching forward feeling close to throwing up. I rub my face thinking I should call Dad. Then again, why not give him five more minutes of happiness? My brain is spinning like a slot machine; the first wheel lands on a skull and crossbones; death. So does the second. So does the third. It's not just my brain, everything else is spinning too.

The phone rings. I'm startled back into the darkness of the present. I pick up the receiver in the kitchen. "Hello."

"This is the Davis Police Department. Am I speaking with Tom Bross?"

I'm totally unprepared to talk. The police represent an entirely different category of stress. I'm sure my sister means nothing to them. Her death is just another case to sort and file, but not before sharing all the gory details with the public. This is big news for Davis. It will be in the newspaper. Our family's nightmare will be out there for everyone to judge, pity and scoff at.

"Yes. This is him."

"Hold on a moment and I'll connect your call, okay?"

"Okay."

"Hello Tom. I'm Detective Cox." Then he spells it for me: "C-O-X." *Do people with this last name honestly think we're going to spell it any other way?* He asks a few questions to verify that he's speaking with the 'brother of the deceased.' I can hear him tapping on something. We talk about the kids and what my immediate plans are for them. My head is spinning. I have questions too and getting them out takes tremendous effort.

"What about Jeff?" I say, sounding less than neutral.

"Jeff Fowler is being detained voluntarily while we begin our investigation. Cause of death has yet to be determined; no charges have been filed." He sounds as cold as the speech program on my computer.

"You know he has a criminal record, right? He's beaten Chris up before. He's put her in the hospital." I can't stop my voice from shaking. "This time he went too far."

"I am aware of his record. We're waiting for the results of the autopsy."

"How long will that take?"

"A week, maybe more with the holiday. Tom, we would very much like to interview Shane as a witness. Because of his age, it's essential this happens right away." I'm at a loss for words. "The sooner the better," he adds. Caught off guard, I agree to the interview but refuse to settle on the time or date for now. He's still finger tapping as he gives me two numbers where he can be reached. I should be getting more information, but my mind is cluster-fucked by emotion. He ends the call abruptly and hangs up.

How do I process what just happened? I remain leaning against the kitchen counter, stuck in time, holding the phone in my hand wondering what the fuck is going on. *How did my poor sister get caught up with a loser like Jeff?* The answer comes rushing at me like an evil linebacker with death in his eyes.

∞   ∞   ∞

They met at a bar in Davis. She went out with some girlfriends one night. Chris—more than anything else in the world—wanted to have her own kids. But she was living with Allen and knew it wasn't going to happen with him. He already had six kids and a vasectomy. That can happen when teens hook up with sexual predators, including the ones employed by the school system. Sperm-donor-loser Jeff was at the right place at the right time, but he certainly wasn't the right guy.

Jeff was a total hard-ass-dickhead-stoner in high school. I can't remember the details of how she went from Allen to Jeff—maybe she never told me. She just called one day and said she was living with Jeff. 'Not Jeff Fowler!' I yelled. She assured me that he had changed. I tried keeping an open mind, but I also had my doubts. I met them in Davis at a restaurant shortly after they got together. Even though they were in the everything-is-rainbows-and-butterflies beginning stage of their relationship, I could tell he was the same old Jeff I steered clear of in high school. He told me he was making a 'killing' painting apartments and was planning to start his own business.

What my sister saw in him, other than sperm, I'll never know. She must have thought she could change Jeff into something good. A few months after they moved in together, Dad had a writing job that brought him to California. We made plans to visit Chris and Jeff at their new apartment in Davis but ended up visiting her in the hospital instead. Clearly, the abuse began right away. Apparently, Chris got dressed up to meet some girlfriends downtown for drinks and when she got home, Jeff was so jealous, he beat her with one of her own shoes. Both her cheeks were heavily bruised. She had a black eye that was still swollen shut and a large cut across her lower lip. I thought having Dad there might help her see the light. Maybe he could convince Chris to move out; maybe Chris would finally see how much the situation was hurting her family. But no. Chris shocked us both when she said it was her fault. My heart broke again. She said Jeff had every right to be jealous. She said, 'It's never going to happen again,' and, 'Now we're closer than ever.' She even tried to make us laugh by showing us how hard it was to sip water through a straw. Dad went home,

Chris got out of the hospital and went straight back to Jeff. Our visit had no impact and the pattern of abuse continued.

More calls. Usually from Lisa Thomas. 'Chris is in the hospital again.' The panic. The sadness. The frustration of it all. I'd try another strategy, but she had a gentle way of brushing me off. My sister became less of herself the longer she was with Jeff. Over time, he broke her spirit. He beat her down both physically and emotionally.

Then one day she actually moved out and moved in with me! That was six and a half years ago. She arrived at my house determined to leave him for good. I knew she was serious because Chris generally never drove on the highway, yet there she was. Things fell into place quickly. She got a job right down the street from where I was working. We were able to carpool together and sometimes we met for lunch. By the end of her first week, she was the top-selling telemarketer in her office and was earning daily bonuses. Every day she became more like the old Chris; funny, upbeat, confident.

Right when I became convinced that she'd gotten over Jeff and left him for good, she went back. She left a note asking me not to be mad. She said they had a deep and serious talk and that their future was bright. And, just like that, after about a month, she was back in Davis and living with Jeff again—right back where she started; stuck in a shit-storm of drugs and violence. I made other attempts. Out of courtesy, she took the number to a local women's shelter I gave her. I went to a WEAVE meeting, which stands for Women Escaping a Violent Environment, hoping to find her a mentor. I thought if she could talk to another woman who had broken free from an abusive relationship, then Chris would see that she could do it, too. But the right person wasn't there, and I didn't bother going back. I gave her a copy of Narcotics Anonymous. She thanked me for it, but I could see in her eyes that she had no intention of reading it. Things would be okay for a while, and then the same old shit would resurface. Restraining orders were filed and broken. Jeff was sentenced to *anger management courses that had no effect. It was a horrible life that was only getting worse, and she tolerated it. We all did. But I lived the closest to her. I could have and should have done more…*

∞   ∞   ∞

Call dad. He's had the same phone number for years. I know it by heart. My father might be home, or he could be overseas working on a travel article. He answers the phone. I get it over with and tell him the news, which is still painful but less dramatic than telling Mare. He's not as connected to Chris. He loves her, but he also lives three thousand miles away. We grew up seeing him once a year—if that. Now we hardly see him at all. His response is more panic than pain. He's flustered but not floored. He's not choking back the tears like I am as we talk about Shane and Skyler. He's composed while we talk about Molly and how this will be especially hard on her, since her husband, Kurt, just passed away four months ago in March after battling cancer for years.

"Molly and her family are already in the middle of a major loss—and now she has this to deal with?" I say.

"You're right. She's going to have to be a strong little girl. Listen, I'll get out there as fast as I can. As soon as I know my flight details I'll be back in touch. I do have to finish a story before I can leave. It might be a day or two."

"That's fine. Just keep me posted. Are you sure you don't mind calling Molly? I can do it if you want me to."

"That's okay. I'm her Papa. I'll call her as soon as we're off the phone. Promise you'll stay in touch."

"I will."

There is nothing else to say. You don't call your father, tell him that his daughter died, and then ask about the weather. Molly should be getting the news from me, but I tell myself it doesn't really matter who delivers the awful message. About ten minutes later the phone rings again.

"Hi Molly."

"How'd you know it was me?"

"Just did. You know… bad news travels fast."

"Dad just called. He just dropped the bomb. No warning. Nothing. Chris is dead? Are you fucking kidding me? First Kurt, now Chris? That's how it's going down? Oh shit. This is a catastrophe. It's sad, so unbelievably sad…" Her voice makes me cry again.

"Can you run out of tears?"

"You can," she says, "but it doesn't stop you from crying."

We talk about how fragile life is, the vice grip of death and how it affects the people they leave behind. She tells me about the roller-coaster ride she's been on with her husband's cancer, how she would reassure her kids that this was going to be daddy's last treatment, only to have him come home and continue to deteriorate right before their eyes.

"I don't know if I can keep it together in front of my kids. I'm not kidding, Tom. This is too much. I'm falling apart."

Poor Molly. My sweet little sister. I've managed to shuffle her struggles to the bottom of the deck and for the most part, out of my mind. I've never fully grasped what she and her family were going through until today. We talk about Chris and how much we looked up to her growing up; and how naturally beautiful, smart, funny, and caring she was.

"Chris loved to sing into anything remotely resembling a microphone. She did ten things at once and made them all look easy," Molly says.

"She was able to connect with people of all ages, and especially loved the little ones. Every baby, toddler, and kid she babysat or nannied fell in love with her. She always had tremendous love in her heart for children—even kids that weren't her own."

"Chris made us laugh, even in the worst situations, just to make us feel better," Molly says.

"And it was always Chris who checked in, stepped up and took care of us when mom checked out. She was a good person. Through and through."

"Bad things happen to good people," Molly says.

"I guess they do. It makes no sense."

"I love Chris, you know that," Molly says. "I love her so much and I'm heartbroken that she's gone. But I'm also angry at her for not cleaning up her act. She chose to let her situation continue even after she became a mother. That's not right—especially for a person who loves kids so much. Look at the mess she created; for herself, for us and especially for her own children."

"It's hard to pull yourself up when someone is pushing you down."

"I know. But ultimately it was up to Chris to know she wasn't being responsible and to want the change enough to make it happen—and she didn't. And the truth is I'm fucking pissed off at her for that right now. Of course, I love her. But I'm very angry, too."

"I see your point. You're right, she wasn't perfect. Nobody is. She could have made better choices. I guess I'm a little angry too. But I also know I could have tried harder to help her. I should have tried harder."

"Tom, don't blame yourself."

"I can't help it. I know Chris didn't want to die. She'd never want to leave her children."

"No. She didn't want to die. But she didn't want any help, including yours either."

"The kids will be here this evening."

"Everyone's making plans to get to your house as soon as possible. I'll call you back tonight when we figure it out. Can you pick us up at the airport?"

"Of course."

I hear my little sister take a deep breath. "You should have called me, Tom. Not Dad. Mom could have called. Anyone but Dad."

"I know. I'm sorry. I was so overwhelmed telling Mom that I didn't want to go through it again."

"I understand. Dad was just so matter-of-fact about it. It was cold and shocking. I'm still shaking. I love you brother. Be strong for Shane and Skyler."

"I'll do my best. I love you, too."

I feel a lot of things right now but none of them have anything to do with strength. Those poor kids. Skyler is less than a year and a half old. He'll eventually forget his mother. But Shane just turned five and he'll probably *always* remember her. I don't know which is sadder. How on earth are you supposed to tell a little boy that his mother is dead? Shane is so smart, aware and sensitive; he's an old soul and I can't imagine how he'll feel getting this devastating news. Just thinking about it brings more tears.

Second

July 3rd, 1996

Feeling worthless, restless, and miserable, I go to the backyard for a change of scenery and lean against the trunk of the almond tree for support. Looking up at the blue sky through the branches and leaves, I happen to see a hummingbird resting on a twig. It's the first time I've seen a hummingbird at this house. While focusing on the subject, I notice the most subtle movements; a turn of its head, a twitch of its wing, the sun dances on its iridescent feathers. The bird remains perfectly poised and appears to be glancing back at me with mutual curiosity. We remain locked in a soothing stare-down for a full minute before the bird suddenly lifts off, hovers momentarily and then darts directly skyward in a high speed vertical climb like a tiny jet. I lose sight of it in the sun.

That was cool.

I let go of the tree, close my eyes and stretch. When I reopen them, the hummingbird is back and it's even closer. I hold my breath for a moment and freeze. At this range, I can see much more; individual fan-like turquoise and teal feathers, the delicate structure of its tiny feet, even the sun's reflection in the curve of its eye. The bird begins chirping pleasantly, which, for some reason seems directed at me. I mimic the sound back, perfecting my technique, as we converse back and forth while the sun warms my back and shoulders. I study the creature with primal wonder. I'm amazed at its scale, its beauty and astonishing power. To fly with that kind of precise agility is nothing short of miraculous. There must have been generations of people before me who were equally amazed by this masterpiece of nature. It's pure. It hasn't been altered by mankind in anyway. It's the same now as it was then and will continue to be into the future. This tiny bird is in creation's simpler scheme, its own most precious thing.

I desperately need to believe that the bird somehow embodies my sister's spirit; and so, it does. *This hummingbird is Chris. She's a part of everything now. Her soul has been released into the universe and she can take any form. A hummingbird suits her perfectly. This bird harnesses my sister's energy. It's Christina.*

Real? Unreal? Rational? Irrational? It doesn't matter. Because for a brief moment I feel an undeniable connection to Chris and just knowing something still exists between us calms me to the core. Suddenly, the bird lifts off—a coruscating spark of pure energy—and darts to another branch, higher in the tree but still relatively close and begins chirping even louder. I close my eyes to picture my sister's face in my mind's eye.

"Oh Chris, I love you so much. You're going to be missed by so many people. It hurts to go on without you. Don't worry about Shane and Skyler. We'll take care of them. We'll find a way. I believe you're in a better place now. No addictions. No pain. No abuse. No more suffering. There's a giant hole in my heart and you will always be my sister and I will never stop loving you. Ever."

The hummingbird chirps on cue at the end of my quiet monologue. I open my eyes slowly to see if I can relocate the bird. The moment I do, it zips into the air, banks left and then hovers behind me somewhere close. There's comfort in the vibrating sound of its almost-invisible beating wings. I twist to get a better look as it jets away, cutting confidently through time and space, leaving a scintillating trail of lingering color in its wake.

"Please visit again," I whisper, clinging to that delicate sense of precious connection.

I feel grateful, honored, and humble. I could feel my sister's spirit and it took my mind off the pain for a few precious moments. Chris is not completely gone. I know a part of her still exists. I sensed her unique vibration in the beating of the bird's wings. This encounter was more than a coincidence. It just had to be. The unexpected calming sensation was magical. For the first time since getting the news, I'm breathing normally.

Thank you, Christina.

I go inside the house to assess the spare bedroom. In order to make room for the kids, I'll need to put some things into the garage. I'm moving slowly and methodically on autopilot mentally telling myself to just keep going because doing something is better than doing nothing. Using a camping pad covered with clean sheets and blankets, I make my nephews a bed. I roam the house moving potentially dangerous items out of what I imagine to be Shane and Skyler's reach. The house needs cleaning. *Keep moving.* The windowsills need dusting, the rugs need vacuuming, counters need wiping and the microwave needs scrubbing. As I'm working, that beautiful bird comes to mind and it actually feels like I'm channeling Chris's neat-freak energy.

The front door opens, and slams shut. I hear a set of keys sliding across the kitchen counter.

"Dude, are you home?"

"I'm in here," I say, from the bathroom. "I'm cleaning."

My roommate, Monica, springs down the hall and braces herself at the door. I look up, our eyes meet and straightaway, she knows something isn't right.

"Dude, what the fuck is wrong?"

"Nothing." For a second, I consider not telling her.

"Dude." Her voice is nine octaves lower now. Her bug-eyes are big and serious.

"Chris is dead. I found out at work. She died at the hospital this morning."

"What? Are you fucking serious! How?"

"It sounds like Jeff beat her to death." Just telling another person what happened makes my eyes pool up with tears.

Silence. Then she slams her hand against the wall. BAM!

"Well that fucking sucks!" She leaves the doorway, marches to the kitchen and returns holding two cans of Coors light. "I hate that motherfucker. He won't get away with this."

"The worst part is Shane and Skyler."

"Holy shit! Their mother!"

"I know. It's bad. Really bad."

"Well, if there was ever a time to drink, this is it!"

"A silver bullet," I say.

"That's right, a silver fucking bullet, dude. For the pain." She opens both beers, hands me one and raises hers.

"To Chris." She tips her head and drinks half the can.

"To Chris," I say, and take a sip.

Monica is an almost welcome distraction from the grief ricocheting in my head.

"That's it," she says. "Now take a big drink like me."

Monica is always looking for a party—and new ways to bulk up. She's a living paradox. She works at the gym. She does some personal training with clients and spends a good part of the day lifting weights on her own. She's all wheat grass and self-discipline at work but one foot out the door and she's a completely different person. When training is over, it's nothing but beer, cigarettes, and steroids. She has both incredibly good and incredibly bad habits. I have a history of attracting strange roommates.

Deep down, Monica is a good person with a good heart—metaphorically speaking—who knows what damage the black-market drugs made from bull testicles have caused? She just wants to help, and this is her way of trying. I take another sip of beer.

"I haven't eaten since breakfast. I should eat something," I say, setting down the can.

"Beer is food… cereal, grains, hops and yeast. And you don't have to chew it." She laughs hysterically at her own joke. I manage to force a trembling smile.

"I need to call the hospital and get all the details I can. I should call Brad and tell him what happened. I just can't get myself to use the phone right now. I've been cleaning like a maniac just to keep moving."

Monica claps her hands and springs into her motivational training mode. She holds up her index finger motioning for me to wait, dashes into her room and returns with a pack of Marlboro reds. She waves the box in front of my face.

"First we'll have a smoke. Then we'll make those calls."

I'm not a smoker. I don't buy cigarettes, but I do smoke socially. When I'm out partying, I tend to bum them off pretty girls. There are worse ways to break the ice. The clubs are so smoky, I figure it's better to smoke and look cool than just sit there slowly dying from second-hand smoke. Plus, there was that one occasion when I asked a pretty blond for a cigarette and ended up sleeping with both her and her drop-dead gorgeous girlfriend. Funny how a once-in-a-lifetime wild threesome can create such a positive association with such a negative habit.

I follow Monica outside. The cigarette burns my throat and tastes disgusting. It makes me dizzy. I really don't enjoy anything about smoking but then something remarkable happens. For a fraction of a second, I feel lightheaded and am able to put my misery on hold. It's not a deep, mental feeling like I experienced with the hummingbird. It's more of a physical distraction—and yet it worked. I already know I'll smoke again in search of this sliver of escapism.

"Things are about to get crazy," I warn Monica. "My family is on their way from all over. Shane and Skyler will be staying here until we figure things out."

None of this fazes her in the least. Monica cannot comprehend how I feel. She makes a lame attempt to pump me up for the phone calls I need to make, but it's the same cliché phrases she uses at the gym. We put our cigarettes out and go inside. I pick up the phone, turn around and she's standing right behind me. I pause before dialing so she can leave the room but doesn't take the hint. She just stares at me with her Graves'-diseased, protruding eyes.

"Get psyched! C'mon Tom! You can do this!"

"I'm… well, I'm psyched. But can I have some privacy please?"

"I'll get more beer!" she yells, stomping off on foot to the corner liquor store.

While she's gone, I call and leave messages at the hospital, with my best friend Brad, and with his mother—who is kind of my mother, too. I consider calling Peggy but decide to try her later when there's a better chance of catching her at home. I finish cleaning the bathroom. The house is quiet and then gets loud again when Monica returns. She wants me to drink another beer with her, but I'm still not ready to open up a new one. She slams down three more, then retreats to her room to nap.

I know I should eat something, but I have no appetite, so I take another cigarette from the pack she left on the counter and light it up outside. I look for the hummingbird but don't see it. This time the cigarette does nothing for me. I could get stoned but fear it will only make me feel worse—if that's even possible. I go back inside. The steady drip of depression brings time to a crawl. I keep getting up to look at the clock and sitting back down. I lie down on the floor and stretch my back. I'm shivering even though I'm not cold. I get up and pace through the house like a caged animal. Then I sit back down and flip through the dismal daytime TV shows with the sound off in a trance. My mind begins to wander. Memories of my sister drift upward in my mind like bubbles breaking the surface of a body of water.

∞   ∞   ∞

We lived on Castro Street in San Francisco when we were little. Our neighbors, Keith, Kerry and Evan were all college photography students. They welcomed us kids to play in their apartment pretty much whenever we wanted because we were the perfect subjects for them to photograph. They developed the film in their bathroom, which, when the door was locked, was also a dark room. They lived on the third floor in the building next to ours. We could go wild there, mess up the place, play anywhere with anything we wanted and never get in trouble, which was the opposite of what we could do at home—especially when John was present. Shelley was in a thrill-seeking stage. Chris and I watched her climb out the kitchen window, scale upon the smallest piece of trim on the side of the building all the way around to the bedroom window, where she climbed back in.

Perfect subjects are clueless to the camera's lens.

"Now you gotta do it," she says looking at me and Chris. "I double-dog dare you."

Chris peeks out the window and turns white. I can see the fear of God in her eyes. I know she's afraid of heights. Mom and Peggy took all of us kids to a carnival they'd set up in Golden Gate Park one day and Chris wouldn't ride the Ferris wheel.

"I don't want to do it," Chris says.

"Ha, ha! You're chicken!"

"Don't make her do it. Remember when she wouldn't ride the fairest wheel in the park?" I say to Shelley who looks at me like I'm dirty toilet paper she'd just wiped her butt with.

"For your information, it's called a *Ferris* wheel, Retard."

"He's right. I don't like heights. I'm not doing it."

"I triple-dog dare you!" Shelley says pointing her finger at Chris who crosses her arms and considers her options.

"Well," Shelley says, "Well… ?"

"I'll go for her," I say.

"You'll do it?" asks Shelley.

"Tom. You don't have to—" Chris starts to say.

"I'll go if you let Chris off the hook."

"Okay," Shelley says. "Funny. I thought you'd be the first to chicken out."

"No. But if I die, Mom's going to be really mad at you."

"So, what. Just do it."

"Fine. Move out of the way."

I ease myself out of the window reaching with the toe of my PF Flyer tennis shoe to feel the little ledge. Fortunately, it feels slightly more secure than I expected.

"Don't look down!" Shelley shouts and then adds, "Now go!"

I move slowly carefully placing my hands and feet in the right places. When I peek at what's below, my heart skips a beat. About twelve feet down is a broken fire escape and then it's another twenty feet down to the alley where all the garbage collects between the buildings. Chris runs to the bedroom window and calmly encourages me to move carefully. Once I'm within reach, Shelley suddenly appears and slams the window closed. I hear Chris screaming at her. She's frantic and begins to cry. Shelley opens the window and they both grab ahold of me and help me back inside.

"You closed the window on me!"

"I wasn't going to keep it closed forever."

"That was mean. Way too mean," I say to Shelley.

"You're fine. Relax."

"I'm never doing *that* again!" I say, still laying in their arms on the bedroom floor, and then I start to laugh, even though there was nothing funny about what just happened. I think I was just happy to be alive. They start laughing too. And in the end, we agreed to never do this again.

Not long after this death-defying stunt, in the very same place, Molly, Chris and I were all jumping on the bed having the time of our lives. Molly landed at the perfect moment, which boosted my momentum sending me skyrocketing upwards. But I wasn't going straight up. I was heading directly towards the open window. There's a fleeting moment when several things simultaneously go through my mind, including the fact that I am about to die. Maybe it was my life flashing before my eyes and it was a short flash because I was only five years old. It happened so fast. I didn't have time to block the opening with any part of my body—I was essentially a five-year-old human-missile heading directly for my demise. Then I felt something wrap around my torso and stop me in mid-flight. Half of my body was out the window. The other half was being pulled back in and I landed on the floor with a thud. Feeling confused by the whole life—death—life again cycle, it took me a moment to realize what had happened.

Chris saved my life.

There was no surviving that fall. Miraculously, Chris was at the right place at the right time and had the presence of mind to react with lightning quick reflexes.

"I thought I was dead."

"Yea. That was a close one."

"I think you just saved my life."

"I think I just did. But don't tell anyone or we'll get in trouble."

"Okay."

"We should scooch the bed away from the window."

"Yea. Let's close the window, too."

"Good idea."

Then we went right back to jumping on the bed trying to time our jumps to boost each other ever higher and more out of control because everyone knows that's what makes you laugh the hardest.

Nearly dying always cracked us up.

∞   ∞   ∞

I really don't want to look like an emotional mess when the kids arrive. *I've got to control my emotions and put Shane and Skyler's needs first.* I get up to look at my face in the bathroom mirror. It still looks like I've been crying my eyes out. *I wish they were here already.*

Finally, when I hear cars pulling up to the house, I jump up, open the front door, and wait for them to come through the gate. What little excitement I've managed to drum up is quickly washed away when I see their faces. Skyler is on Kelly's shoulder. He looks at me with a sorrowful and drained expression. Shane looks straight down as he walks past me without even glancing up. *They're so vulnerable and fragile. They have no idea how much their lives have changed.*

Kelly and I introduce ourselves, we shake hands, then her boyfriend extends his and says, "Steve." Kelly sets Skyler down, along with some bags strapped to her shoulder. Shane takes his brother into the living room and they settle on the floor in front of the TV. The blank expressions on their tired faces don't change as I flip through the channels. I offer Kelly and her boyfriend a beer–*no thanks*, then juice–*no thanks*, then water–*no thanks. They're not staying long.* Everyone's understandably edgy and wiped out.

I get down on the floor and put an arm around Shane.

"I'm glad you're here. It will be fun having you guys spend the night."

He sees right through my charade. He knows something out of the ordinary is going on and knows it's not good. He can feel it; the stress surrounding him is as inescapable as his shadow. I think Skyler can too. Shane is content staring at the television. Skyler wanders into the kitchen to explore the cabinets. The second I get up to follow him, Kelly intercepts and steers me outside whispering, "We need to talk."

As the sliding glass door is closing, an avalanche of words spills out from her and all I can do is let them carry me away. She's trembling, crying, smoking, and spewing forth her guilt, shame, and despair. The more I listen, the more I start to think Kelly *was* in a position to help my sister. But that's probably my own guilt mixing with hers. I'm the family member who lives the closest to Chris. I knew the lifestyle she was living. I knew it wasn't getting better, even after the kids were born. I'm her brother. I could have done more.

Apparently, things took a drastic turn for the worse for Chris when Jeff's father, David, moved in about two months ago. According to Kelly, he's an unemployed, alcoholic with a criminal record that includes domestic violence, forgery, DUI's, and robbery. This was Jeff's role model growing up. I'm sure Chris had no choice but to welcome this asshole into her home, and knowing Chris, she did it with open arms. About a month ago, Kelly and her boyfriend were at my sister's duplex partying with the glass pipe. Jeff locked himself and Chris into the bedroom and began beating her up. They could hear Chris screaming, begging for mercy. Jeff's dad just read the paper and tuned the whole thing out. Kelly called the police. Jeff was arrested, but not before shoving Kelly so forcefully to the ground, that she still has bruises on her shoulder. She shows them to me.

"I looked into his eyes and there was no sign of Jeff. He was a whole different person," she says and then shudders at the memory. The weight of her words continue to bury me until I'm unable to move, trapped in them like quicksand.

"I think Jeff was issued a restraining order that night," she says, and I make a mental note to find out for sure.

"Chris and I were serious about quitting. The last time we partied, we swore it would be our last. It was Saturday night. Four days ago. That's the last time I saw her. Now she's gone. I'm never going to do meth again. We should have quit months ago. If we had, Chris would still be alive. I'm done. And if Steve doesn't quit too, then I'll leave him and move away. I can't take it anymore. She shouldn't have died. I saw this coming…"

Kelly cries into my shoulder, still talking, still needing to expunge herself of the pain. Once she's calmed down a bit, I ask when she picked up the kids.

"Jeff's dad, David called me this morning. He sounded so serene. He said, 'Chris just passed away at the hospital,' like it was no big deal. Then he asked if I wouldn't mind meeting him at the duplex to get Skyler and then go pick up Shane at school. When I got there, he was dragging a garden hose out of the house. I went inside and the carpet was soaking wet. The bed was stripped. I grabbed Skyler, the car seats, some of his things and got the hell out. Jeff's dad was hovering over me the whole time. He's creepy. Cleaning must have been taking him longer than expected. He didn't intend for me to see him in action."

"That's so fucked up. Then what happened?"

"I drove to Shane's school and told his teacher that there was a family emergency. When we got in the car, Shane said he wanted to see his mother. I had to tell him something, so I told him she was resting in the hospital. He asked about Jeff, too. He thinks his dad is in a lot of trouble. Sooner or later, Shane has to know the truth. Someone in your family has to tell him."

"What happened next?"

"I drove back to my house, settled the kids and called Lisa. She knows your family better than I do. This is the worst day of my life… I knew this was going to happen and didn't stop it. I deserve to die."

"Has Shane mentioned anything about last night?"

Kelly looks up and wipes her eyes. "We talked about it at my house. I asked him if he had a rough night. He looked at me and nodded. His eyes were so sad. I almost started bawling. 'She was knocked out,' those were his exact words. He said he didn't understand why Jeff was so angry. He heard screaming and yelling. He saw his dad drag his mother through the house. He saw Jeff trying to wake her up by pouring water on her face and kicking her stomach while she was passed out on the floor."

"That's horrible…" I say, closing my eyes, thinking about Shane, wondering if this will be his last memory of his mother. Kelly is visibly shaking but no longer talking. I can sense she doesn't want to utter another word. We go back inside. She hands me the keys to the Honda.

"Be careful with the brakes. They're a little uneven. Oh, and Skyler is just about out of diapers." She hugs the boys and is getting ready to leave when Monica emerges from her room, all gussied up for a party.

"I'm think I'm too drunk to start my car, but not too drunk to drive it. Will one of you blow into my breathalyzer for me?" She's dead serious and stands motionless blinking her bulging blue eyes at us waiting for an answer.

After a long pause, Kelly's boyfriend says, "Sure, why not?" They all head out the front door, leaving me alone with Shane and Skyler. It's just the three of us and it feels so strange and void as if I'd been arrested in a foreign country.

I have no idea what to say, or if I should say anything at all. Normally, I'm great with kids but this isn't a normal situation. We watch television for an hour then I offer Shane something to eat before bed.

"No thank you," he says politely.

"Then let's get ready for bed."

"It's still light outside."

"I know. Aren't you tired though?"

"Okay."

I sift through their bags and find pajamas. There are no toothbrushes, so I give Shane my spare.

"Does Skyler brush?"

"You gotta do it."

"Skyler turns to me, opens his mouth revealing about eight teeth that I begin to brush. Clearly hating the taste of adult toothpaste, he spits it out all over me and then the mirror.

"Well, that's probably good enough for tonight."

I take them into the spare room and put them under the covers.

"Skyler gets a bottle at night," Shane says.

"Cold milk or warm?"

"I don't think it matters."

"Okay."

I come back from the kitchen with a bottle of cold milk, lie down and look at the pictures in a National Geographic magazine.

"I need my pappy."

"Your what?"

"You know. My pappy," Shane says.

"A pacifier?"

I dig into the deepest corner of the clothes bag and am relieved to feel what can only be a 'pappy.' It's covered in lint but before I can offer to rinse it off, it's in his mouth. After a few more pictures, Shane rolls over and away from me. I run my fingers through his hair trying to think of something I can say to make him feel better.

"Everything is going to be all right. Get some sleep, because tomorrow we're going to have lots of company." I ease myself up and out of the room, only to return a minute later because Skyler isn't sleepy and he's bugging Shane.

I take the little guy into the living room. From there, he wanders off to explore the house. Then it occurs to me that he's looking for his mother. He starts to whimper so I pick him up and walk him around, but he cries harder. *There must be something I can do.* I try giving him another bottle. He promptly throws it to the floor. I set him on the couch, turn on the TV, turn down the volume and he still cries. I turn off the TV and he throws himself on the floor weeping. I fetch a cracker from the kitchen. He sees it and looks away, same with a slice of cheese, a photo album, a book, a tennis ball, and a flashlight. I try music. It fails. I try the bottle again. Fail. Check his diaper. Turn off the lights. Turn some back on. The more he cries the worse I feel. Nothing I do is working. I just want to cry with him. The best I can do is hold him until he wears himself out. It only takes ten minutes, but it seems like an eternity. He finally falls asleep, exhausted. I wait a long time to make sure he is all the way out. Then I lift myself up steadily, carry him like nitroglycerin back into my room and ever so gently, set him down on my bed.

An hour later, even though I know I won't be able to sleep, I crawl into bed anyway. Every now and then, the silence is broken by the sound of fireworks. *Stupid Fuckers. Don't they know there are children here trying to sleep? And who lights off their fireworks on the third of July? The premature ejaculators of the world, that's who.*

I listen to Skyler's steady breathing, hoping it will calm my brain. An hour goes by, then another. He wakes up crying. Again, everything I try fails to bring comfort. What he wants, I cannot give—his mother. I try singing, whispering, and rocking him back and forth. Nothing, nothing, and nothing. He is crying so hard that he loses his breath and cannot catch it. I begin to cry, too. I'm crying for his loss and mine. I'm crying because I feel completely useless. I beg for my sister's help.

"I miss your mother, too. I can't bring her back. You have every right to miss her. I'm so sorry. I'm so sorry. Chris, we really need you right now. Skyler needs your love. Talk to him. Comfort him. Please Chris… Please Chris… Please…"

His cries are breaking my heart. Suddenly, I can feel my sister. Not in the room and not completely inside of me, but in the tips of my fingers and under the skin on my arms. I feel the joy and pain of a mother holding her baby for the last time. Chris loves this baby wholeheartedly. I can feel it. Skyler feels her, too and begins to settle down. He's able to catch his breath and falls back asleep in my arms. I carry him, again ever so gently, to my room and ease him onto the bed. It's been a living nightmare of a day and yet he's so perfect, pure, and beautiful—a living miracle.

Third

July 4th, 1996

For a sliver of time, right before I open my eyes, everything is fine. It's just another day. And then yesterday's catastrophe comes crashing back down in full force leaving me gasping for air. Next comes the realization that this is the first day of the rest of our lives without Chris in it. It's no wonder I just want to lay here and shut my eyes. But then my mind starts racing in circles around one thought and I know what must be done; I need to get my sister's personal belongings—the things of hers that need to stay in our family. This is my one chance to get it done. I have no choice but to pull down the blanket and open my eyes. Rolling my head to the left, I'm greeted by Skyler's smiling face. My eyes focus on his gap-toothed grin.

"Mornin' Pal."

"Dacu luna shem, mo-mo," he says softly, seriously, and in a voice so high it makes me wonder where he got the helium. He obviously can't talk, but his pacing and inflections are spot on. It may be gibberish, but he delivers it with the skill of a master linguist.

"Yeah. Let's go eat some cereal."

I peek at Shane in the spare room. He's sprawled out on top of the blankets sound asleep. His cheeks are red and there's droplets of sweat on his forehead. I close the door quietly and continue down the hall. Skyler plays on a swivel chair in the dining room while I get the cereal, milk, spoons, and bowls situated.

"We need to get you a highchair."

He's sitting across from me, kneeling in the chair to reach the table and we chat about the weather, traffic, and TV shows between bites of our cereal—all of which is very surreal.

"No-no hoozie shigs."

"I agree. It's hard to sleep when it doesn't cool off at night."

"Aidee con ebby… Chinch."

Chinch? I turn into Bill Murray from Caddyshack. "Chinch bugs. Manganese. A lot of people don't even know what that is."

A few minutes later, we hear Shane using the bathroom. He joins us at the table in his underwear, scratching his belly like a little old man. His disheveled hair is an amazing feat of physics. He plops down and proceeds to grind away as if it's his regular routine. I gaze back and forth at them, feeling how vital they are to our family; they're our living links to Chris, a part of her that lives on in her absence. Shane turns the cereal box and reads the skinny side. Skyler is using his spoon to make it rain milk and Quaker Oh's on his head. I should stop him but he's having too much fun and I don't want to ruin the moment. Shane looks at his little brother then looks at me and rolls his eyes.

Must be genetic.

"You sleep, okay?" I ask.

Shane pushes the box of cereal away and looks directly into my eyes.

"Is my mom still in the hospital?"

I'm on the spot—dumbfounded and unprepared. Now is not the time to tell him the truth, but I don't want to be telling lies either.

"Yeah, she is. I'm going to Davis to check on her today," I say, fabricating an enormous lie.

"Can I go with you? I want to see her too."

"You and Skyler can come to Davis with me, but you can't see your mother… yet. I'm sorry sweetie, only grownups can see her now." *I am a lying sack of shit.* His face is blank, but his eyes are like a vice grip. "She's still unconscious," I add, unable to stop my stupid mouth. "You have to wait until she wakes up." *Why can't I shut the fuck up already?*

"Is my dad in jail?"

This kid cuts right to the chase.

"I honestly don't know."

Another lie.

"He's been in jail before," he says, with a serious expression.

"I know."

He finally unlocks his eyes from mine. My guts are in a knot from lying.

He shrugs his shoulders, which are carrying the weight of the world, and begins reading the box again. I'm clearing the table when it hits me—a funk so strong it slaps me right upside the head.

"Woah!"

"Skyler needs his diaper changed," Shane says, nonchalantly.

"And we need a case of Lysol."

One second; no smell. Next second; suffocation. This is a burn-your-eyes, breathe-through-your-mouth-and-you-can-still-kind-of-taste-it smell. It feels like an emergency situation, so I race into action and fetch the diaper bag and throw the changing blanket on the floor wanting to get this over with as quickly as possible. I position Skyler on the blanket, pull the side ripcords of his diaper, which opens like a giant evil clam shell releasing wet, green sludge and its pungent odor in its full hideous glory.

"Holy shit!" The funk permeates my pores. I want my mask and snorkel. I wonder if this stench will somehow trigger the smoke detector. "Good Lord sweet mother of Jesus, you have got to be kidding! How can so much crap come out of one baby?"

I'm gasping for air. Shane is thoroughly enjoying my genuine state of shock. The sticky goo is as thick as wall spackle. Skyler keeps moving around, making him hard to clean. Soiled wipes litter the floor. He grabs the dirty diaper I failed to place beyond his reach. As I take it back, he kicks his legs upwards sending the loaded diaper dangerously close to my face. As it plops on the floor, a glob of green tar lands on my hand.

"I've been hit!" I yell, snatching more wipes. It takes another minute to secure the new diaper.

"Wrap the dirty diaper into a ball and seal it shut," Shane says casually.

"Thanks pal. You're the best."

"You're welcome."

"Unfortunately, Sac County Disposal doesn't accept hazardous waste, so I'll have to sneak this in with the regular trash. Wait here, I'll be right back."

I march out the front door in my underwear holding the mess as far from my nearly naked body as possible. Back inside, I start scrubbing my arms like a doctor preparing for surgery, wondering how often he goes number two. *Twice, maybe three times a week?*

After the shit-show and before getting dressed, I call Kelly and tell her my plan. She agrees to watch the kids while I complete my all-important mission. Not knowing what they might need during the day, I stuff as much food, beverage, and clothing into the baby bag as I can fit.

The thought of entering the duplex repulses me, but the thought of not collecting my sister's personal things is even worse. I want her pictures, her record collection, baby books, and anything else that's meaningful. I buckle Skyler into his car seat and make sure Shane's buckled up as well. We hit the road with a sense of urgency though I'm driving extremely slow. I know I've got precious cargo on board and questionable brakes. For the first time in my life, I am the slowest and most cautious driver on the road.

The causeway between Sacramento and Davis is constructed in such a way that it creates a rhythm in your car as you cross it. Something in the hum of the road retains an echo of the past. This familiar pattern of sound and motion lulls me into thinking about the last time I saw Chris. It was at Shane's birthday party a couple of months ago. I shot some video that I haven't watched yet. Some clips come to mind; Chris putting lids on sippy cups, talking to friends, carrying Skyler on her hip. She always looks relaxed doing ten things at once. There was nothing special about my exit that day. She was busy. I wanted to get home. I didn't know it would be the last time I saw her. We barely hugged goodbye.

Sacramento's modest skyline shrinks in my rear-view mirror. The kids are perfectly quiet, content looking out the window. We can see for miles. Beyond the curvy, soaking fields of rice, Mount Diablo rises in the distance on one side, the Sutter Buttes on the other. The rhythm of the car moving forward sends me back in time again to when we attempted an honest to God intervention with Chris. Fair to say it didn't go entirely as planned.

∞   ∞   ∞

I was driving with Dad in his rental car on this very stretch of road to Davis. The fact that Dad flew out from Boston was monumental. Chris was pregnant with Shane at the time. Dad and I were on our way to meet up with Shelley in the Safeway parking lot before going to Chris's apartment. Shelley thought it was important for all of us to arrive together. She's the one who orchestrated this 'tough love' event and she did it for all the right reasons. Drug-addicted babies were headlining the news at the time. Chris had admitted to taking drugs while she was pregnant with Shane. Everyone was concerned. Early in the pregnancy, Jeff arranged for Chris to have an abortion, but they couldn't locate the free clinic in Oakland and had to reschedule. Then, on their second attempt, Jeff's truck broke down en route to the clinic—leaving me to wonder if Chris messed with his truck because *she wanted* the baby. Either way, it was enough to make one believe that Shane was simply meant to be.

Everyone agreed that an intervention was necessary, and we all wanted to help however we could. Well, almost everyone; Mare and Journey couldn't participate because their pot plants were just about ready to harvest. And Alex would have helped but couldn't take any time off work.

It seemed simple enough. Step one; confront Chris and tell her why the family is taking control of the situation. Step two; remove Chris from her toxic environment and relocate her to a safe and loving place. This was to be at Molly's house in Idaho, where Chris would have her baby. Step three; everyone lives happily ever after. It looked easy enough on TV but making it happen in real life proved to be… challenging.

Shelley told me that she was driving down from Mendocino with a friend who owned a vintage limousine. I thought it was a rather classy addition to our intervention. Dad and I were on the lookout for a 'late '50's Chrysler Crown Imperial limousine with fresh black paint'.

"There they are," I say, pointing at the vehicle that was impossible to miss.

"Wow. That's quite a car," Dad says.

Shelley introduces us to a skinny red-haired teen. He looks exactly like Chaka, the ape-boy, who spoke Pakuni on the TV show *Land of the Lost.* They share the same Cro-Magnon brow, sloping forehead, jutting underbite and horse-like teeth. His wild red hair jets out from his silly chauffeur hat. He's wearing a 1980's-era thrift store black and white checked jacket with massive shoulder pads, and on his feet are oversized red and white checkered Converse shoes. Picture a circus orangutan dressed for a music video. His name is Joaquin. Shelley calls him King for short, but I just can't. He's a little boy in an ape-man's body. The intervention is already off to a strange start.

Shelley and Joaquin follow us to Chris's apartment, which is only a few blocks away. Jeff is off at work painting apartments somewhere. Chris wasn't expecting Dad and is genuinely surprised. For the next hour, we enjoy each other's company and almost forget why we're there until Chaka-Joaquin starts pointing at his watch signaling that we had better get going. It's time to start the intervention. Dad and I look at Shelley nodding our heads; a signal that's it's time for her to speak up and say something.

"We're having a family reunion up at Mare and Journey's place! Road trip!"

Dad and I are baffled. A family reunion is no way to describe an intervention. That's like calling a mass suicide a meeting of the minds. Plus, Mare and Journey would never allow Dad to set foot on their property. We're not even allowed to mention our father around Journey. Surely Chris knows she's being bullshitted. I grab Shelley by the arm and lead her into the kitchen.

Shelley and I must have seen different TV shows on how to perform interventions. I saw an episode of Oprah called *Tough Love*. Once you get everyone in the same room, you explain to the addict that the family is stepping in to tackle the problem with the honesty and conviction to solve it. This usually happens against the person's will, and they're more or less forced to oblige. Shelley saw an episode of *Cops* in which you kidnap the victim, drive them across state lines, and pray no one witnesses or reports the felony.

"We need to be honest. We have to tell Chris the truth. She needs to know exactly why we're here. What we intend to do and why. Duh! This is all about honesty," I explain to Shelley. "Starting off with a giant lie is wrong. It's called an intervention not a road trip."

"Shut the fuck up, Tom! You're not equipped for this situation. I have way more experience with drug addiction than you. I know what to expect and how to handle withdrawals. It's going to get intense. Trust me. We need to get her ass in the car and start driving. She doesn't need to know precisely where she's going—yet. That can happen later when the time is right."

"The right time is now! Lying undermines the point of tough love. We're trying to help our sister because we love her. She needs to know that. We gotta be up front with her so she can start dealing with the plan. Step one, confrontation."

"I disagree. Everything will fall into place on the way. You'll see. What matters now is that we get her out of Davis."

"So, you're just going to keep lying to her?"

"For a while. Let me worry about that. Let's get her and her things into the limo. You and Dad can follow follow us for back up support. If we stick together, this will all work out. Okay?"

What's strange is that while Shelley and I are arguing, Chris is quietly packing for the trip. I'm pretty sure she knows we're not going to Blue Moon Ranch, but apparently, she's up for a ride. And off we went; our fuel-efficient compact rental car, following the big old black limo north on Interstate 5. Dad and I wonder what kind of baloney Shelley is feeding Chris as we pass the cut off to Mare and Journey's place. Maybe Chris has accepted this as her fate. Or maybe she's just playing along, waiting for the right moment to escape. We have no way of knowing. We stop somewhere near Redding for gas. The limo windows roll down. Smoke billows out of the car. There's time to use the restroom and buy some snacks, but no time to get an update from Shelley or hear from Chris. As soon as everyone is back in their seats, we continue driving north.

We drive for hours, past Mount Shasta, across the Oregon border, over Grants Pass and beyond. Then around 10:30 pm, we follow the limo into a Denny's parking lot somewhere near Yoncalla. The doors fly open. Chris jumps out and lights up a cigarette. I try talking to Shelley, but she hustles inside saying she has to pee. Dad and Chaka-Joaquin follow her into the restaurant, leaving Chris and I behind. She takes a puff off her cigarette and blows the smoke directly into my face.

"This isn't going to work."

"What do you mean?"

"Your stupid plan. I don't know where Shelley thinks she's taking me, but the only place I'm going is home. I'm not riding in the limo anymore. After we eat you and Dad can drive me back to Davis. I'm done. I'm tired. End of story."

At this point, I have no choice but to tell Chris the truth and spill my guts. I begin to do what we should have done in the first place and explain to her that this is a family intervention and that it's for her own good—and for the good of her baby.

"We believe you'll be better off out of Davis, away from Jeff, with Molly and her family. Yes, we're taking extreme measures, but only because we love you so much. You need our help right now. Even if you don't think you do." She listens patiently and takes another drag off her cigarette before speaking.

"Well, I appreciate everyone's concern but it's not necessary and I'm not going all the way to Molly's house to have my baby under any circumstances. No offence, Tom, but you, Dad and Shelley can take your tough-love-intervention plan and shove it up your asses. I'm exhausted. Let's go inside, eat a good meal, have a visit and be civil. Then I'm going back to Davis; either with you and Dad, or with Shelley and Joaquin. Or I'll fucking hitchhike! There's no changing my mind. Where I have my baby is my decision, and I'm not having my baby in Idaho."

Chris has never expressed herself more clearly or with such conviction. I know there's nothing I can say that will make her change her mind. For now, giving it some rest and eating is the only logical option. Maybe we can broach the subject later with calmer minds. She crushes out her cigarette with her foot, and we go inside, looking like a nice couple about to have a baby. Think of this exchange as, *Act One*.

Act Two: Stepping into that Denny's is like freefalling into a bizarre dream. Despite the hour, it's bustling with truckers and lumberjacks. Immediately, I notice at least three people in the room who have less than all their fingers, but it's our group that's standing out like a sore thumb. I'm thinking, *Sawmill Accident Survivor convention in town?* We're road weary and emotionally drained; our sallow expressions exaggerated by the fluorescent lights. We sit at two tables pushed together in the middle of the room, as if on stage, surrounded by people in booths who can't take their eyes off us. Tensions are high. None of us are talking. When the food arrives, we eat in silence.

After a few minutes, Dad ceremoniously clears his throat, wipes his chin, and says, "I think now would be a good time for us to have a rational conversation about what's going on. Chris, you're my daughter, and I love you…"

He's interrupted by the crash of Shelley's fists hitting the table.

"Dad! No!"

Dad turns his attention to Shelley as she chucks her salad directly at him. It happens in slow motion; the expression on her face, the bowl of salad leaving her hand, flipping in the air, the contents flying horizontally across the table. Time snaps back to normal when everything hits his chest in a creamy explosion of Ranch dressing.

"Well, that was unnecessary," Dad says as calm and cool as the cucumber slice sliding slowly down his shirt.

I'm shocked, jump up and yell at Shelley, "What the fuck is wrong with you?"

"Fuck off!" She yells. Just then, Chaka-Joaquin stands up and throws water in my face.

"What the fuck is wrong with YOU?" I yell at him.

I reach across the table and grab his shirt by the collar. He slips away snagging a butter knife off the table. We lock eyes. He's tossing the knife back and forth between his hands, like we're about to rumble. Our four-fingered waitress marches to our table.

"Hey folks! Take it outside! Right now!"

Everyone, except Chris, heads for the door. We're cussing at each other all the way out. Shelley's pissed because we're not following her plan. I'm pissed at Shelley for what she did to Dad. Chaka-Joaquin is pissed at me because he wants to protect Shelley—also because he had to cough up his knife to our waitress. Dad is angry at all of us for losing control. Once outside, we scream at each other even louder until our tempers reside and calmer minds return. Then we begin to laugh at ourselves, apologize to each other and agree to go back inside to finish our meal without talking about the situation until later.

Act Three: We re-enter the restaurant. All eyes are upon us, and several people point—though not with the finger you'd expect. All the knives have been removed from our table. Shelley orders another salad. "I promise not to throw it this time," she says, smiling politely. We chuckle pleasantly, perfectly civilized and composed. Dad cleans himself up the best he can in the restroom and returns to the table. Chris is unusually quiet. She's the only one almost done with her food. Everything is reasonably normal for the next few minutes and the people at the other tables go back to grunting, talking, and enjoying their food.

"We're officially in the middle of nowhere," I say, just to lighten the mood.

Chris looks up and says, "I'm not going any farther."

Shelley loses it again, this time throwing the remainder of her Eggs Over My Hammy sandwich at me. Before I can respond to her assault, I am being doused with Chaka-Joaquin's ice-cold Coke.

"You   mother-fucking-beverage-throwing-ape-boy!   I'm gonna kick your ass!" I yell at him fully enraged. His eyes dart back and forth under his Cro-Magnon brow. He grabs a spoon off the table, exchanges it for a fork, then crouches, ready to fight.

"That's it! Enough! Get out right now!" Shouts our waitress. This time, several large customers offer assistance in seeing us out. Dad throws a wad of bills on the counter where the cash register is. We're still yelling obscenities all the way to the door. Chris is still inside. We realize we have no precious cargo.

Act Four: Chris finally emerges and waddles confidently down the walkway in front of the restaurant. Shelley lures Chris back in the limo by promising her that they'll go straight to the nearest hotel for the night, and then drive her home in the morning. Shelley orders Dad and I to leave immediately.

"Just go. That's the best thing you can do. You're not helping anymore. I can handle this."

"Are you really taking her home in the morning or are you still trying to get her to Molly's?"

"Well, that's pretty much up to me now, isn't it?"

"We can get a room too. Maybe that's the best plan. Tomorrow we can start over. We'll talk to Chris and do this right."

"You're weak and stupid. She'll be going through withdrawals by then. I'll get her to Molly's house. That's all that matters. This is real life, brother, not some TV show."

"I have the windows down you idiots. I can hear every word you're saying," snaps Chris, from inside the car. I throw my arms up in frustration.

"She knows you're still fucking with her."

"That's my problem not yours. Now go!"

Dad and I are too exhausted by the miles and drama to put up much of a fight. Bewildered and spent, we watch them disappear into the night, wondering about the type of adventure they're in for. I'm worried; Chris is pregnant and determined to get home; Shelley is in full commando mode and Chaka-Joaquin the ape-boy, is all cranked up on who knows what, so he can drive straight to Idaho without falling asleep.

They actually make it to Molly's house the following afternoon. Apparently, Chris had mind-fucked Shelley and Chaka-Joaquin into a state of paranoia by telling them she called the police from a pay phone in Washington, and that they were being tracked. The three of them arrived like an atomic bomb. The scene they caused minutes after reaching Molly's place was so over-the-top intense and out-of-control crazy, that Molly put her kids in the basement for protection. Molly's husband, Kurt, was at a cancer treatment facility in Colorado. Molly called a drug rehabilitation center, and they told her to bring Chris in immediately, but there was no way to make that happen during the shit storm of chaos. More bad craziness spread through the house until Molly couldn't take it anymore and threw everyone out. They were there for twenty minutes, which was long enough to make a lifelong impression on Molly's kids. Then Shelley and Chaka-Joaquin got back in the limo and drove Chris home.

End Scene. Fade to black. And that's where our sad little play ends.

Five years later, Shelley still blames the failure on me and Dad for deserting her in Oregon. She has no recollection of ordering us to leave. It doesn't matter. The whole thing was a fiasco. Our intentions were honorable, but our execution was horrible.

Everyone was both excited and deeply concerned about the baby's health when Chris went into labor. Mare and Journey drove down, and I met them at the hospital in Woodland. Once her contractions became intense, Chris had everyone leave the room except Mom. Her screaming was tortuous. Fortunately, the baby came quickly. Shane was born on May 7th, 1991. He was big and beautiful and had all the right parts in all the right numbers. There was something special about him the moment he came into this world, and I just *knew* he was a perfectly normal, healthy baby boy.

"Time will tell if he has a learnin' disorder or brain damage," Journey said, like a Danny Downer, which almost ruined the moment. Mare thanked the universe for blessing Chris with a beautiful child of her own, something she wanted more than anything in the world. Right after Shane was whisked away to be cleaned up, Chris asked the nurse if she could go outside for a cigarette. Not only did the nurse agree, but she also wheeled her out and lit one up as well. Why do so many people in healthcare smoke?

Jeff already has two kids; Ryan and Rachel from an ex-girlfriend. He wasn't nearly as awe-struck as we were. This was a very big deal for our family and Mare seized the moment to make an important point.

"Listen Jeff, you're officially part of our family now and we welcome you. We love you. Chris, you have the baby you always wanted. We know you'll love and take good care of this precious soul. Now's the time for both of you to come together and make a change. It's time to clean up your act and live relatively drug-free. Give up the heavy shit. A little pot, maybe shrooms, and other natural hallucinogens, hash—and some booze now and then, is all you really need. Be healthy. Be happy. Let Shane be your reminder to get and stay clean. Do it for your child."

Of course, Chris and Jeff proceed to make sincere, heartfelt promises and we believed every word they said. For a while, things actually did get better. Jeff found steady work. They moved into a nicer apartment. They stopped asking to borrow money. We stayed in touch more, over the phone and with more regular visits. I loved my nephew and loved listening to Chris gush about his latest accomplishments.

Then it happened again. Jeff beat the shit out of Chris, and I found myself back at the hospital visiting her wondering how many other times she was beaten or hospitalized without anyone in her family knowing? I enter the room feeling sick to my stomach. I notice her hair right away. Her long brown, beautiful wavy hair is gone.

"You cut your hair."

"Yeah. Jeff didn't like it long anymore, so I cut it off. I kind of wanted to try something different anyway."

Bullshit! He wanted you to cut your hair, so you'd be less attractive to other men.

"It looks good."

I cannot describe how uncomfortable, helpless, and sad I felt seeing my sister battered and bruised, or how much hate I felt towards Jeff for doing this to someone who was so much smaller and so undeserving of his violence. Invariably, she felt it was her fault, that Jeff's violence was somehow justified. The pattern of abuse left me empty and unable to understand how or why her brain would think this way.

"I got busted hanging out with some old friends from high school. One of his friends saw me at the restaurant and told Jeff he saw me out having a good time. I didn't want to tell Jeff; I knew he'd get mad, so I lied and that just made him even madder. He hit me a few times and later we made up. I shouldn't have lied. He wouldn't have been so mad if I didn't lie to him. It really was my fault."

With bruised cheeks, another split lip, and swollen eyes, she tells me she's taking him back. "In a way, this will bring us closer. We really communicated on a deeper level and worked it all out. I know it will never happen again. We're better than ever now," she forces a painful smile. "I learned a lesson—the hard way." She says, laughing at herself, but I'm unable to join her.

"Come live with me again," I begged. "You owe it to Shane to get out of there, right?" I have tears in my eyes. But Jeff had broken her spirit, her soul. She acted as if this was the life she deserved. There's no reasoning with her, no rescuing her. Seeing someone you love slowly slip away is both heartbreaking and incredibly frustrating.

I never knew the specifics of their drug use. It wasn't something we discussed openly; we sort of tiptoed around it. When I did bring it up, she would belittle their consumption, claiming it was just recreational and no big deal. They did crank and crack, though I never understood the difference. She jokingly referred to it as 'poor man's cocaine.' I liked to believe they only did it once a month, on a Friday night, to let off steam. I was just fooling myself. It was a depressing subject, so I tried not to think about it.

When Chris announced that she was pregnant again, nobody was exactly overwhelmed with joy. Despite her excitement, I was filled with dread knowing that with another child in the house, things were likely to get worse not better. Still, there was that chance that another child might be the wake-up call Chris so desperately needed.

Skyler was born on January 18th, 1995. Again, Mare and Journey drove down in the bus, and we converged at the hospital in Woodland. Mare gave Chris and Jeff the same clean-up-your-act-speech she knows so well. Again, they promised that their drug use was over, a thing of the past. Again, we believed what they said because it was easier than accepting the truth. Again, we were all rooting for them. And again, they weren't strong enough to quit and the violence tethered to Jeff's drug abuse continued.

∞   ∞   ∞

We're off the causeway—back on smooth pavement, which snaps me back to the present. I take the Covell Boulevard exit, drop the kids off with Kelly, drive to my sister's duplex and park behind a dented-up pickup that I assume belongs to Jeff's dad. There are no cop cars on the street, no yellow police tape to indicate a crime scene. There's nothing out of the ordinary at all. If anything, it's impossibly normal…

Were the police even here?

Being here is making me anxious but I'm determined to get the job done. Inhaling through my nose, exhaling with pursed lips, I take two deep breaths before getting out of the car. I take another deep breath before knocking on the door. No one answers, but I can hear the TV blaring inside. I knock again, louder and wait, then knock even louder and wait some more. Nothing. I try the door. It's unlocked. I open it slowly and step inside. It was so bright outside and so dark inside, that it takes a moment for my eyes to adjust. Then, an eerie shadow on the other side of the room materializes into the form of a man holding a large bottle of beer. He's standing so perfectly still, frozen in time like a statue.

"Hey. I guess you didn't hear me knocking," I say to the silhouette. He lifts the beer to his lips, takes a drink while keeping his eyes on me. "I'm Tom, Chris's brother."

I glance around the room. The walls are void of all pictures. He pokes his tongue around his mouth and rubs his murky brown eyes with the back of his hand. He grunts but doesn't offer his name or extend his hand. I open the door to let more light in. He coughs, takes another slug of beer and steps toward me.

"Where's the Honda?" he says. His voice is laced with rust and decay.

"You mean my sister's car? It's out front. I drove it here. Kelly picked it up for me yesterday because I need a car I can fit the kids into."

"Kelly shouldn't have done that. That car's registered to Jeff."

"Okay. But I know for a fact that my dad bought that car for Chris. It's her car."

He clears his throat. "Check the registration. It's in Jeff's name."

"So what? It doesn't matter."

"You and him can work that out later." His pallid skin is aged from years of smoking and drinking. The closer I get to him, the meaner he looks. "I'm here to get my sister's things."

"Figured you might. I packed it for you," he growls. "Check the hall."

I look down the hall expecting to see a sizable collection of my sister's belongings but there's only a couple of half empty trash bags. *Trash bags? What a fucking asshole! My sister practically left this place in a body bag.* I'm furious, but I also need to hear his side of the story. *If I become confrontational, he won't talk.* I swallow my anger and steady myself.

"What happened yesterday?" My voice is calm.

"Which part?"

"The part about my sister." *You fucking animal!*

"Oh Christ… how would I know?" he sputters. "Do I look like a doctor? All I know is that Chris came home from her job about three hours late, so I had to babysit the kids. She was drunk and reeked of booze when she got here. Completely wasted—slurring her words. She hit her head on the wall on her way to the floor. She passed out and Jeff took care of her. He was real sweet—put her to bed and took care of the kids. I just went to bed."

"She hit her head on the wall falling down?"

"That's what I said."

"Did you see her again that night?"

"No. Like I said, I went to bed."

"Then what?"

"I fell asleep."

"And in the morning…?"

"I got up early and read the paper. Chris was up too. Of course she wasn't feeling good—bad hangover. She asked if I'd take Shane to school. I said no problem. I don't mind helping out."

"So, you took Shane to school. What time was that?'

"Not sure. Sometime around eight I guess."

"Then what?"

"When I got back, Chris was passed out again. Jeff was working on her. He looked so sad. I told him to call 911."

"Why? Was she bleeding or something?"

"No. No. No. Just very tired and sick. She wasn't breathing normal. We kept her calm and comfortable until the medics came."

"Really?"

"Oh yea. They got here fast and started working on her right away. They put her in the ambulance and went to the hospital. Jeff rode with her. He's heartbroken that she's gone. He loves her, you know. He has feelings too."

"So do her children."

"Look, my boy did nothing wrong. You'll see. The police will sort it out. Jeff didn't kill her like you think he did."

"I didn't say he did. But he does have a history of beating her up. There was a big fight here about a month ago. The police came to break it up. Were you here for that? Jeff was issued a restraining order."

"I must have missed that."

"He's obviously a suspect."

"No, Jeff tried to help her. We both tried to help her. She overdosed on something. Or got alcohol poisoning. That's the truth. I'll take that to my grave."

"How exactly did you help her?"

"By waking her up in the middle of the night to help her use the bathroom and change clothes. Later Jeff noticed she was struggling to breathe. He gave her mouth-to-mouth and CPR and finally woke her up with ice water. Then she was fine. She told him she was feeling better, just tired and wanted to go back to bed."

"And you helped Jeff do all this?"

"No. I was in bed for the night, and I sleep like a rock."

"Of course, you do. Who called 911?"

"Jeff did. The medics got here, got her settled into the ambulance and Jeff rode with her. He was real sad. I stayed behind with Skyler. Later, Jeff called me from the hospital, and I knew it was bad news. That was it. Jeff said the docs tried everything they could."

"He might have done more harm trying to revive her on his own. Does he even know CPR? If someone is barely breathing, you don't wait for hours, you call 911. You wasted precious time. You took too long calling for help." I'm losing my temper. "Shane saw some really bad shit go down that night."

"There was nothing to see."

"Tell that to Shane." Somehow, his eyes get even meaner. I have to look away and catch my breath before continuing. "Okay. What happened after Jeff called you from the hospital?"

"Nothing. He told me the police wanted to keep him for voluntary questioning. It's standard procedure. He asked me to call Kelly and have her pick up the kids."

"Did the police want to question you?

"They came over in the afternoon and we talked. I told them what happened. When they were done with me, I just got out of their way and read the paper in my truck out front so they could do their job. That's everything."

"How long have you been living here?"

"What difference does that make? Look, this is just as hard for me and Jeff as it is for you. He loved Chris. He really did."

"Right. He loved her to death."

He lifts a crooked finger in my face and is about to say something but changes his mind. Instead, he just tries to look sorry but fails. I take another breath looking down the hall at the trash bags.

"So what's going on now? Have you heard from the police? Do they still have Jeff?"

"I bet they're about done. I'll call and check soon." He takes a big swig of beer, walks through the kitchen, through the sliding glass door and outside to the patio. He digs his lighter and cigarettes out of his pocket and lights up.

His only concern is for his son. There is not a hint of remorse for what happened to Chris.

I shake my head and go down the hall to look inside one of the bags. It's mostly clothes. I find a small box with some old Christmas cards and letters inside. There's a worn white vinyl purse, with a candle stub, a pair of scissors, and a couple of busted cassettes spilling their skinny brown guts inside. This isn't what I'm looking for.

The other bag is full of Shane and Skyler's stuff. There are some clothes, a few diapers, shoes, and a tackle box full of toys; two metal cars and a bunch of McDonald's Happy Meal plastic junk. It's about the saddest thing I've ever seen—a toy box filled with sorrow. This also isn't what I'm looking for.

Our mother, Mare had kindly divided up our family photos, school pictures, and the other random shots taken over the years and gave each of us a couple stacks bound with rubber bands during one of her downsizing phases as she prepared to live in the bus–because, 'Gypsies don't rent storage units.' What I'm looking for are my sister's photo albums and the old black-and-whites that each of us have. This is the first thing on my mental list. *I have to find Chris's pictures. Now that she's gone, these are what matter most to the rest of us.*

The bedroom door is closed. I don't want to enter but have to and turn the knob. I feel sick. Bad vibes. Something terrible happened here. There are damp areas on the walls and places where the texture has been scrubbed smooth. *To remove my sister's blood.* I can almost hear her screaming. The carpet is wet. The bedding is hanging over the fence in the backyard. The pictures they had are gone. The dresser and night table are bare. None of the normal clutter that comes with life is anywhere. Even the worst cop could tell this room, this entire apartment has been tampered with.

Jeff, or more likely, Jeff and his father, did their best to sterilize the room. I'm spinning. I need to get the fuck out. *Focus. Find her stuff.* I look in the closet and dresser drawers but see nothing. *Where is her make-up, jewelry, girly soaps and lotions? Where is her jacket, her shoes and her sunglasses? Where is her real purse, her checkbook, her record collection and driver's license?* I go into the bathroom in hopes of finding her hairbrush, a toothbrush, something, anything of hers, but there's nothing—except for a stack of Jeff's dirty magazines under the sink. I look everywhere and find nothing. As I am walking out, Jeff's dad walks in.

"Where's the rest of her stuff?"

"I have a few more things in the kitchen. Come on. I'll help you load up."

He hands me a manila envelope that includes my sister's driver's license, some bill stubs, letters from Welfare, Shane's and Skyler's birth certificates and other papers.

"I want her photo albums. I want the picture that was hanging right there of Chris with her sisters and our father. I want the rest of her things! Now!"

"I don't know what's hers and what's Jeff's. And I've never seen any photo albums in the house."

"Look. You shouldn't have touched any of my sister's stuff. Her personal items belong to her family. They're worthless to you, but they mean the world to us. Do the right thing. Please!"

"Well, Jeff is her family, too, and when he gets back, he might know where she keeps more stuff."

In desperation, I bend down and look under the couch. Then I go into the kitchen to see if there's anything in or above the cupboards.

"There's nothing else. I already told you." He wants me to leave. He follows me to the laundry room that has a door leading to the garage. It's locked. I look at him, asking with my eyes to open the door.

"Bring it up with Jeff later," he says. I can smell his sour breath.

There is no later.

"Please open the garage door," I say, trying to sound as calm as possible.

"No can do. You are more than welcome to come back later and bring it up with Jeff. This isn't your house. You should go now. I got things to do."

"This isn't your house either."

"I'll tell Jeff you came by. So long now."

I walk away angry, overwhelmed, and barely in control. I want to slug this wretched old man in the face. I want to kill Jeff for what he's done. He deserves to feel what he did to my sister—the fear, the helplessness, the complete lack of mercy. I take the trash bags and the envelope to the car completely frustrated for failing my mission.

Kelly can tell I am not happy when I pick up the boys. I skip the details and tell her that I wasn't able to find everything I was looking for. She helps me buckle the kids into the car. I drive home feeling disheartened and totally defeated. It takes a long time for my anger to subside, and when it does, I begin to wonder who the first family member will be to arrive.

Fourth

July 4th, 1996

My little brother Alex is the first to arrive. He goes by 'Al' now. He shortened his name when he joined the Army four years ago. He was twenty-six at the time, as old as you can be and still enlist. The fact that he changed his name wasn't surprising news in our family. Growing up, at her request, we could no longer call our own mother 'Mom' and had to address her by her name, Marilyn. And as soon as we got used to that, she changed her handle to 'Mare'. What surprised us was that he volunteered to join the Army. Growing up, Alex was our resident animal lover, a gentle pacifist, a pot-smoking hippie-kid. He had a glow in the dark shirt that he was too scared to observe in the dark. He didn't play sports or play rough; he mostly played with four-legged animals. He generally preferred the company of our pets to his friends and family. Sometimes he'd lie on the floor, letting the dog or cat lick the inside of his mouth, nose, and ears for hours, which was pretty disgusting.

Growing up, he was drawn to all the TV shows about animals. He stumbled upon a PBS documentary about the baby-seal-clubbers; brutes slaughtering seal pups in the name of fur. It made him miserable and yet he couldn't look away. He wouldn't let me change the channel or come outside with me. I left him crying silently in front of the TV. At one point or another, he came home with dogs, cats, lizards, snakes, baby birds and an occasional insect, like a praying mantis, a colorful moth, or a butterfly. The Army was looking for a lean mean killing machine. What they got instead was a gentle giant—a mellow fellow with an inherent love for all living things.

About seven minutes into boot camp, he wanted out, but it's not that easy. He was 'counseled' into staying on and managed to graduate. His soft heart was set on being stationed in Germany, at a picturesque military outpost in the country, taking leaves to explore Europe's animals accompanied by beautiful Fräuleins. He ended up in Fort Hood, Texas.

Mare stayed in touch with him more than the rest of us, which was nice until her letters became an issue. Alex, I mean Al, said she was subtle at first; she'd sketch a heart or a peace sign on the back of the envelope. Then her embellishments became more colorful and controversial. Eventually the envelopes became her canvas to make anti-military statements about our government. She drew tanks with peace signs, pot leaves, and flowers coming out of the turrets. She drew the nuclear explosion mushroom cloud, added a rainbow over the top and the words, *Make Love not War*. Every letter arrived stamped with first-class humiliation. Al was perfectly clear. He reminded Mare that her letters are opened and read by his superiors before they're delivered. Her doodles and anti-government statements caused a stir. People started calling him names like, Flower-Power-Boy, Star Child, and Junior Moonbeam.

My little brother begged her to stop but of course she didn't because these declarations weren't directed at him; they were part of her agenda with *The Man*. Mare got off on it. He laughs about it now, but at the time he was mad as hell, wondering how our mother could be so insensitive. Their relationship migrated to the telephone. He called her once a month from a phone booth far from the base—one he was sure wasn't tapped.

I think my brother was just looking for a fresh start. After high school, he and a buddy formed a punk band called *Critic Eyes*. They became well known on the central coast then moved to LA in hopes of a record deal. Their biggest gig was opening for *Black Flag* at a music festival in front of thousands of people. When the band fizzled out, he tried drumming with other groups, but nothing ever came of it. His rock-star days were behind him, along with the tours, the groupies and heavy partying. It must have been hard to let it all go. He began looking for something new, something that would change his life—so he wouldn't have to. Joining the Army was the complete opposite of joining a band. He had nothing to lose; well, except for the life he knew, the name he grew up with, most of his freedom and nearly all his hair.

Soon after enlisting, he sent everyone in the family a wallet-sized photo of himself in uniform. The look on his face is not one of pride or patriotism. I would describe it more as tepid apprehension. His nervous grin and the shell-shocked expression in his eyes seem to be asking—'What the hell did I do?' He looks like he's about to jump up and run out of the photo. For the next three years, he lived what I imagine to be, an incredibly banal existence in and around Abrams M1-A1 tanks. With practice, focus and determination, he became an expert armory loader—maybe one of the best ever. Unfortunately, there's very little demand for this particular skill in the civilian world.

Sometimes our first thoughts are second thoughts .

He was elated to get out. I picked him up at the airport; he was in uniform, sporting a fresh crew cut. That's how they send soldiers back into society, looking as out of place as possible. We drove up to Mare and Journey's for Christmas. He made me laugh the whole way telling me his stories, imitating his commanders and the characters he lived with. When we got to Blue Moon Ranch, he smoked joint after joint as if making up for lost time. I left him there and returned to my little world. After a month of consuming their weed, Mare and Journey sent him home to Morro Bay. He got his old job back at The Cliffs Hotel parking cars and started surfing again. The Army is helping pay for school. He's taking a smattering of unrelated classes like pottery and German at Cuesta Community College, which eventually will earn him an associate's degree in fifteen to twenty years.

I study his face as he parks in my driveway. My little brother is a good man—sensitive, generous, and funny. He's also book-smart like his father. He has an inquisitive mind that wanders easily from topic to topic. His vocabulary is astounding. He can pretty much read something once and remember it forever, a skill that makes me writhe with envy. He has a firm grasp on just about everything, except himself. The Army didn't help him, but it didn't ruin him either. Fortunately, he's still the same person, a little lost, a little shy, and a little shithead who's funny as hell. I love him just the way he is. While he was serving, he saved enough money to buy his Toyota pickup—one with only 287,000 miles on it.

He takes out the key and holds it up for me to see.

"She'll keep running for another minute or two," he says, chuckling.

"Your hair is still so short. Why don't you grow it out?"

"I like it this way," he says, getting out of the truck, rubbing his head. "I don't worry about lice."

We laugh and hug. Al is tall like his father and as solid as a Greek pillar. We're happy to see each other but neither one of us can conceal our pain. He hoists a giant duffel bag from the back of his truck.

"Bring enough stuff?" I ask, sarcastically.

"Be prepared."

"There's no preparing for something like this."

"You're right about that, Bro."

We go inside and play with Shane and Skyler for a while. Then we go out back to smoke and I tell him about my trip to Davis, how strange it was being in the duplex and what an asshole Jeff's father was. After listening carefully to my account of the last twenty-four hours, he starts to hypothesize.

"It sounds like Jeff and his dad didn't call 911 until they were good and ready. They had time to tamper with the scene. Not just that night, but the next morning too. Jeff's dad stayed behind when the ambulance went to the hospital, even more time to cover their tracks. If Chris had marks on her, that's a red flag signaling suspicious circumstances. That's enough to declare it a crime scene. It sounds like the paramedics botched it."

"The police sure took their time getting to the duplex," I say. "And they didn't stay long once they got there."

"We need to see how it's written up in the papers and keep an eye on the news. There's this street-trick lowlifes do when they want to throw off the police. You can force drugs into the deceased making it look like an overdose. These are easy open and shut cases, just another junkie who went too far and crossed the line. Who knows? They might have done something like this to Chris."

"Jeff might have been under a restraining order at the time of her death."

"All the more reason for him to get rid of any evidence. And another thing," Al says, taking a drag off his cigarette, "when a body dies it releases everything inside. In other words, Chris soiled herself. I want to know if they changed her clothes before calling 911. We need to know the exact time of death."

He asks for a pen and paper. "We should keep track of what all parties are saying."

"Jeff's dad mentioned that Chris's clothes were changed that night."

"That's suspicious."

"I think in the end, justice will prevail. I still have faith in our legal system," I say.

"Don't count on it," he says. "So far, it sounds like the authorities haven't done one thing right."

Mare, Journey and Shelley are the next to arrive in the faded yellow Chevy Nova. I still have to get used to the idea that the yellow bus is no longer in our family. A few months ago, Mare and Journey traded the bus for the Nova, an electric guitar, and a killer batch of pot-oil infused brownies. I got the news during a phone call, and it bummed me out because the bus had been in our family for almost twenty-five years. It was our mascot, stuffed with memories—not all good, not all bad— but all ours. And now, with no warning, it's gone forever.

Mare looks better than I expected. She hasn't been crying recently. Shelley, on the other hand, is a hot mess. She's in pajamas and has incredible bed head. When I hug her, she feels limp and spongy. She excuses herself, wipes her eyes and disappears to the back of the house. Journey is a couple of years younger than my mother but looks at least ten years older. Today he looks exceptionally tired. We spend some time with the kids trying to act light and happy beneath the weight of our sad reunion.

Later in the day, Al volunteers to take the Nova to the airport to pick up Molly and her kids, Ali, Willie, and Joey. Under normal conditions, I'd be ecstatic to see my sister. Today, I'm wondering how she's holding up. The Molly I want to see is the one in my mind's eye; radiant, smiling, and cheerful. The Molly who walks through the front door is drained, defeated, and lost. There's a limit to how many deaths in the family a person can endure especially when they're back-to-back. It's easy to see the pain she's holding back in her eyes. I'm grateful she's here. We need her and she needs us, and it's all too clear she's going through hell.

"Who are these enormous kids?" I say, hugging her children. "I guess that's what happens when I only get to see you every few years. Do I look any taller?" They laugh politely. Ali is thirteen now and looks a lot like Shelley, Willie is ten, and Joey is seven. Molly's great at sharing pictures but seeing them in person really makes you notice how fast they're growing up. Willie and Joey take Shane and Skyler into the backyard. Ali is content to hang with the adults. As I'm helping Molly bring in their luggage she asks if they can all share a room.

"We've been sleeping in the same room since Kurt died and it's really helping."

Her words leave me speechless. I move Shane's bedroll to my room and give her the guest room. Then I hear Monica's Jeep skid to a stop out front. She charges into the house wearing a neon-pink bikini top and cutoff shorts, holding two 12-packs of Coors Light under her muscular arms with one thing in mind—partying.

"Everyone, this is my roommate, Monica. Monica, this is everyone."

"Happy fucking Fourth of July!" she shouts, smiling at all the faces in the room.

Monica makes sure we all have beers as Mare goes into her full joint-rolling mode. Shelley comes out of her shell and joins the party. After all, it is the Fourth of July—celebration time. Never mind that there's been a death in the family. Drugs and alcohol are great for numbing the pain. Besides, we always party when we're together; why should this time be any different? It feels borderline inappropriate, and yet I reluctantly join in the festivities. As soon as we finish the last beer, Monica starts hustling one of us to blow into her breathalyzer. Ali takes the bait and Monica takes off in her Jeep to start another party someplace else.

In the evening, as it's getting darker, we bring our fireworks to the curb. I'm holding Skyler in my arms at a safe distance, while Al and Journey coach Shane and Molly's boys on how to light the fuses. It's a hollow celebration. I used to love everything about the Fourth of July, from the sulfuric smell of gunpowder to the sweet taste of watermelon. Now the whole thing feels like a colossal waste of time. It's just a pointless, loud, and dangerous ritual that scares the shit out of dogs. And for what? So, we can celebrate something that, according to history, didn't even happen on this date? I'll never feel the same about the Fourth again.

Once it gets dark, Molly lovingly puts Shane and Skyler to bed in my room. In the back of my mind, I'm hoping her maternal instincts will kick in, so she'll want to adopt them. She's a fantastic mother. But now's not the time to be thinking ahead; it's party time. We drink. We smoke. We drink and smoke some more. It's actually very sad how hard we're trying to get wasted to forget the pain. We're pathetic.

Journey's tongue starts flapping. "When Jeff goes to prison, all I'z got ta do is pick up da phone, ta get him killed. I got connections in da big house, you know," he says out of the blue, to no one in particular.

Al bites his tongue to keep from laughing. I make a mental note to laugh later. Ali giggles. I catch Molly rolling her eyes. Shelley looks at Journey seriously. Mare nods her head in mindless agreement to everything he says, no matter how lame.

I'm stoned and let myself drift back in time to 1977 when Mare enrolled at UC Davis as a forty-one-year-old freshman. That's when and where she met Journey. Only he wasn't Journey then. His transformation hadn't taken place yet...

∞   ∞   ∞

"This is David. David Leader. These are my kids. Well, most of them. I mean they're all my kids. One of them moved out.

She's not here right now," my mother gushes like a drunk cheerleader introducing the stranger she found at school to us. "What's far out about David is that he's a full-blooded Creek Indian who grew up in Oklahoma."

"Nice ta meecha," David says, about as insincerely as humanly possible. He didn't even glance up to look us in the eye.

"David's studying to be a veterinarian. We have a class together. We're going to study here tonight."

Study? Oh, really…

We studied him. At the time, Charlie was essentially living with us, but he also had a room on A Street and spent some nights there. Mare must have made sure he wasn't around that night because we woke up to find David sitting in our breakfast nook drinking coffee wearing tighty-whities. I closed my eyes. I rarely pray but when I do, I really mean it.

God, please let this be one of my mother's one-night stands.

And just like that, Charlie was out, and David was in. I felt crushed and so did my siblings because we *LOVE* Charlie, and he *LOVES* us. I know my mother loves him too. But not enough. She likes that he's crazy in love with her. She likes that he can make all of us laugh. She likes the fact that her children adore him. But her love for Charlie is based on convenience, which must suck like shit if you're Charlie.

David is so clean-cut he simply doesn't look like my mother's type. He's not much of a talker and when he does speak, he sounds like a redneck, which is the opposite of what my mother likes. Nevertheless, we start seeing much less of Charlie and much more of David. Then my mother set out to change him into her kind of man.

"I'm taking David on a vision quest," Mare announces as if it's a common thing study mates do.

"Where to?" asks Molly.

"The coast," Mare says with authority pointing west.

Molly, Chris, Alex, and I watch them pack the bus. We wave goodbye as they back down the driveway and disappear down the street. Every time a new man drives the bus, I feel like I'm going to puke. A couple of days later they're back.

"What an amazing trip!" Mare says. "We had a life-changing experience!" Translation: *We took some heavy drugs.* "It started as a nature walk. And it turned into raven talk. We had a close encounter with one. Well, he did. I could tell he was tripping in a wonderfully deep trance. His breathing became super slow. That big black bird just hung out on his shoulder for almost an hour. Then it started pecking at his ear and David opened his eyes and we watched it hop to the ground before flying away. A major mind-blowing experience, right?"

"I guess so," I say shrugging my shoulders.

"When I got close to his eyes, they seemed different. Something changed," Mare says.

"Dat's right," David says.

"That night, I ceremoniously pierced David's right ear and put one of my earrings into the hole. That's where it must stay forever. Then I looked into his eyes that were still strangely different and asked him what his true name was."

"He paused, blinked slowly and said, 'Journey.'"

There are a few seconds of silence. I wasn't expecting a new middle or last name. Journey is like 'Cher'. One name is enough. We were all just trying to digest what we were hearing, and it felt like we had eaten rocks.

"Wow," I manage to say.

"We both understood. He never really *was* David. He's always been Journey. We just needed to unlock his *true* spirit to reveal his *true* name."

At this point, I remember thinking, *My mother has infected him. Her insanity is contagious.*

"Well sure," I say, trying not to laugh because this is funny shit to a sixteen-year-old.

"Life's a Journey," Journey says.

"Journey is life," my mother adds.

They sound as corny as a Hallmark card designed for hippies.

Next there's a hostile takeover of our furniture. Mare dumps our funky velvet couch and trippy coffee table for his 1970's bad-taste floral couch and glass lamps right out of a Levitz commercial. For some reason I'm convinced his stuff smells like Oklahoma, which I've never been to, but would be willing to bet, stinks.

They've lived all over the place after Davis. Fort Bragg, Little River, Casper, Albion and Westport on the northern coast. They tried living in Mulegé in Baja California but couldn't get along with the locals or the tourists, plus there was no way to grow weed. They moved to Oklahoma and tried growing it there, but Journey's parents would have none of it. That was a short trip. They moved back to California settling in Ocean Beach outside of San Diego so Journey could go back to work welding. To get on his health plan, Mare needed to marry him so they 'tie-dyed' the knot five years after the vision quest.

This was no normal wedding. No one was invited except maybe a waitress as a witness. They chose to get married on Halloween. The event took place at the San Diego Courthouse. The entire staff was in full costume. The judge dressed up like a clown and had a giant tarantula on his polka dot tie. The city clerk was Wonder Woman. Mare and Journey wore clothes they bought at Goodwill. Their Halloween/wedding costumes made them look like normal people, which was quite a change.

What are you going to be for Halloween this year?

A member of society.

Cool.

Journey's suit was three sizes too small, and Mare wore professional business attire: an Ann Taylor blazer with a matching skirt. Unfortunately, there were no photos taken. I'm sure they looked adorable.

I was going to college at Chico State in northern California at the time and enjoyed visiting them in 'So Cal'. They lived near the beach. The weather and people watching was always great. Plus, there were lots of fun places to go that were a short drive away. But getting to those places was a problem. It was extremely annoying to be in a car with Journey. Why? Because every radio tower, ship, storage container, metal pipe and bridge we encountered, Journey—forever proud of his occupation—had to say, "I built dat."

I get that welding is an integral part of construction, maintenance, and repair. I respect welding as a worthwhile skill, but Journey didn't build every man-made iron object we encountered. Things would randomly come up in conversations, like when I mentioned that Alex doesn't like living so close to the Diablo Canyon Power Plant. Journey found it necessary to interrupt me so he could inform everyone that, "I built dat."

It got to the point where I would landmine our conversations with stupid things just to hear him chime in.

"Thank God they have a guard rail on this road."

"I built dat."

"I can't believe how big those cargo ships are."

"I built dat."

"Is that an offshore drilling rig?"

"I built dat."

"I've been to the top of the Eiffel Tower."

"I built dat."

"Why sure."

Journey was a connection welder and one morning, he fell through the floor and landed on another one, two floors down. Ouch. It was a serious accident that's left him in chronic pain ever since. His prescription Vicodin bottle is a comic's prop. Who knew prescription pill bottles came in *Land of the Lost* size? I poke fun at Journey, but I also respect him. He's intelligent. Journey patiently played his cards right and received a generous compensation package with more than enough cash to buy their own piece of land.

Seen from above, the property would appear as a sliver; one acre wide and ten acres long. One end borders Ten Mile Creek and the other backs up to a large parcel of government land at the top of a hill. Blue Moon Ranch is isolated, covered in dense growth, has great soil, gets lots of sun and has access to free water. This makes it the perfect place to grow weed. Not so much on their land, although they do have some plants, but on the government land where they can grow anonymously. I read *Dune,* in which the most valuable thing in the universe was a drug—so I shouldn't be shocked. Still, I'm amazed that it's the pursuit of drugs that shapes so many lives.

∞   ∞   ∞

I'm exhausted. The pot and beer have amplified my grief, sorrow, and guilt. Mare hands me another joint, and I pass. This insults her.

"What's wrong?" she asks.

"I don't know. I just don't want to party anymore."

"Chris would want us to party. This party is for her, so shut your mouth and party."

You don't know what Chris wants; I think to myself.

"Fine," I say, taking the joint just to get her off my case.

"Go on now. Have another hit."

I inhale deeply. "There. Satisfied?" I say, holding my breath.

"Nice," she says, taking back the joint so she can bring it to the next person.

Later that night, Shelley, Molly, Al, and I form a huddled ring in the backyard. We have our arms over each other's shoulders and our heads are nearly touching. We focus all our thoughts on Chris and take turns talking to her. We laugh. We cry. We laugh and cry at the same time. Tears are streaming down our cheeks as we sing parts of her favorite songs and call out our favorite catch phrases to her. For a moment, everything we need is inside our little circle in my little backyard. When there's nothing else to say, we let go slowly and sink down to the grass quietly collecting our thoughts.

"I can't stop thinking about Shane and Skyler," I say.

"What if I move back to California, buy a big house, that we can all live in together?" Molly says.

"Tom could sell this house, move into the bigger house and we could help you raise all the kids," Shelley adds.

"Stranger things have happened," I say, optimistically. "I mean, why not?"

"If I got fired or quit my job, then I might move in too," Al adds.

"You should buy a house near me. Property is skyrocketing right now," says Shelley. "Plus, you'd be near Mare and Journey."

We daydream about the house for the next few minutes and just as I'm starting to see it in my mind, Molly admits it's out of the question. "I can't leave home right now. Kurt passed just three months ago. My children come first and what they need right now is stability."

Our lovely little fantasy quickly evaporates away. I hear the sliding glass door open. Mare is standing in the doorway.

"We're having a family pow-wow before going to bed. Let's meet out front in say… twenty minutes."

We knew a family meeting was inevitable. We take turns using the bathroom, freshen our drinks and check on the kids, who are sleeping peacefully. When the time comes, Ali joins us outside. She's wearing makeup and looks much more glamorous than the rest of us. We instinctively form a circle under the maple tree. It's a warm night and the damp grass feels good. Mare and Journey spark up dueling joints and pass them in opposite directions.

"We're all going through some heavy shit right now," Mare says. "It's going to affect each of us differently. We need to help each other through all this the best we can. The pain we feel is a form of love we all have for our beautiful Christina. She's no longer with us in our world. She's out there now, on another plane, continuing her journey."

She has our attention and we're listening to every word.

"There's something else we need to deal with—her wonderful, beautiful kids. A part of my daughter lives on in Shane and Skyler. They're my grandchildren, your nephews, and your cousins, and it's essential we keep them in the family." She pauses to take another hit. "Is everyone ready to talk about this now?"

"Oh, we've been talking about it," Molly says. "It's on everyone's mind. We fantasized about me moving to California, buying a big house and all of us moving in together and taking care of the kids."

"That's *soooo* beautiful," Mare says, grinning

"But it's not going to happen," Molly says, erasing Mare's smile. "We're not moving to California—someday maybe, but not now. I can't uproot my family. My kids need me too much right now. There's no way I can take on two more kids at this stage in our grief. No way. We were just daydreaming."

"She's right, Mare," Ali adds, genuinely concerned. "Our lives are already upside down right now." She tucks a string of hair behind her ear and smiles sadly.

"Molly and Ali know what's best for their family and we can certainly respect that," Mare says.

We sit silently for a long minute, and then Molly says, "The boys are very bonded to you, Tom. Skyler already looks to you for security. What do you think, bachelor-boy? Has the thought crossed your mind?"

"What are you talking about?"

"You know what I mean," Molly says. "Have you thought about adopting them?"

It's just like Molly to put me on the spot. I'm not all that surprised or the least bit angry. I glance around the circle. Everyone's eagerly awaiting my answer.

"I just happen to live the closest to Chris, so I get to see her and the boys more than the rest of you. They know me. Have I thought about adopting them? The first thought I had when I got the news was, *what about Shane and Skyler?* Losing a sister is bad. Losing your mother is a thousand times worse. Imagine how hard this is going to be for them. This is about the most traumatic thing that can happen to a kid. Their mother, the one who took care of them, the one they turned to for comfort and love, is gone. One thing's for sure; Shane and Skyler have to stay together. I need family more than ever right now. Don't you? They need each other the same way—to get through this together." I pause, hoping to be interrupted, but everyone remains silent.

"Of course, the idea of raising Shane and Skyler has crossed my mind, but I don't think I can do it. I can see by the look on your faces that you wish I would. To you, I must be the obvious choice. I have a good job, and I'm responsible. I have a house—there's even an elementary school right around the corner. Problem is, I'm a bachelor, and I'm very happy that way. I love my life the way it is, and I don't want kids. I've never wanted kids. What kind of parent would I make if my heart isn't in it? Not a good one. I have no idea how to take care of them. Ideally, kids have a mother and a father. I'm neither. I'm just Uncle Tom."

There's now a variety of expressions staring back at me. "I know that what I'm saying is selfish, but it's the truth."

"We're just exploring options. This is about keeping an open mind and an open heart," Mare says.

"Well, what about you? Have you thought about raising Shane and Skyler?" I ask.

"Yes and no."

Leave it to my mother to answer a simple yes or no question so vaguely.

"What do you mean?"

"We have, but only since yesterday. This is happening so fast. I remember the first time I found out Jeff hit Chris. I told her to leave him right now. Send a clear message. Any man who hits a woman is unworthy of her love. Eventually, we had to accept that she was sticking with Jeff, so we tried to make the best of it. We even welcomed him into our family under the conditions that he clean up his act and treat Chris with the love and respect she deserves. But crank is very addicting, and it fucks with your brain—and your behavior. Journey and I got all caught up in that shit-scene when we were living in Ocean Beach. It's a gnarly mother fucker. We told her to stop using because the heavy drugs will wipe you out. We called them out on their shit several times. They promised to change. Sometimes they did but never long enough or for good."

"Dat's da truth," Journey says.

Is she ever going to get around to answering my question?

"From her most recent letters, Chris was doing great. She was becoming more independent. She loved her job. She was making money and getting out of the house more. She might have realized that she needed to get out for good. The fact that Chris was starting to flex her independence might have drove Jeff over the edge. So, to answer your question—yes. Journey and I have thought about raising the kids. We certainly could do it and do it well, but there are other options as well."

"Like what?" I ask.

"I've been thinking of a way for all of us to share them. Maybe you could have them during the school year, Journey and I could have them for the summer and Shelley could take them during the holidays. When things settle down with Molly, they could spend a year or two in Idaho… that sort of thing. It would be such a righteous way to keep the boys in the family by moving them around."

She's finger-painting a circle in front of her face while she speaks. All she has to do is turn her head and she'd be making the crazy gesture.

"That's beautiful," Shelley says.

Molly and I glance at each other, knowing this is a God-awful idea. You can't timeshare kids like condominiums. Considering that everyone, including my mother, is still in shock about Chris, I manage to stay calm and choose my words carefully.

"That's one option," I say, "sharing the children. I just think they might need something that feels more permanent and stable, like—"

"We're all stable," Journey interrupts. "You're stable. Your sisters are stable. Your brother's stable. So dey'd go from one stable place to a-nudder."

"I know. I'm just concerned that rotating them around might make them feel like they don't belong anywhere. I could be wrong. What do I know about kids? I'm no expert."

"No, you're not!" Journey snaps. "Hell, I raised tree-boys and a girl, which makes me more of an expert dan you."

"It would be up to each of us to make them feel loved," Mare says calmly. "If we do it right, they'll have the benefit of feeling loved by more than just one set of parents. There's all kinds of better ways to raise kids these days. Take a look around. You'll see tons of fucked-up kids who come from so-called normal families. It's hard to raise good kids. I managed to do it, but not everyone's so lucky. If more people got involved in the process, kids would turn out better. That's a common-sense fact."

Wait. Mare actually believes she was a good mother?

"I don't know. It's a thought…" Molly says. Just to say something.

"I could raise them for a couple of years," Shelley adds.

We smile and reward her generosity. Her heart is certainly in the right place, but Shelley is incapable of raising kids. She's a tad irresponsible when it comes to life. Ever since she lost her job at the Heritage House three years ago, she's been drifting from bad jobs to worse. For the last couple years, she only works seasonally when the marijuana buds are harvested. Dad's been paying all her bills, which isn't helping Shelley get any better. I don't know if she's bipolar or manic-depressive, or what— but she certainly has her highs and lows. The truth is, I don't really know Shelley anymore. We rarely talk on the phone and never write and hardly ever see each other. We've grown apart. Shelley's an artist and lives her life submerged in emotions. She's a beautiful person, but not mentally equipped to handle major responsibility. She can barely take care of herself.

Mare's voice takes on a familiar cosmic tone. "In time, the universe will present us with a righteous solution." Everyone nods in hopeful agreement. "We need to get away from here and get in touch with Mother Earth. I want everyone to come to our place, so we can grieve, heal, and have our own private wake for Chris."

"We need time to process all this heavy shit," Shelley says, nodding in agreement.

"We can have our own ceremony," says Journey.

"I can take more time off work," Al says.

"Journey is a medicine man," Mare says.

"I got me some eagle feathers," Journey says, "legally for ceremon'al purposes."

"I want to see where you live," says Molly.

"Me too," says Ali.

It bothers me to be leaving in the middle of the crisis. "Maybe I should stay behind. There's a lot of stuff going on right now. I want to know if Jeff's out of jail, and if he has any rights to the boys. Do we need an attorney? What about the funeral? We haven't even talked about that yet. I want to see the police report, the coroner's report."

"That's why we need to get away for a few days. How can we think straight, let alone grieve, with all this bullshit? I'll deal with Chris's death on *my* terms," Mare says. "This is our crisis, not theirs and we'll handle it the way we damn well want to."

There is no point in protesting. Mare is understandably in a highly emotional state, and we know better than to challenge her in these situations. She begins to cry quietly. "I lost my daughter... I'll do what I want."

One tear, and I completely crumble. "You're right. Let's go to Blue Moon Ranch. It's a great idea."

Don't fight it. This isn't my crisis. It's our crisis. Just go with the flow...

Fifth

July 5th, 1996

It would be nice if the brain came equipped with an on-off switch.

It's late. I'm exhausted. But can I sleep? Nope. Our family meeting under the maple tree didn't exactly calm my mind. I can't shake Mare's crazy idea of time-sharing Shane and Skyler like a vacation condo in Cabo. I've tried deep breathing and slowing down my thoughts but neither has helped. Everything is happening too fast to process. Leaving in the midst of this crisis for a 'ceremony' at Blue Moon Ranch is crazy. I should have insisted on staying behind.

Shane's on the floor, Skyler's in the bed, both are breathing peacefully in unison fast asleep. I feel like a different person—uncomfortable in my own body. One minute everything is hunky-dory and the next, it's a wild shitstorm of pain, suffering and loss. Death changes everything. It makes you realize just how dark and painful life can be. I live in another world now—one I never knew existed, and there's no going back to what I had before. Against my will, I've joined a dire, sad club that I'll be a member of for the rest of my life. Losing Chris has changed me. It's altered my outlook on life and darkened my worldview—forever.

Skyler wakes up at 2:22 in the morning, crying. I carry him to the kitchen and heat up a bottle of milk. I wake up to see the clock at 3:33, 4:44 and 5:55. I fall back asleep and wake up to Skyler manually opening my eyes with his little monkey fingers. His hair is a wild mess. The sun is just starting to rise. I'm pleasantly surprised to see he's happy. His gap-toothed smile makes me smile. We get out of bed being careful not to disturb Shane and go to the bathroom. Skyler looks up at me while I relieve my bladder.

"You want to pee like a big boy?"

He appears to nod so I finish, shake, flush and then tug his diaper down and hold him over the toilet. Sure enough, he fires away. "Oh, you're so ready to be potty trained," I say, yawning.

Mare and Journey are up. She's pulling a brush through his hair. My mother's hair is all poufy on one side and yet, she still looks good. She hands me a joint as I'm walking by. I hesitate. I know today will require clear thinking and mental stamina. I'm already wiped out, sleep-deprived and depressed. On the other hand, nothing sounds more appealing than escaping this dismal reality just like we all did yesterday. I take the fat sticky joint from her skinny fingers, hold it to my lips and inhale deeply—it burns the back of my throat, but I still hold my breath while I count to ten slowly in my head. Then I exhale a plume of thick smoke like a blown head gasket.

"Wake and bake," I say catching my breath.

"Yes, my son. It is the wake and bake time of day," she declares, deliberately, with the cadence of a monk. This is her morning ritual.

The milky smoke filling the room becomes spiral galaxies swirling in the morning sun. I'm already high as fuck and regretting it. When I get stoned on good dope first thing in the morning, my entire day is altered. Taking a shower, eating, napping, and drinking coffee makes no difference. It can be the only weed I smoke all day, yet I never feel completely sober until the following day, after a good night's sleep. If I take even one toke in the morning, I've committed myself to being stoned all day. Therefore, wake and bake is something I rarely do. Mare and Journey, on the other hand, wake and bake every day. Even before their first sip of coffee, they're already high. I know marijuana affects everyone differently, and considering their tolerance to THC, maybe they don't get as high as I do. But then again, with the mass quantity of marijuana they consume, it's more likely that they're constantly as high as the northern lights.

Pot doesn't mellow me out. It may be classified as a downer, but for me, it's the opposite. It recharges and energizes me for hours. Unfortunately, this rush is accompanied by laziness, anxiety, starvation, and various degrees of paranoia, leaving me to wonder why I even bother. No, I have not forgotten that getting high has widened my depth of understanding—and misunderstandings—of this wacky world we share. It has equally expanded and reduced my world view. Despite having this love-hate relationship with weed, I sure smoke a lot of it.

I have huge lungs and an unusually small head. All I need is one or two hits for the maximum effect. Any more is just a waste. Wake and bake for Mare and Journey is just the beginning. They continue to smoke pot all day and all night, right up to the time they risk catching on fire in bed. I know that if they didn't get stoned first thing in the morning, their entire day would be as equally altered as mine is when I do. *Ha! Imagine Mare and Journey sober. I can't!*

Later that morning, Molly and I take off in my car to rent a large enough vehicle to haul everyone up to Blue Moon Ranch. We park and march toward the largest van on the lot.

"This will work," Molly says peeking through the window.

"With a roof rack it will," I say visualizing all our luggage.

I rent the van and a cargo box for the roof. Normally, I would have declined the all-inclusive-no-hassle coverage, but considering my state of mind, my gut feeling is to buy it for the van and the box. When we get home, Willie, Joey, Shane, and Skyler are playing in the sprinklers.

Ali suddenly appears by the front door and is beckoning me inside. She points at the phone on the kitchen counter. "It's for you."

"Hello Tom?"

"Yes."

Is this Christina Marie's brother?"

"That's right. Yes."

"This is Stephanie Santoro. I'm a psychologist specializing in helping crime victims. You can call me Steph."

We're crime victims. Weird. I knew it was true, yet it sounds so odd to hear it said. *Why did I have to wake and bake?*

She's with the county health department. I'm unclear why she's calling. When she asks about Shane and Skyler, I figure she's associated with child protective services. I tell her that the kids are doing fine—considering. I bring the phone into the garage and sit in the sanctuary of my Z giving her my full attention. *Damn, I wish I had not gotten stoned.* I bring her up to date on the kids, my family, and our immediate plans. Then she asks, "What can I do to help?"

It's a simple question that I struggle to answer. So instead, I ask questions about her and the agency she works for.

"I've been with the Victim Services Unit for three years. We're a state-funded organization that helps people immediately following a crime."

Hearing this confirms for me that Jeff, in addition to being an enormous pile of shit, is also a criminal.

"I need to tell Shane that his mother has passed away. How do I go about that in such a way that causes the least amount of harm—if that's even possible."

"I can help you with that. First, help me get to know Shane and your family a little better."

She begins asking direct questions about the very things people, let alone two strangers, normally avoid when conversing. I'm trying to be candid and brief but can tell I'm rambling. I wasn't prepared for such poignant questions. It's challenging to neatly summarize one's position on religion, politics, the human soul, life, death, evolution, and the meaning of life, without starting to ramble—when you're stoned. And yet, we dive headfirst into a deep discussion in which I feel more and more comfortable speaking freely about these exact things.

First, we talk about Shane. I describe his personality, his environment, how he gets along with his brother, mother, and father. I tell her everything, including what a great kid he is—smart, polite, funny, imaginative, sensitive, athletic, I go on and on.

"He's also got a serious side." I tell her about the direct questions he asked during breakfast yesterday. "He likes to know exactly what's happening and you should see the way he takes care of his brother." I describe the life I imagine he's been living with Chris and Jeff.

"Can you tell me what Shane has said, about the situation?"

"Shane saw them fighting the night before she died. He couldn't understand why his dad was so mad. He knew that his mother was in bad shape. He watched his father kick her and throw ice water on her in a lame attempt to wake her up. Right now, Shane thinks his mother is still recuperating in the hospital."

There's a long pause. She's probably taking notes.

"That's awful."

"I know."

"How does Shane get along with his dad?" She asks.

"I think most of the time just fine. Kids his age tend to blindly look up to their dads no matter what. Chris never mentioned Jeff being physically abusive to the kids. It's safe to say Shane, and Skyler for that matter, witnessed some domestic violence. They must have seen the black eyes and the bruises their mother tried to hide."

I told Stephanie about my visits to see Chris in the hospital and convey what little I know about their drug abuse and its consequences to their lifestyle.

"My bet is that Jeff's an absentee dad. Meth gives you insane energy. You don't sleep. You can't live a normal life without sleep. I bought a couple of lamps Jeff refurbished to help them out. You could tell he put an insane amount of time into making and especially painting them. When I got home and plugged them in, only one worked and not for very long."

"Shane's concerned and confused; he knows something bad happened. My whole family has suddenly gathered. I'm trying not to let him know how I feel about his father. I'm fairly good at hiding my feelings. But the same can't be said for the rest of my family—and Shane is highly intuitive. We have a lot of anger directed towards Jeff… it's hard to be neutral when you believe he's responsible for her death."

"I understand. It is going to be hard to keep those feelings from Shane, but you need to try. Look at it from his point of view. He's about to confront the loss of his mother. Let him cross that bridge first. As of now, Jeff is only a suspect, and we don't know for sure what happened or if he's responsible in any way yet. It's important that Shane knows his dad is ok. Knowing his father is safe and still loves him is pretty crucial right now. I'm sure Shane has mixed emotions regarding his father, but he does need him."

"I understand."

"Where is Shane's head at?"

Normally, I'd have said something silly like, the usual place, on top of his torso, but this isn't the time and we're making progress. "He's so intelligent. He probably already knows something is terribly wrong—maybe even that his mother isn't coming back. He must be wondering, just like the rest of us, who's going to take care of him and his brother. He's got a lot on his five-year-old brain right now."

"Has Shane ever experienced the passing of a grandparent, relative, or anyone close?"

"No, not that I know of."

"Hmm. What about a family pet?"

"Yeah. They lost their little dog, Pepper last year."

"Okay. You can start a conversation by letting Shane tell you about Pepper's death. Then you can reassure him that Pepper is no longer in pain and that even though he's gone, he'll be remembered. Talk about the things that made Pepper special. Just be clear he understands that Pepper can never come back. If you talk about heaven, be clear. Kids often see it as a place people can visit and come back from. This creates false hope and can prolong healing."

"Okay…"

"Five-year-old kids are actually pretty darn smart and well-equipped to handle what life throws at them. Generally, they can deal with things better than we give them credit for. Children are resilient. He needs to know the truth."

"It's going to break my heart."

"It's going to break your heart like never before and you need to allow yourself to feel what you feel. Shane will see that you're capable and comfortable expressing your feelings. That's good. It will help him express his."

"I guess."

"Follow through once you start. Then be prepared to talk about it more if he comes to you later with questions."

"Wow. Okay…" *I sound stoned.*

"You can expect Shane to go through the same five stages adults do: denial, anger, bargaining, depression and acceptance."

"Wow. Okay…" *I still sound stoned!*

Our conversation turns to Skyler; his emotional development, his sudden lack of routine, his dependence on his brother and the separation anxiety he's sure to experience. Then our discussion takes an odd turn when she asks about my core beliefs.

"Tom, where do you see your sister now?"

This is exactly the type of lofty question that's difficult to answer on the spot when your brain is sleep-deprived and pot-fogged. My meandering reply starts by telling her how we were raised as Catholics when we were young. Next, I explain how my mother married a scientist, who was an atheist; and how being the doubting Thomas I am, I found it easy to accept a world in which that type of God does not exist.

"Not that I have anything against God or Jesus. To the people who believe in God, God is real. The same goes for whatever religion or higher power you have faith in. Blind acceptance freaks me out though. How can you deny evolution and believe the Earth was created in seven days or that the universe is only five thousand years old? I don't accept the traditional Christian definitions of heaven, hell, purgatory, or final judgment, but I do believe something like heaven and hell exists within each of us—and that some kind of karmic universal balance exists."

Fuck! I sound like Mare!

"The more we learn about the universe, the more mysterious it becomes. When you get down to the subatomic level into ten, eleven, and twelve dimensions, nothing makes sense anymore. Ironically, it's science that makes me feel spiritual. The flip side of all this quantum chaos is that anything is possible."

"I remember stargazing with my stepfather when I was a kid. He taught me how to find the blind spots in my own eyes. I learned that sometimes you can see things better by not looking directly at them. He told me about the big bang, and I believe it's true. I've come to accept that everything came from nothing. Everything includes time, matter, religion, creativity, Mother Nature, life, thoughts, dreams, even our souls… it all came from nothing. If you break down a living organism into smaller and smaller parts, eventually what you have is a small pile of atoms, none of which are alive. Yet here we are. Somehow life animates out of this inanimate material. That's miraculous. That's the soul."

Fuck! I sound like John!

I can't stop now. I talk about how, after my mother's second divorce, we were exposed to a lot of different religions, philosophies, and cultural ideologies.

"I noticed many similarities and some universal truths among them. Treat others as you would like to be treated yourself… don't kill or steal or sleep with your neighbor… these make perfect sense. But the minute you declare others damned just because they don't believe in the exact same things you do—the whole thing falls apart. Religious wars in the name of love? Give me a break. As far as the big questions go… *Why are we here? What's my purpose? Is there a soul?* I don't have a definitive answer. And from what little I've learned about world religions, despite what they may claim—neither do they. I cling to a smidgen of a feeling inside that says it's not all in vain, that there's a purpose and meaning to our lives, that we're a part of something bigger. And that's enough for me. I know I haven't answered your question." I add, catching my breath.

"That's okay," she says politely. "Go on…"

"I believe there's a physical and spiritual side to people. I think the unique energy that makes each person who they are cannot be destroyed. Energy is always transformed. The spiritual side of a person transcends into something else that is indefinable and yet undeniable." —I stop just shy of telling her about my visit from Chris in the form of a hummingbird.

"Chris is okay now. I can still feel her. She's a part of everything." I wonder if anything I've said made any sense at all.

"Share these exact feelings with Shane—even if he can't keep up with you conceptually, you'll be amazed at how helpful it will be."

"What about the funeral? This morning, my mother informed me that she wants an open casket so she can see her daughter one last time. I don't think the kids need that at all. But what about the rest?"

"That's up to you and your family to decide. The kids can attend the wake and skip the viewing. It's something to think about."

"Okay. We'll see…"

"How do you feel?"

I take a deep breath. "I'll talk to him today."

"You'll do fine."

"I hope so."

"I'll follow up in a few days to see how you and the kids are doing. Please extend my sorrow for your loss to the rest of your family. I also have some very helpful resources—free resources you should know about and take advantage of. I'll give you more details when we talk again soon. Okay?"

We end the call. The good doctor has given me a shot in the arm. All I need now is a little alone time to collect my thoughts. *The river.* I bolt back into the house to tell Molly that I'm going for a quick float down the river and to watch the boys until I get back.

I take the shortcut through the elementary school field. Down the street, around the corner of a dead-end street, I find the narrow trail that slices through the towering dry thistles leading to the river's edge. It's a holiday weekend and the water is polka dotted with rafts, colorful inflatables and ice chests of beer floating in their very own inner tubes. The girls are in their teeny tiny bikinis. Many of the guys have water bazookas made from PVC plastic pipes to engage in water wars along the way. Just a couple of days ago, I was one of those fun-loving people without a care in the world.

That already seems like a lifetime ago. I find a clearing above the river where it's deep enough to dive in, take my shirt off and wait for a break in the floating parade so I can drift peacefully along with my thoughts alone. Clutching my shirt, I leap headfirst toward the water inhaling deeply on my way down. I love the initial shock of cold water; breaking the surface, creating a churning swish of bubbles as you go under and the sudden change in sound.

∞   ∞   ∞

This is the same river that swept Chris away years ago. It was only a mile or two upstream from this very spot. All five of us kids were playing along the bank of the river near our house in Fair Oaks on a typically warm spring afternoon. The deep blue sky was peppered with clouds that looked like paw prints. We took off our shoes and waded into the cold water in our shorts. The current was as high as we've ever seen it. The rocks we normally hop, jump and step upon out into the river were under water and slippery with slime. I liked placing sticks and chunks of bark in the moving water as targets I'd try to hit with rocks. Suddenly there was a SPLASH! and I knew someone had fallen in.

I turned around and see Chris being pulled into the river. I chucked my handful of rocks and raced along in the shallow water. The rocks hurt my feet knocking me to my knees a couple of times, but I kept moving. Once I got a good angle, I dove in and started swimming as fast as I could toward Chris who was keeping her head above water and yelling for help. She looked frightened and didn't know which way to swim. I stopped, looked for her, adjusted my direction and yelled, 'I'm coming!' as loud as I could. I finally got close enough to see the panic in her eyes. She must have thought we both were going to drown and hesitated before reaching for my hand. We were both breathing heavily as I side stroked her out of the main current and eventually out of danger. By the time we got to the river's edge, we were too exhausted to speak.

Shelley, Molly and Alex had been watching the rescue while running along the bank. The river carried us about a half of a mile downstream. Another fifty feet or so and we would have encountered a long section of rapids that would have worn us out. My chest is still heaving when our siblings catch up. Chris is exhausted and yet she starts to laugh. I remember thinking, *Why is she laughing?* She made us start laughing, too. We seemed to do this after every good joke and near-death experience. I think she loved the sound of us laughing. I coughed up some water and we laughed some more.

"I guess we're even now," Chris said smiling.

"For that time, you saved my life in San Francisco?" I asked.

"Yep. Exactly."

∞   ∞   ∞

That first breath of air. There's nothing like breaking the surface and refreshing your lungs when you've been underwater a long time. I swim further into the river searching for the feel of the currents full power. And then it finds me. Surrendering to the flowing force, I'm swept away. My body is perfectly relaxed. The unconstrained forces of nature will take me where they will. Water, gravity, temperature and all my thoughts begin to drift away in the slowly swirling current caressing me like a newborn baby in a mother's arms.

Life is like a river. Our lives begin as pure and simple as falling snow. The smallest drops of icy melt, weld the mightiest rivers—as are all children who are born with infinite potential. The many forms of water like; rain, snowmelt, brooks, streams, and meadow springs are all tied together. They're the tributaries that combine to change the very nature of the river. They'll eventually define its course. Our lives move in unique paths altered by the experiences we encounter along the way, which shape who we become. Rivers are in a constant state of change; so are we. A rivers character is defined by the environment they flow through. We're equally shaped by our surroundings. Occasionally, supernatural forces like landslides, tsunamis and earthquakes can reverse a rivers direction. Life is full of unexpected surprises that affect, redirect, and change the course of our lives, too.

Some rivers have lots of rapids; some are smooth. Some people's lives are riddled with bumps; others lead an essentially unruffled existence. Life is so begrudgingly linear—a beginning, middle, and end. All rivers flow in one direction; downward. They too have a beginning middle, and end. Their final destination being the sea, where they become part of something bigger than themselves. We might become part of something larger when we reach our final destination. Our boundless oceans are endlessly evaporating, which transforms moisture into clouds. Clouds that are then carried by wind, back over land where they release their mass in the form of rain, snow, mist, and fog. All this moisture eventually returns to the rivers in an endlessly repetitive cycle. Do our spirits perform a similar journey in a circle that never ends?

I'm literally up to my neck bobbing in water drowning in my own deep thoughts when I suddenly come to a gentle stop on a submerged sandbar.

Ride over.

I've never drifted this far before and it takes some time in my squishy sneakers to find the trail. It feels good to walk and quiet my mind. Now each step I take seems to feed the mental strength I need to talk to Shane. For a night of shitty sleep and a morning wake and bake, I feel relaxed and surprisingly clearheaded. This is a first. For the first time in my life, despite getting stoned in the morning, I feel 99.9% sober.

I get home, take off my shoes and change into dry shorts. When the opportunity arises, I pull Shane aside and bring him to the garage. We get in the Z, shut the doors, and roll down the windows. He looks small in the bucket seat next to me staring straight ahead as if we're moving down the road. I take a deep breath and close my eyes. I'm searching for the right words to get me started but come up empty. I open my eyes and tell myself; *I can do this. The time is now. Here we go.*

"Shane. Oh, Shane, I love you so much. I do. And what I have to say is really difficult. But you need to know exactly what going on." My voice is dry and weak. "I'm talking about what's happened to your mother." *So much for opening with Pepper.*

He nods.

"Your mother passed away at the hospital yesterday. They tried to keep her alive, but they couldn't." His head sinks even lower into his chest. I swallow hard.

Without looking up, he asks, "She's dead?"

"Yes. She died. Do you know what that means?"

"Yes."

"Can you tell me what it means to you?"

He finally turns his head and looks at me with his big sad eyes. "She's never coming back."

I start to shake. A tear leaks from my eye and rolls off my cheek. "Right. But we can still love her and that's exactly what we'll do. Even though she's gone, we can still love her, right?"

He covers his face with his hands and starts crying.

Every sad conversation has to start somewhere. It feels good crying with him. He lets me hug him. We talk. We also just sit there with nothing to say, which feels perfectly natural. I listen to him describe what he saw that awful night, when his dad was so mad, and what he was doing to his mother. It's not easy to contain my anger. Such an innocent child experiencing such a horrific event is heartbreaking.

Stephanie's words stick. I know it's more important to help Shane and his brother deal with their loss than it is persecuting his father.

"Your dad loves you very much. Please don't worry about him. He's going to be fine. You can talk to him on the phone if you want. Just let me know and I'll make that happen."

I'm sure my jaw is semi-clenched but I'm still glad I was able to offer him that. Part of me still wants to kill Jeff for what he did to my sister and his own children. I do my best to let go of my anger and finally mention Pepper. I listen to Shane's interpretation of what happened and where he believes Pepper is now.

"I think your mom is something extra special now," I say. "Not only is she in a better place where she feels happy and free, she's become part of a larger world. I believe her spirit is a part of everything now. She's in an extraordinary place where she can visit with other people that have also died. When we feel the sun on our back, that's her. Every time a bird drops in for a surprise visit, that's her. I'll be reminded of her every time I see a beautiful sunset and skies with amazing clouds. I know she'll want to make sure you and Skyler are being taken care of. She'll be around. Not in person—but in spirit. We'll feel her presence."

No false hope.

Shane shifts his position a little and wipes away some tears.

I tell him, "Even though she's not coming back, it will be easy to feel her in our hearts. We can remember her forever. I'll tell you what a great sister she was, and you can tell me why she was such a great mom. Every person has their own story that's unlike anyone else's. That's what we are, a collection of stories; the things we did, the places we lived, the people we loved. As long as we remember your mom, by telling her stories, she'll be here in our hearts. She's kind of like a book now. That makes me feel a little better. What about you?"

He nods slowly.

"You can still feel her love for you, even though she's gone. I believe she can feel yours in return."

"She's like a book?"

"Absolutely. A one-of-a-kind book. There's a lot of people here, including me, who love you very much. Everyone's here to make sure you and Skylar are in good hands. You have enough on—"

"I want to live with you."

What?

He catches me completely off guard. Part of me reaches out to hug him; another part leaps from the car and runs down the street.

"I guess maybe you and Skyler can live with me while we figure out a permanent plan," I say, rubbing his shoulder. Comforting him makes me feel better, too. I still can't believe what he just said.

"Where am I going to go to school?" he asks.

Another zinger!

"Well, if you're staying with me for a while, then you can probably go to the school behind my house."

"Okay."

He feels unsettled. I know that feeling all too well. He's so relaxed. I'm expecting much more of a reaction. And yet, it's because he's so strong, brave, and composed that I'm able to be so open, honest, and loving. Shane already knows his mother is gone. He needed to hear it from someone else, but he knew. He's bright. He knows it's final—that nothing will ever be the same.

We hug the best we can over the car's center console and wipe our eyes. Then we just sit silently for the next few minutes.

"I keep thinking about our lives as books. Some are tragic, some are comic. There's so many kinds; travel, romance, adventure, fantasy, thrillers, science fiction, classics, graphic novels and more. But almost every life is a combination of many genres all mashed together."

I'm probably talking over his head.

"That makes sense."

Maybe not. I'm completely humbled by Shane's composure.

"You and me, we can talk about anything. Anytime you want," I say leaning in for one more hug. We get out of the car. He reaches the door into the house before me. His cousin, Joey, intercepts him with a soccer ball and takes him outside to play. Mare wanders into the kitchen from another room.

"So, how'd it go?"

I replay the conversation I just had with Shane. When I finish, she closes her eyes and sighs, "Heavy shit."

"I was blown away. Shane is an old soul. He's a remarkable kid."

"So are you, my good son. So are you."

"Don't call me that. You know I don't like it. Unless you have an equally kind nickname for Alex, I mean Al, I don't think it's fair."

"See what I mean? You're always so considerate of other people's feelings. You are the good son, so shut the fuck up and get used to it." She laughs. I roll my eyes. We hug. She smells like a bag of pot-pourri; comprised of high-quality Mendocino sticky, stinky buds.

Molly waits for Mare and Journey to leave the room before telling me that Dad called while I was at the river.

"He's in San Francisco and wanted to drive to Sacramento today, but I told him to wait until we get back from Mare and Journey's."

"Smart. I feel bad that he flew three thousand miles to be with his family, and now that he's here, we're pretty much ditching him."

"I pretty much told him that, but he said he's okay with the plan," she says reassuringly. "We'll see him soon enough. He's in his favorite city. Besides, there's too much shit going on right now, including what we can and can't say around Mare and Journey, if you know what I mean."

"Unfortunately, I do."

Talking about our dad is forbidden. Journey claims to be protecting my mother from painful memories, but the truth is, he's jealous, and we don't like having to edit what we say around Journey one bit. It's our past not his. We're the culmination of our past; the present-moment is a result of our life experiences—all of them. You can't edit history to make it tolerable for someone. I own every good, bad, wonderful, horrific, miraculous, mundane, tender, and tragic moment I've ever experienced.

At first, we rebelled. *We can't just eliminate our pasts to appease Journey!* Journey does not want to hear about any of the men Mom was with before he came along—especially

Charlie. God forbid I mention Victor the circus clown. Mare took Journey's side, declaring that she wants to live fully in the present moment unfolding before her and that the only way she can do this is to never mention or think about the past. Begrudgingly, we go along with this rule, though it certainly limits the depth of the relationship we have with both of them. One day I'll call them out on their bullshit. But now's not the time even though it makes no sense whatsoever.

Mare, Journey, and Shelley are itching to hit the road. At the last minute, Ali gets Molly's permission to go with them. So, the plan is for Mare and Journey to drive Ali to Shelley's house and then on to Blue Moon Ranch this afternoon. Al, Molly, Willie, Joey, Shane, Skyler, and I will drive up in the van tomorrow. Shelley and Ali will meet us at Blue Moon Ranch sometime tomorrow afternoon.

Several joints are passed around as four members of our group prepare to depart. It's a lengthy farewell. I spy Mare giving Al a warm hug. She tenderly tucks a joint behind his ear. It's good to see my brother getting some much-needed attention from her. The moment they leave, the house takes on a mellower vibe. Their absence is relieving. With fewer people in the house, it's easier to focus on Shane and Skyler. Molly's motherly touch makes putting the boys down for the night a snap. Once Willie and Joey are asleep, Al, Molly and I decide to watch the video from Shane's birthday party. I put the tape into the VCR and sit between my little sister and brother on the couch.

It begins outside with some kids running about. The adults are chatting in a semicircle of chairs. I pan the camera to the right and catch Chris coming through the door. She has Skyler in one arm and is carrying a bag of chips and a stack of cups in the other. Seeing that she's on camera, she smiles and shouts, "Happy Birthday Shane!" It's surreal seeing her alive and well in my living room.

Molly and I look at each other feeling the same thing—a mix of wonder, joy, and sorrow—but say nothing. Al isn't blinking. I captured the spin-art machine in the garage, the birthday cake, and the piñata swinging from a branch in the front yard. Mostly, I shot video of Shane and his friends. As soon as there's another shot of Chris, like when she ties the blindfold over Shane's eyes, we lean in and pay extra-close attention. Jeff spins him around two times and aims him at the target—a swing and a miss, another swing, and a miss. Shane peeks from the bottom of the blindfold up at the target and whacks it squarely. Candy flies everywhere. Swarming children appear out of nowhere with their greedy little hands picking up as much as they can.

Chris and Shane on his 5th birthday.

We see our sister, on the phone, scooping ice cream, taking pictures, smoking a cigarette, and laughing with her friends. She looks beautiful in the shot I got of her lighting the candles. She tells Shane to make a wish and he easily blows them all out. There are a few seconds of Chris pulling him in for a big hug. Someone yells, "Stay right there!" Chris and Shane turn towards the voice and smile on cue for the camera's multi-fire red-eye flash. Even though they're not looking into my camera, it's a powerful moment.

Parts of the video make us smile—we even laugh a little. But sitting in the dark glow of the TV watching her holding her kids is also extremely heartbreaking.

Oh, how she loved her boys.

Seeing our sister in living color is peculiar. On one hand, it makes us feel closer to her, on the other, it magnifies her absence and the cold brutal fact that we will never see her alive again. Molly reaches out and squeezes our hands. We watch the last part in silence encased within our thoughts. Even when the screen goes black, we remain still. I look over at my little sister and brother. Their cheeks, like mine, are polished with tears.

Sixth

July 6th, 1996

When Mare and Journey first moved to Laytonville, a couple of years ago, she told me it was next to Wavy Gravy's Ranch—as if that would help me pinpoint the location. I told her I haven't been hanging out with Wavy Gravy and fetched a map. Willits is a black dot on Highway 101, which represents a small town. Laytonville is an outline of a dot, which indicates an even smaller town. There's about a half inch of separation between the two, which equates to roughly twenty miles. Other than Willits, there isn't another dot of any kind, in any direction, for quite a ways. Mare and Journey live in the middle of nowhere.

I like maps for all the obvious reasons. I like a birds-eye view of where I'm going and how I'll get there. Knowing the geography makes me feel more connected not just to the trip on hand, but to the entire planet. A map will let you know the ocean is on the left, there's a mountain pass ahead and a river to cross at some point in the journey. In addition to the vital information they provide, maps can also be works of art that inspire the imagination. Great paintings can generate deep emotional feelings; they can even transport you to a different time and place—and so can a map. A musician sees more than the spattered ink of notes on paper. They actually hear the music they represent. With a good map and some imagination, you can get a feel for the landscape, terrain, foliage, fauna, and climate. Our brains fill in the rest—down to the colors you'll see and the scents you'll smell. A good map will tell me exactly where I am, even when I'm feeling so completely lost.

We're in the rental van heading northwest on Hwy 20 passing some nice views of Clear Lake out the left side windows. We're a little more than halfway to Mare and Journey's place, known as Blue Moon Ranch. It's already been a long drive, and everyone needs a break. I stop at a gas station in the little town of Lucerne on the north shore. While I'm pumping gas, Al goes to the restroom and returns wearing his Army fatigues—a camouflage ensemble with lots of pockets and hulking black boots.

"Why'd you change?" I ask.

"So, I can freak out the hippies."

"Well sure."

He pats my back so hard; I release a fart. "Are you talking shit?" He asks, laughing. My brother is a funny guy. He offers to drive the last leg of the trip, which is thoughtful. I'm sitting shotgun with the trusty map folded across my legs. It's nice to be out of the driver's seat. My finger is on the map casually tracking our progress. Another beautiful stretch of the drive begins as the highway carves a path through rolling mountains generously sprinkled with evergreens. We travel up and down long grades of smooth road, navigating perfectly engineered curves that push and pull us from side to side. It's dry and scorching-hot outside. The air conditioner is blasting. Al is driving with the cruise control on. I call it the 'cruise-out-of-control' button. He refers to it as his autopilot.

"Ladies and gentlemen, this is your captain Al speaking to you live from the cockpit of flight 4-20. Oh, we'll be flying high today so please buckle your seat belts and enjoy the view. RRRERK! We're currently experiencing no turbulence and anticipate a smooth ride all the way to our final destination."

He's holding an imaginary microphone and adding his own static. He reaches behind his ear and grabs one of the joints Mare gave him and pops it between his lips. Then he fishes into his shirt pocket for a Bic and lights up. He takes a puff before continuing.

"RRRERK! We know, when it comes to flying, you have a choice. That's why we'd like to take this opportunity to spark up a fatty and thank you for choosing us." He takes another hit. Holding his breath, he says, "Please enjoy the rest of the flight," and hands the doobie to Molly. A skunk-smelling cloud system forms within the van. Molly takes a toke and passes me the joint. While I'm hitting on it, Willie starts tapping my back. He wants me to hand it to him while Molly isn't looking. I shake my head no.

Molly catches on to what's happening and says, "No way, Willie. No way."

"May I *please* have one little, teeny-tiny hit?" He asks.

"Absolutely not!" Molly says, scolding him. Willie throws himself back into his seat and huffs. "But thanks for asking so politely, sweetie," Molly adds, kindly.

"What's the big deal? You let me get stoned yesterday."

"Yes, you did get stoned… behind my back. I didn't *let* you. There was just so much going on and I got distracted. I'm really mad at Mare and Journey for smoking pot with you. It's not up to them. I'm mad at you because you broke your promise to me. You're *my* son and you will do what I tell you, because I know what's best for you. No smoking pot. Got it? So, when we get up there and the joints are being passed around like Halloween candy, you are not to partake. Is that clear?"

"Fine," says Willie, turning his gaze out the window.

"No trick-or-treats for you," I add, siding with my sister.

"That goes for any other drugs, too," Molly says.

"Good point. You never know with M and J."

A little farther down the road, Molly moves to the space between the front seats to get a better view.

"Imagine Chris seeing Grandma and Grandpa." She says softly.

"I'd like to think she's sharing a joint with Charlie," I add. And since we're on the topic of death I ask what her husband's funeral was like. She closes her eyes for a moment before answering.

"Kurt chose a beautiful place to be buried in the mountains…"

I had to let this sink in. Imagine knowing you're going to die and selecting where you want to be buried—such a sad thought.

"There was a family wake at the church Kurt's mother belonged to. After that, I cooked his favorite dinner at our house for about twenty of his closest friends and family. We took turns sharing memories of Kurt. The kids and I put all these great pictures of Kurt up all around the house for everyone to see—happy pictures of a healthy man enjoying life. I put pictures out that the kids drew of our family as well. It was all about remembering the good times. We celebrated his wonderful life."

"Wow. It sounds… perfect," I say.

"We laughed and had a good time because that's what Kurt would have wanted. Since you have no choice, right, you eventually learn to accept death and celebrate the life. Kurt was in a lot of pain near the end. I'm happy he's not suffering anymore. We knew he was going to die, but it was still a shock when it happened. I'm just not that far along with Chris yet," she says, "I'm still getting used to the fact that she's gone."

"Oh Molly. I feel for you. I can barely endure one death in the family and you're handling two—plus trying to be strong for your kids. I wish I could do more for you."

The next few miles are quiet because sometimes words are utterly worthless.

We see a sign that we're entering in Laytonville. Al lets up on the gas for a second and then it's gone. That was the outline of the dot on the map. We're in the northern part of the state and even though it's like a pizza oven outside now, it also snows here in the winter. Laytonville is loaded with extremes. You see it in the people and the lifestyles they lead.

We reach the almost black wooden water tower precariously pitched at an angle, barely standing in a meadow. It is Laytonville's own Leaning Tower of Pisa, except this one is covered in moss, and looks like it can be toppled by a hefty sneeze. According to Mare and Journey, there's a contest to see who comes the closest to picking the date it collapses. The pot, they tell me, is a pound of pot. The water tower is the closest landmark to the turn off I'm looking for.

"Slow way down," I say.

"Copy that. Over," Al says back.

We crawl along the highway in search of a side road that is as elusive as the entrance to the bat cave. "Right there!" I yell, socking my brothers arm and pointing to the left. Al turns onto a rutty dirt road through a meadow of towering dry weeds that ends at a creek and stops.

"Ladies and gentlemen, as we make our approach to Blue Moon Ranch please remain buckled up until we reach our final destination and come to a complete stop. RRRERK! Please be sure to enjoy the river view. Flight attendants, prepare for landing."

Al tiptoes the van into the creek and then drives through it slowly. The kids have their noses pressed against the windows, awestruck that we're driving through moving water. During the winter this creek becomes a raging river that further separates Blue Moon Ranch from the rest of the world. You have to leave your car on one side and cross the river on foot. The narrow bridge is a tangle of decomposing rope and weathered scraps of wood. It swings, sways, cracks, and bounces as you traverse step by careful step to the other side. It would be a great location to shoot an Indiana Jones action scene.

Mare in the middle of nowhere.

Having made this drive more often, I help Al navigate the forks in the road. The scenery is beautiful. Across the valley floor, the coastal range climbs upward. I've seen this patch of land in every season and it's always breathtaking—probably because I'm always high. We pass a series of weather-faded signs: *Keep Out, Not a Through Road, and finally, Dead End.* Al's been gradually increasing our speed. The dirt road has deep potholes and tangled roots sticking up. Now he's driving too fast and steering wildly, like he's playing a video game. We're being tossed like a salad.

"Slow down!" I yell, right before we hear a loud thump and come to a sudden stop.

"What the fuck?" Al says.

"Ouch, my head," says Joey.

"We hit a branch," I say, pointing out the obvious. "Turn off the engine."

"That was so cool," says Willie.

"Where'd that come from? I didn't hit that, it hit me. It's one of them freaky trees from *The Wizard of Oz.*"

We get out to inspect the damage. There is a good size dent in the corner of our roof-mounted luggage rack. "Well at least it's covered," says Molly.

"You bought the no-hassle insurance?" Al asks. I nod my head. "Bravo, brother! Let's get our money's worth and do it again!"

"Settle down, Ram-bro. Slow down and get us there in one piece."

We continue another quarter of a mile and stop in front of a green metal gate. *Private Property, No Trespassing, No Outlet*, the sign reads. But the warning is softened by the little peace signs Mare painted on the inside of the O's.

"I'll get the key," I say, jumping out. It's hidden under a nearby rock. Al pulls forward so I can relock the gate. Locking the gate is a 'must-follow' rule at Blue Moon Ranch. I get back in and we drive another hundred yards or so to their home.

Mare and Journey live in a hippie museum.

The structure was originally just a roof to cover an RV, but Journey framed in the sides and added a kitchen. My mother can make any space cozy and this humble structure is a tribute to her talent. Almost all hippies practice the same art of interior design, which is amazing, considering there are no periodicals, catalogs, or TV shows devoted to promoting the style. I've often wondered why most hippies dress, eat, speak, think, decorate, and smell with such remarkable consistency.

My mother is the Martha Stewart of hippies because she is so adept at expressing her hippie-ness in every aspect of her life. She's spent countless hours arranging and reshaping an odd collection of pictures, album covers, photographs, cartoons, posters, breakfast menus, letters, postcards, tokens and tidbits into every nook and cranny of her dwelling. The result is a three-dimensional, ever-changing collage they call home.

Shane and Skyler are enthralled. I've never seen them this focused before. No matter how many times I visit, the initial effect is mesmerizing. After our hugs and greetings, we take our time meandering the exhibition. The window over the sink is festooned with gnomes and fairy figurines. We see small jars, some full and some not so full of unidentifiable herbs and dry seeds. One appears to contain the eye of a newt. An origami swan sits proudly next to a green plastic soldier crouched down on one knee firing his crooked rifle. Small candles, a glass tetrahedron, metal stars, and rocks with faces painted on them compete to be noticed. I spy a map of Tibet, a color copy of Shelley's latest painting, and a Bob Marley poster that have been added since my last visit. We examine tiny mouse skulls, buttons, beads, and delicate dream catchers. There's a stack of abalone shells; the smallest is no bigger than the fingernail on Skyler's pinkie. We discover a miniature disco ball hanging from a length of fishing line and then marvel at the slivers of rainbow-colored light it casts on the counter. Skyler reaches for the God's eye that once hung in our yellow bus. Some things are familiar, others are new. Their space is in a constant state of change.

"What time will Shelley and Ali be here?" Molly asks Mare.

"Oh, I forgot to tell you. Shelley kind of freaked out at the last minute yesterday. She didn't want to be responsible for Ali—something about her brakes going out in her car. For some reason, Ali didn't want to stay with us, so we dropped off Shelley at her place and took Ali to Sapphire's house."

"You what? Why didn't you call me yesterday? This is *not* cool Mare. I need to call Ali right now."

"You can call her. I just forgot to tell you. Besides, Ali is fine. She's with one of your old friends, your buddy. Call her after dinner." Molly is not pleased with Mare's who-gives-a-shit-laissez-faire attitude.

"I want to talk to her *now*. This is the worst possible time for Ali to be dropped off with a person she doesn't know!"

Mare rolls her eyes, something she learned from us—or did we learn it from her? As soon as Molly reaches Ali on the phone, she's much more relaxed. Molly, Ali and I coordinate a pickup time and place for tomorrow. Once that's settled, there is copious amounts of sticky bud to smoke in bongs, pipes, and joints. Right when the munchies start to kick in, Mare serves a dinner consisting of brown rice, tofu, tortilla chips, salsa, hard-boiled eggs, raw zucchini, and monster Kit-Kat bars. As we're smoking the after-dinner joint, we decide to hike to Skull Point for the sunset.

Journey thoughtfully grabs a hand-truck from the shed and some rubber bungee cords, then attaches Skyler's car seat to the dolly. Now we can pull the little tyke up and down the trail instead of carrying him. Skyler gets it right away; gets in and is ready to go. Mare made some fantastic trails that crisscross their ten acres of property. Some of them take you where you want to go; others meander aimlessly—designed for the journey, not the destination, as Mare likes to say. Our tour begins right in front of their house.

"Welcome to the Buddha Garden," Mare says, pointing to the three statues. I feel a moment of pride that the cement Buddha I gave them is the biggest, followed immediately by shame for being so egotistic and shallow in the presence of all these Buddhas. Mare has brightened my statue up with day-glow paint, beaded jewelry and a strategically placed incense holder rising from his groin like a mystic erection. "That's the boner-Buddha," Mare says.

White speckles of bird shit adorn his rounded shoulders. One of the other two Buddhas is carved from ebony wood. The weathered surface adds to its character, which is starting to split right down the middle. "And that one is my bipolar Buddha," Mare says. Cats in need of luck have left claw marks on his bulging belly. The smallest Buddha in the garden is cast in metal and corroded in seven shades of green patina. Mare glued a feather to the back of his head. "And this little guy is our Shama-Llama-Ding-Dong-Indian-Healer-Buddha."

"I love your Buddhas," Molly says.

"I'm a born-again Buddhist," Mare says rather seriously, smiling proudly. She's such a lunatic, it's impossible not to love her.

"Amen ta dat!" Journey says.

Mare and Journey adopted Buddhism into their eclectic mix of spiritual beliefs about five years ago immediately after they read, *Essential Teachings* by the Dalai Lama, which she made available to me as well. Of course, Mare and Journey are their own kind of Buddhists, taking what they like, leaving what they don't, combining it with other spiritual beliefs and adding their own ideas as they see fit. Actually, they're anything but Buddhists. They just like to think of themselves as awakened. This is also when they created their own brand of transcendental meditation.

∞   ∞   ∞

Two years ago, I was dating my psycho ex-girlfriend, Nadine. We took a road trip and arrived at Blue Moon Ranch a couple of hours earlier than planned. When we got to the door, it seemed unusually quiet. We pressed our ears to the wood and could hear music faintly playing on the other side.

"They're home but I think they might be busy," I say.

"Getting busy," Nadine says, with a devilish smirk.

"I don't want to barge in on them," I say.

"Oh, don't be a pussy. Let's open the door, peek inside and see if there's any action."

"Worst idea in the history of mankind. Do you know how many times I walked in on my mother while she was having sex growing up?"

"How many?"

"Too many."

"Then one more time won't matter," she says, easing her hand onto the knob.

I know better than to try and stop her. She opens the door quietly just enough for her head to fit through. When she looks back at me, she's smiling like a five-year-old on the Peter Pan ride at Disneyland. She tips her head, signaling me to follow her inside. All the shades are drawn, and the lights are out.

My eyes seem to take forever to adjust. The first thing I see that makes sense is the dim glow of the stereo. Their ethereal music includes nature sounds; a blend of birds chirping, rain falling and waves crashing. Then the two human silhouettes of Mare and Journey solidifies in the shadows. They're facing away from us sitting in the traditional lotus position with legs crossed and backs straight. Their hands are resting palms on their knees, index fingers and thumbs touching lightly. They're clearly in a deep stage of meditation and I find their dedication and focus absolutely astounding. They certainly know what they're doing and the last thing I want to do is disturb them. I'm about to leave, but the music, lighting and mood is so relaxing I pause to enjoy the moment. Soon, I've become very relaxed as well. I glance at Nadine, who also appears unusually calm and relaxed. I think we're experiencing a contact-trance just from being in the same room with them.

It's incredibly beautiful. I'm both impressed and bewildered by their commitment and level of inner peace. But then my mother rolls one of her butt cheeks off the floor, spasm slightly and rips a quick little fart—the kind that sounds like sandpaper tearing. Our eyes get huge, and we cup our mouths to keep from laughing. Journey is undaunted by my mother's fart and then, he lifts a butt cheek, twitches and lets out an even louder fart—the kind that sounds like a couch leg scraping on a wooden floor. My admiration is fading fast. *Do they know they're being watched? Are they fucking with us?* They continue to meditate and fart as if the two go hand-in-hand. Nadine and I can't take it any longer and slip back outside, running far enough away from the house where we can't be heard as we fall to the ground laughing.

"What the hell was that?" she asks, cracking up.

"I believe we just witnessed the mystical art of transcendental farting." I reply.

"Beautiful," she says.

"And smelly," I add.

"I guess you can't reach that level of inner peace without getting some shit out."

∞   ∞   ∞

"What's a more relaxing religious symbol? A tortured Jesus on the cross bleeding out his life, or a fat smiling Buddha sitting in peaceful mediation?" I say.

"Good point," Al says, poking his finger a little too hard into my chest. Like his father, I don't think he realizes his own strength. Meanwhile, Skyler is babbling away. Maybe he's speaking in tongues. Even though no one can understand a single word, it sounds like he really knows what he's talking about. He's a master of inflection. Then, in the middle of all his gibberish, he says clearly and with emphasis, "Oh! Buddy Ebsen."

Mare repeats what she hears, "Oh! Belly up son!" She laughs and adds, "You tell 'em, Skyler!" It doesn't matter if he was talking about the Beverly Hillbillies or chubby Buddha bellies or nothing at all. Everyone is amused and laughs—out loud. I almost forgot we were capable and how good it feels. "Okay, and on that cute little note," Mare says, "let's move on." She leads us to a level clearing with no trees where the weeds have been cut low. It looks like a crop circle. "Can anyone guess what this is?" Mare asks.

"Where you park the flying saucer?" Al says.

"Very funny—but no. This is where we'll have pony rides one day. Imagine the kids' taking rides on a real live pony… or donkey…"

"…Or llama," I add, for no reason other than there's a lot of them in this area. I'm not sure why. I'm not aware of people eating llama cheese or a fad involving genuine llama fur apparel.

Our next stop is in front of a hand-painted sign that reads *Blue Moon*. Even before Mare speaks, I can tell by her body language that she's about to go overboard. This is the first time Molly and her kids have ever visited and Mare wants to make it a magically memorable experience.

"This is special," Mare begins. "Journey and I made this sign while we were camping in Mexico back in '83. Our dream was to have our own land one day. The first step in making that dream come true was creating this sign. We're always looking for signs, right? Why not just create your own and make things happen—kick the universe into gear, right? We did our part and let good karma take care of the rest. This sign has been everywhere: Oklahoma, San Diego, Albion, Casper… Now it's here. And we're here, standing on our very own land. Dreams will come true if you make even the slightest effort. The universe is magical. You just have to put it out there."

"That's so awesome," Molly says.

"Everything in the universe begins as a thought," Al says.

"Includin' da universe itself," adds Journey.

I don't know if I should laugh or deeply ponder what's being said.

"I should make a sign that says gull-wing Mercedes," I finally say.

"The less selfish the wish, the more likely it is to come true," Mare says.

"Who comes up with these rules anyway?"

A sign of things to come.

She smiles and shrugs as if it is obvious that *she* does, and we continue along the trail. The route takes us under a canopy of giant oaks with twisted, moss-covered branches looming overhead. Small birds flutter from tree to tree as a lone vulture circles high overhead. The occasional lizard scurries off the trail disappearing under dry leaves. Journey unlocks a make-shift gate in the barbed-wire fence, and we carefully pass through to the other side.

"Nice trail, Grandma," Willie says. Then I hear my mother asking him to call her Mare instead. I shake my head and roll my eyes. *Really?* I take a turn pulling Skyler in the dolly up the path to the next sign, which is marked with a large wooden fork—Mare's literal fork in the road. To the left is Skull Point, to the right, Ranch View. We go left, heading around a bend where the hill levels out. Al notices some pot plants growing in hollowed-out areas beneath the manzanitas.

"There's a few of those around here," Mare says smiling.

Journey chuckles, in his deepest voice, "Haw, haw, haw…"

Skull Point features a long warped wooden bench that's as gray as Journey's beard. The unusually deep patterns in the grain commands attention but so does the view overlooking the canyon. It's vast, untouched, and full of life. Mare removes her backpack and starts to roll. She looks as natural as the scenery itself.

Mare hands the joint to Journey, who fires it up and passes it along. She rolls another and then another after that. I take hit after hit until my toes are stoned. Willie, Joey, and Shane wander down the trail to explore, giving us a chance to talk about Chris. I'm practically in a cannabis induced coma.

"This spot is sacred," Journey begins.

"This is sacred pot," I mumble.

"No. Sacred *spot*," Journey says, clarifying. "See da skull behind you?"

I've seen the skull before but force myself to stand and take a closer look with Molly. Jutting forward from the trunk of the tree, about eight feet up, is a bighorn bull skull. Mare painted the night sky on the cranium. From one of the horns, a leather thong with eagle feathers hangs. From the other hangs a beaded necklace. On the jaw, she painted zebra stripes. It's a mind-blowingly trippy piece of art. Especially when you're on drugs.

"This is where Journey and I want to have our ashes spread one day," Mare says, which sort of shocks me at first as being a little morbid, but then again, death is on everyone's mind right now.

"I want Christina to be cremated and we'll spread her ashes here." She adds.

Molly, Al, and I glance at each other, each of us wearing matching shades of sorrow. Our mother's pain is real. We can feel it in our bones. As much as I miss Chris, as miserable as I feel; I know my mother's pain is even greater.

"When it's time for Journey and me to be with Christina, it's up to you to make sure we join her here. This is where our Earthly trip ends and where our next journey begins," Mare says, profoundly in a voice that's also sad and broken.

I picture my mother releasing Chris's ashes into the wind, wondering what it will be like to come back here one day and do the same with her remains. My eyes begin to tear. I look out over the rolling hills and imagine my mother's spirit reuniting with her daughter's.

"Parents aren't supposed to outlive their children," Mare says. Her pain is contagious. "I think each of you should have some of her ashes. That way, Chris can stay connected to her brothers and sisters." Her voice is unsteady. Al wipes his cheek. "We'll have Chris's funeral in Davis. It will be for immediate family. No one got to say goodbye to her, so I want an open casket." Molly puts her arm around Mare. "I want to see her one last time. I need to…" Her voice is as fragile as melting ice. Molly and Mare weep. My little brother and I cry quietly into the vast nothingness of the canyon.

When the boys return, we get up, dry our eyes, stretch, mask our sorrow with smiles and continue the tour. Journey leads the way, pulling Skyler behind him. We proceed up a steady slope, step-by-step, to the apex of their ten-acre universe. At the top, you can practically see the Earth's curvature, across a vast valley, to the next chain of mountains, past another valley to an even higher mountain range and beyond.

It's the magic hour and everyone looks beautiful in the amber glow of the setting sun. Feathery clouds are turning shades of pink and orange. I find myself shaving the curled bark off the manzanita bush next to me, which is oddly comforting because what's under it is so smooth. It's pleasing—like removing wax or rubber cement off your fingertips. After the sun sets and the colors fade into grays, we follow a different path zigzagging down the hill. It's lined with thousands and thousands of acorns. Mare must have been stoned out of her mind to do such a thing. Maybe that is why it bothers me so much. It's just the kind of project I could lose myself in—given enough time and weed. I don't want to be like her, but in so many ways, I know I am.

We get back to the house and hang out listening to music and looking at pictures until our thoughts turn to sleeping arrangements. I've hardly slept at all the last three nights and have been smoking so much pot that my blood feels as thick as maple syrup. Mare, not so thoughtfully, suggests that Shane, Skyler, and I should sleep in the tool shed.

"You'll get wheezy if you spend the night inside," she says. "We still have Not."

"I haven't seen your cat," I say.

"Wait. Not is a cat?" Molly asks.

"Yes. We have a cat named Not. Why Not? We were living in Albion and our neighbor's cat had a litter. This one kitten kept hanging out at our house all day and we kept taking her back. 'This is not our cat,' we'd say. But the kitten liked us more and eventually we had to accept that the cat was ours. So, instead of 'This is not our cat, it became, this is, Not. Our cat."

"That's a cute name," Molly says.

"I don't feel wheezy," I say.

"You guys will be really comfortable sleeping in the shed."

That statement will never be true for anyone anywhere. Ever.

I'm too tired to argue. She probably wants us out there, so we won't wake them up during the night. Al helps me move our bedding into what looks like a doghouse on stilts. Holding a flashlight in my mouth, I move the clutter around to make room for a bed. It smells like dust and gasoline; a combination that always brings me back to Cliff's garage. There are big spooky webs hanging in the corners made by what must be freakishly large spiders. My brother sees them too and asks for the flashlight.

"That's got to be from a Calisoga longitarus spider," Al says.

"Super."

"That particular species is not highly poisonous."

"Duly noted. Thanks Bro."

The floor is barely large enough for the three of us. Shane and Skyler fall asleep quickly. I listen to them breathe, the babbling creek and the subtle, spontaneous sounds emerging from the woods. I'm physically exhausted but my mind will not rest. I drift—not into sleep but along a series of thoughts that seem determined to find me. It's like being carried in a current and around every bend an old memory appears. It's hard to tell if I'm drifting by them or if they're coasting by me. Faces flash in and out of the darkness as in my imagination. Some are familiar. Some aren't. A few of them catch my gaze and look directly back at me—through me—if only for a millisecond. It's as if they've been waiting for me for hours, for months, for years—forever. And now that I'm here, they certainly won't let me sleep. The smell seems to get stronger with every breath. I give in to this endless, unwavering tide of thoughts and let them take me where they will.

∞   ∞   ∞

That fucking smell. Gas. Oil. Dust. The smell of depression. The smell of Cliff's garage. I'm lying on a couch that feels like it's concealing an anvil looking up from my crusty blanket into the shadows of the ceiling wondering how long I'll be stuck here. I feel empty and hollow. Not just from hunger but from chasing the same circle of thoughts endlessly in my head. *When is Mare going to find a place for all to live? What am I going to eat today? When will Charlie bring my bike? How long can I keep this a secret from my friends?* Then it happened. Mare found a place and we were all together again. That nightmare was over and reuniting with my family is the best day of my life!

Next, I'm on a hard floor. But now, in my minds' eye, it's on the dust-smelling shag carpet of the townhouse apartment in Davis. This is where we all lived together again after our brief and disastrous move to San Anselmo. Thanks to my brother, we call it the 'Avocado' Parkside Apartments instead of Alvarado. It's not that far off with its green shag carpet, green countertops, green fridge, oven sinks, tub, and toilet. We smoked a lot of green in there, too!

Everything is wonderful at first. We're so happy to be living together again, that for the first few weeks we get along like a TV family. But the honeymoon doesn't last. The place is much too small for all of us. Our mother's waterbed takes up most of the living room. There's no privacy and we start getting on each other's nerves. Our mother offers a solution.

"I'll live here but spend my nights at Charlie's. It will help keep the peace."

The new arrangement works fine at first. But then she stops spending her days with us and her absence creates a stress-filled void. Those familiar unnerving feelings about our long-term security creep back. Even when she is home, joining us for an occasional dinner or stopping by to get high with us on the weekend, there's more tension than ever before. Most of it's still between Mare and Shelley. They've figured out how to bring out the worst in each other. Sometimes Chris can calm them both down but even that becomes more rare as time goes on.

Their verbal assaults often escalate into shoving matches, which they were evenly matched for. Sometimes I'd step in to talk them down, smooth things out, get them to share a joint and think they were fine. But minutes later, they'd be going at it again and I'd storm off in frustration. If they would just pause long enough to see the look in little Molly or Alex's eyes, they'd see how hurtful their fights were to the rest of us. The tension they stirred was as toxic as nuclear waste. Everyone knew it was only going to get worse.

Meanwhile, I'm in the seventh grade trying my best to get in and out of the shower as quickly as possible so no one finds out about my little secret. I don't enjoy being naked with the boys I go to school with, the ones who spit wads of paper at the English teacher, the ones who bully others in the cafeteria. But the showers are mandatory, so I do my best to act like they're no big deal. Oliver Wendell Homes, at the time, is a 7th, 8th and 9th grade middle school. Some of the guys I have P.E. with are two and even three years older than me. Some already look like men with muscular physiques, long sideburns, and mustaches. There must have been other late bloomers, but my case is so chronic that I still look very much like a little boy. My hypothalamus gland is either hibernating or on hiatus. To make matters even worse, I happen to have a mole on my left butt cheek. It's a shit-colored spot and close to the crack. It's big enough to be on the 'Could be A Speck of Pooh' spectrum. That's the spectrum near the rectum. To be honest, it's very difficult for me to see the damn thing even with a mirror but I know it's there. My own brother and sisters spotted it years ago when we all used to take baths together and of course they loved teasing me about it.

When I shared this dilemma with Chris, first she laughs in my face, then she tells me to think of it as a beauty mark and reassures me that I have a nice ass, which was very kind and very strange coming from my sister. Her suggestion doesn't help at all. I'm convinced someone in the locker room will notice the blotch and everyone will start chasing me around snapping their wet towels at the target on my bare-ass behind. Hiding my backside means exposing my boyish frontside package, which is just as awful. All I can do is arm myself with defensive logic and perfectly phrased comebacks. Look at my unit longer than necessary and you be smacked with a line like, "You know what they say. It's not the worm, it's the wiggle."

"Your worm's too small to wiggle." Apparently, they had comebacks of their own.

I had another line about it, not being the pen—but how you sign your name, but honestly, I really just wanted a bigger pen. Worst case scenario: I resort to telling peers about my father's penis and how one day, I'm likely to be just as huge. Of course, I know better. Penis discussions in locker rooms are generally forbidden, so I cover up the best I can with my hands, foamy bubbles, and slivers of soap. My time in the shower generally lasts between eight and nine seconds. So far no one has noticed my shit-stain mole or said anything regarding my tiny package. Still, I won't let down my guard—I'm convinced that it's only a matter of time before I literally become the butt of everyone's joke.

Chris along with Della Williams and Orlando Gonzales rehearse for the Junior High Talent Show in our living room for weeks. While other kids plan their senseless cross-dressing skits, or sharpen their baton-twirling skills, or rehearse for a dreadful euphonium solo, Chris Bross the Great is preparing to steal the show with a much higher form of entertainment. She chooses to sing *Operator* by the *Manhattan Transfer*. They practice for hours and really polish their act. The trio buys thrift store clothes from the 1940's, complete with hats, furs and an opera-length cigarette holder. The rest of us love getting high with them and watching their progress. I'm a little nervous about the song choice. It isn't very popular—especially with teenagers. Still, I can hardly wait for the big day so I can root for my big sister.

When it's finally show time, they shuffle us into the gym, dim the lights and introduce the first act. Marcus Hatfield rides his unicycle in a circle seven times then wipes out. He gets up, pulls three juggling balls out of his fanny pack, and attempts to juggle while balancing in place on the wheel, which he manages to do on his second attempt. He's pretty good. It just goes on too long and looks less impressive after a while. He needs another trick or two. Still, the crowd rewards him for the effort. After another five moderately neato acts, the MC finally introduces my sister and her friends. They trot into place under a spotlight, bow gracefully and then strike a pose and freeze.

The song begins very slow; just voices softly harmonizing together. I can feel confusion and some tension in the crowd. She's taking such an incredible chance. The school is either going to love it or hate it. And if they hate it, Chris's popularity will take a hit. *What a risk-taker! She's so brave!* I think. I'm barely brave enough to watch. Then, the tempo picks up and Chris begins belting out the song in a voice that gives everyone in the gym, and anyone outside close enough to hear, the kind of chills you get by witnessing greatness. Chris looks completely comfortable and absolutely beautiful in the spotlight, so confident, gutsy and talented. She rocks that gym right down to its strange rubber floor. And when the song ends and the lights go back on, everyone jumps up and starts clapping and yelling and pounding on the bleachers with their feet. The roar of approval is ten times louder and five times longer than any other act. They aren't the last to perform, but it's clear they won't be topped.

As they're taking their final bows, I'm doing my best to make sure everyone around me is aware that Chris, the school's newest super star, is my sister.

"That's her. Right there. That's my sister. We're directly related. So, if you think she's cool, well then, you know... genes. We're *a lot* alike." The weird thing is it actually works. My sister's performance is so good, that I, against all odds, get noticed for the first time. And by the end of the following week, I've managed to find myself in a surprisingly deep relationship with my first boner-fied girlfriend, Barbara Dunn. So what if it only lasted five and a half days? A lot can happen in a week—especially when raging hormones are involved.

I knew things were getting serious by the way we kissed. When we started pushing gum back and forth into each other's mouths with our tongues, I figured it was time to settle down and get married. Barbara Dunn is the first girl to suck on my neck hard enough to leave a monstrous hickey even though I had warned her about my sensitive skin. She's the first woman to grab my ass and ask, 'Where is it?' She's the first girl I spoke with on the phone for over an hour and then couldn't recall a single thing we talked about. Barbara is also the very first girl I ever took on a romantic date.

I only had one shirt worthy of monumental events like school dances and romantic dates. It was as slick as a snot rag made from super thin material consisting of polyester, rayon, and shame. It's covered with night scenes of Las Vegas; neon colored casino signs, liquor stores, and adult hotels. The shirt looks so full of life but ironically does not breathe and the sweat stains under the arms have gotten worse with every wear. The collar is enormous; so big that it has plastic sewn into it to keep its shape. Other guys wear white puka shell necklaces. To express my individuality, I go with a shark tooth necklace I bought from a vending machine inside of a supermarket. Needless to say, it isn't real, but it sure makes me feel macho. When it's finally time to pack for the date, I begin with one of my mother's candles and stuff it into the outside pocket of my backpack. From the bus, I grab a shabby picnic blanket, which barely fits into the main pouch.

I thought it would be good to smell nice but the only thing I can find is mouthwash, so I gargle and put some behind my ears, on my chest and down my pants. Wishful thinking. I steal two beers from the fridge and asked Chris if I can borrow her portable AM radio. Barbara meets me at Chestnut Park on Saturday night at 7:00 p.m.

"I don't have to be home until nine," she said flirtatiously. Then she looks at the load on my back, and asks, "Why did you bring a parachute?"

"It's a-a-h-h—b-l-l-l-a-a-a-n-n-n-k-e-t," I say like Dracula, thinking it sounds dangerously romantic with my spot-on Transylvanian accent. She smiles because what other options does she really have with a total geek like me? Then I have to practically perform the chicken dance to shake free from the backpack.

"Where should we go?" She asks in a sultry voice.

I take her hand and we glide toward the circular cement building that, on an evening like this, appears to have architectural integrity. Yes, it's a public restroom but it's a really nice one. The girl's side is probably a bit cleaner and better smelling than the boys. Nothing but the best for my date will do. The park is almost empty and once the dog walker is gone, it should stay that way. The chance of us getting busted is small. I wave toward the entrance like its door number one on *Let's Make a Deal*. She stops, gives me a big hug, pulls away, then looks deep into my eyes and smiles. We enter the sanctuary of our private love-slash-shit-shack. First, we spread the blanket on the sticky floor, then turn on the music and light the candle thus creating a provocative atmosphere. Next, we sit and get cozy under the paper towel dispenser next to a garbage can. We pop open our beers and toast.

"To first dates," I say.

"To last dates," she says, before punching me gently in the shoulder to let me know she's only kidding. We laugh and listen to the continual hiss of a running toilet. For the next fifteen minutes, we're happy just to be in each other's company, sharing the first of many intimate moments we're destined to experience together. Then she reaches into her purse for something.

"This is Maybelline Kissing Potion and it's so much better than Lip Smackers," she says, smearing it on her lips. She catches my eyes and adds, "Everyone knows that."

"Yea. Everyone. Duh." I say, which sounds like the first line of the lamest haiku ever written. Maybe it was the way I said it because she makes the first move. Again. Come to think of it, Barbara always makes the first move. This alone makes her a keeper because I have no moves and need all the help I can get.

We start kissing. Slowly at first, our lips as gentle as butterfly wings—then real hard like we're wrestling, trying to pin down each other's tongues. Next, we start doing the gum thing again.

After ten minutes of gum passing, I pivot on the floor so that my back is against the wall, which is coarsely textured and stings my skin. She scooches in front of me, leaning her back against my chest and we talk about how stupid school is for a while. She asks me why boys spit so much. I have no idea and shrug my shoulders.

Then she says, "I'm bored," leans forward, and lifts her shirt revealing her two-lane bra strap crossing her back and a row of Fort Knox eyehooks that already seem to be laughing at me. I'd seen bras before. I have sisters. How come I never practiced? She lets me fumble with the hardware for a solid minute giggling now and then while I wiggle and pull and push the connecting metal hooks every which way praying they'll magically unclip or break before I die of embarrassment. My brain is lost in another world thinking; *Bar-ba-ra wears barb-wire-bra.* Then, like a sleight of hand magician, she whips an arm around, snaps her nimble fingers over the hardware and unfastens the fortress in a nanosecond. I'm dumbfounded as I watch the remaining straps over her shoulders disappear under her shirt.

"There," she says.

"I was so close to getting it undone," I say, trying to save face.

"No, you weren't. Not at all."

I can't take my eyes off the bumpy bones of her vertebrae. They're poking up from her back and I become extremely aroused—apparently, I'm a spine man. Nothing like a good spinal column to get a man's blood flowing. She adjusts her shirt and leans back again. Using complex stealth technology, I place my hands under her shirt and around her waist calculating the distance to her breasts. My fingers are near the top of her pants and I can feel heat rising from between her legs. It's so surprisingly hot I'm wondering if she's carrying a portable kiln or something. She flips her hair directly into my mouth forcing me to spit several times, which I try to do as sexy as possible. It's now or never time. I've got to grab hold of this opportunity because I may never get another one. An old song comes on the radio, *Little Willie by The Sweet*. I don't really like the song, but I'm nervous and feel the need to say something.

"Oh, I love this song!" I say, lying through my teeth. Barbara Dunn begins tapping her feet to the beat, which I interpret as a green light. I bring my hands up, over her smooth skin, across her belly and finally to the promised land of her breasts. As I cup them gently, I experience a deluge of wonderful feelings that are making me dumber by the minute. It takes a lot of will power to keep from saying something stupid like, 'this one feels slightly smaller than the other one.' As the song goes on, I get a little braver and begin gently caressing her nipples. They get hard! *This is incredible!* Her breathing becomes heavy. She arches her back and pushes into my chest, which will leave a cement stucco-pattern on my skin for days. But at this point, I could care less. You could have knocked me out or sprayed us with a high-pressure fire hose and my hands would have remained firmly, yet gently locked in place. I'm baffled. I simply cannot comprehend how incredibly wonderful her ample, firm breasts feel in my hands.

My little willie was about as big as it gets.

It was the perfect date and I have every intention of being with Barbara Dunn until we graduate from high school and go off to separate colleges. I envision reaching the red-hot kiln of her third base groin and even going all the way with her one day—when our love can no longer be contained, which theoretically could happen in one of many public or private bathrooms.

After our homeroom class on Monday, Barbara breaks up with me. She pulls me aside, which is considerate and says, "I had fun on Saturday, but I just want to be friends now."

"Just friends. Why?"

"Well, I really hate that song we listened to that you love so much. Now it gives me the willies. And this morning on the way to school, Skipper Rosenthal asked me out!"

"He did?"

"Yea. And he's really popular and a grade ahead, so…"

"So that's it?"

"Yea. You and I are still friends. But we're not together anymore. Okay?"

"Barbara Dunn is done with Tom?" I had to ask.

"You're funny and sweet and I'll always remember our date."

"Me too."

"But don't come near me for a while. Okay? I don't want Skipper to get the wrong idea."

"Okay."

I consider telling her how I really feel about the song, but I know it won't make a difference. I can't compete with Skipper. I don't think he would have ever noticed Barbara Dunn if he hadn't seen us kissing at school. I'd make a great talent scout. I see hidden beauty in girls that are often overlooked. I'm like an opening act warming up the room until the star takes over.

Of course, at first, I'm devastated and genuinely hurt and spend hours thinking of outlandish ways to win her back. Then I'm surprised how quickly the pain fades away. I honestly don't miss Barbara Dunn as much as I miss her breasts and I can't seem to get either one of them off my mind. A couple of weeks later, while I'm helping Chris make dinner, without consciously knowing it, I begin sculpting the hamburger meat into the form of Barbara's boobs. My attention to detail is remarkable. I'm standing in the kitchen with my eyes closed, squeezing the hamburger breasts in my hands when Chris walks back in. I don't know how long she witnesses this odd display of male behavior. I'm pushing the meat mounds together and pulling them apart while making little circles with my thumbs on the nipple area. I open my eyes and Chris is smiling ear-to-ear.

"You miss Barbara's tits, don't you?

"I do."

That's all we say. Chris knew what I was doing. She knew what to say and more importantly, what not to say. She seemed to have forgotten all about it until we were washing the dishes.

"Promise me you'll process this one fast because I can't wait to tell everyone about your hamburger tits."

"I'll try."

Just the fact that she gives me time is amazing. I know I'm incredibly lucky to have a sister like her. I'm ready to laugh about it before bed that night and tell Chris as much. We all have a good laugh and add another catch phrase, *Hamburger Breasts* to our list.

Like a dustpan for the dysfunctional, the Avocado Parkside Apartments are filled with misfits, druggies, broken families, and freaks like us—all swept together like sludge from the four corners of the world, inexplicably united by our afflictions and disorders. And it's because we are living amongst dregs and deviants of society that it makes perfect sense I would meet my life-long best friend there, Brad Bargmann.

When Brad's family moves into the same apartment complex, no one pays much attention because U-Haul trucks, trailers, pick-ups, and plain old cars stuffed to the max with junk, with barely enough room to see out the windshield, are a common site. Their townhouse unit is on the other side of the swimming pool, which has seen better days. It looks like it's been through an earthquake or two. It's small, but big enough to cool off in during the triple digit temperatures of summer. There are three of them carrying things inside. It's clearly a single mom and her two sons. I forget all about them. Then about two weeks later, while Alex and I are watching the *Gong Show,* someone starts knocking on the door. I get up to see who it is. Standing before me is a lean and lanky teenager about my age. I recognize him as one of the brothers that had moved in. I assume he's here to see me. He's the new kid in town out to make a friend—a buddy who can show him around and introduce him to other people. I just so happen to have been longing to play Frisbee with someone who can throw as far as me. I'm thinking, *He's spindly as all hell, but he looks nice. Besides, it sure would be nice to have a buddy I could be honest with about my family.*

"Are any of your sisters' home?" he asks.

I'm not expecting this at all. My eager-to-be-your-pal expression drops to the floor like a wet towel. *ANY of my sisters? He isn't interested in me at all. He's already met Shelley, Chris, and Molly?*

"Nope."

"Okay. Bye." He spins and walks away. I was so sure he was here to see me and so glad he doesn't see how red my face is. He's carrying a skateboard. It doesn't look like a regular one. It happens to catch the sun on its metal trucks and the glare burns a spotlight into my retinas, like it's a holy icon that's being blessed by mother nature. And from where I'm standing in the doorway, I kid you not, that skateboard looks like it was designed by Dino Ferrari. Later, I ask my sisters if they know the tall, skinny guy. The *all* know him. He had introduced himself to each of them one-by-one on different occasions. Naturally, Chris has the most details…

"Her name is Susie and she's going through her second divorce. They ended up in Davis because she has a long-time girlfriend here, who's also going through a divorce—though further along. Her girlfriend's name is Lynn. She has a daughter named Kelly. Kelly goes to Emerson junior high. So will he. His name is Brad. He's one grade ahead of you. He's five feet eleven and one quarter inches. He's a Libra like Shelley but they're nothing alike. His little brother is Todd. They're from Berkeley but after the first divorce they moved to Alpine. It's a town in the Cuyamaca Mountains near San Diego. Their stepfather is from Oklahoma. They raised champion bulldogs and monkeys. One of the monkeys was part of the family and wore a diaper and ate dinner with them at the table every night. Susie is good with animals. She tames coyotes too. Her second husband made a lot of money but had addictions to pills, women, danger, booze and embezzling. Sometimes he gardened with only his cowboy boots on. They were married for eight years. Things fell apart. After the divorce, they moved to Arroyo Grande. You know where that is, near Pismo Beach. They have an English bulldog named Cisco. He's a grand champion and his sperm is worth thousands of dollars."

"Their family sounds like ours," I say.

"*A lot* like ours. Brad told me his mom's an alcoholic."

"It sounds like you know him really well. What? Are you two engaged or something?"

"Ha, ha. No. We did make out in the cabana though."

"You like him?"

"Yea. But just as a friend."

"Bad kisser?"

"No. It's just that I like someone else I've already been seeing."

"Who is it? Do I know him?"

"You know him from school."

"Who is it? Tell me!"

"I'll tell you if you guess right. Deal?"

"Deal."

I guess and guess and even get out the Minuteman yearbook and guess some more. She swears he's at Holmes, but I never figure it out because she kept it a secret until her senior year of high school. That's when we find out she's been 'involved' with the art teacher since the eighth grade. It never occurred to me to point out a faculty member in the yearbook. He's at least a couple decades older. So it really was her senior year in more ways than one.

After school one afternoon, Alex and I notice the new kid out in the street doing tricks on his skateboard. We press our faces into the window and watch in awe. He's doing things we didn't know were possible. We do know that everything is about to change. Cue the music. Brace yourselves. A new era in skateboarding is about to begin. Alex and I race outside elbowing each other as we go. The first thing I notice is the lack of sound. Brad's coming toward us doing a one-foot nose wheelie. He comes to a stop, kicks up his board and hands it to me knowing that I have never seen anything like it before in my entire life.

"Behold the future."

My first thought: *Geek Alert!* But as I take hold of it, it's clearly as odd and unique as an alien artifact. It seems to encompass space-age technology. It's unusually slender and flexible and the tail flares gently upward providing leverage for doing tricks. The wheels are made of hard red rubber. I spin one around and it never stops turning. Our boards in comparison are thick, clunky, cumbersome logs from the Stone age. Some of us have progressed from metal to clay wheels, but even with these, the tiniest pebble can send you flying ass over elbows to the ground. Our boards have rigid trucks making it impossible to carve turns. Our oily bearings are exposed and slow because of the dirt and grime they attract. His bearings are packed invisibly behind rubber and are safe from debris. Watching that wheel spinning endlessly sends me into a hypnotic trance.

"Urethane wheels," he says. He's a Missionary from a mysterious land communicating to a primitive, indigenous tribe member.

"Urr-eth-aine…" I moan like a hominoid.

I can see my stupefied expression staring back at me in the glossy fiberglass reflection. I flip the board over and run my fingers along the non-skid tape on top, which sparkles in the sun like tiny bolts of lightning as seen from orbit. Toward the front, the tape is cut away in the shape of a scallop shell for the logo. In two-tone gold and white letters, laminated beneath the surface are the words 'Fiber Flex'.

"It's a G and S Fiber Flex. They're famous for making surfboards. This one has Tracker Trucks and Road Rider four-inch wheels," he says.

I hand it to Alex so he can examine it for himself. "How much did it cost?" I manage to ask.

"Fifty bucks."

"Oh my God!" yells Alex. "That's a fortune!" It was a fortune back then.

This is, without question, the first modern skateboard to reach the town of Davis, maybe the first one anywhere in Northern California. This new kid is like a Spanish conquistador introducing us to the domesticated horse knowing that it will change our lives forever.

"Try it out."

I do, and instantly know our skateboards are obsolete. We take it into the cabana, which has the smoothest cement around. I set his skateboard on the ground, place my hands on both ends, roll forward and push myself into a handstand and ride it across the floor.

"Woah! Radical!" he says.

"Bitchin'," my brother adds.

"By the way, my name is Brad."

"I'm Tom. This is my bother, Alex."

"I have a brother too. Todd. He's helping my mother wash our dog and set up its crate on the patio."

Brad spends the next couple of hours teaching us tricks and enlightening us about the skateboard scene in southern California. Thanks to Chris, I already know a little about him and his family, which accelerates our friendship.

"My mother's an alcoholic," Brad says nonchalantly.

"My mother's a pot-aholic," I reply.

"Sometimes my mother drinks and cries all night long.

"Sometimes my mother takes drug-breaks from her kids and disappears for days."

"My stepfather used to beat us with a stick."

"Our stepfather used his belt."

"My mother had an affair with one of the Mexicans we hired on our ranch," he says.

"My mother did that too, with a hired hand hick when we lived on a ranch," I say.

"My brother eats his own boogers."

"My brother lets cats and dogs eat from his mouth."

"My stepfather had an affair with his secretary, Ava, which lead to my mother's second divorce."

"My stepfather did the exact same thing. Her name was Moe."

"My mother took us to Sea World and made out with a walrus trainer."

"My mother took us to the circus and seduced Victor the clown."

"My mother bought a stupid Plymouth Volaré." And then he sings like Ricardo Montalbán in the commercial, "Volaré, oh-oh-oh-oooo…"

"My mother bought a hippie bus." And then I sing a line from The Partridge Family.

We realize, tit-for-tat, we were essentially equals and two minutes into our conversation I know I have a new buddy for life. We'd both had done our share of coping. There's no need to hide behind false pretenses. Guys our age usually have competitive friendships based on macho bullshit. It isn't like that with Brad. Instead of judging, we support. I don't need to hide our family secrets from Brad—or from his mother and brother. I felt grateful that our paths had crossed and that he's finally more interested in me than any of my sisters. He quickly becomes the only friend I can be totally honest with. Brad not only accepts everyone in my family and our wacky behavior, he embraces it. He actually thinks we're cool, which blows my blonde mind.

Brad has an unusually well-defined cleft in the middle of his chin. it looks like a milk-bloated Cheerio that had gotten stuck there during breakfast. He has ultra-fine, naturally blonde straight hair, parted down the middle that floats away from his head as if he's charged with static electricity. His long skinny arms are always slightly bent at the elbow—I don't think he's physically capable of straightening them all the way out. He leans forward with the top half of his body when he walks so it looks like his legs are playing catch up. He's got a large, aquiline nose that fits his face and looks good on him. It reminds me of the prideful expressions our founding fathers tend to have in the historic portraits that grace our textbooks and currency. He's usually squinting his blue eyes even when it's not bright outside. He has fair skin and mole on his cheek just like John Boy's on *The Waltons*.

Brad's mother is attractive. She's what boys our age call a hottie-boom-ba-lottie. Like my mother, Susie is petite and well proportioned. She also has a distinctive nose that adds a unique stamp to her beauty. She used to teach ballet and still has an athletic and graceful body. Brad's little brother is a looker. He has even blonder hair than Brad, me, or Molly; blue eyes and the kind of chiseled features girls like on a guy's face. Brad and I don't like either one of our little brothers tagging along but when Todd does, it's obvious he's a chick magnet. We bring him along sometimes just to meet the girls who stalk him and sometimes we try and pick up on his leftovers.

Tom, Brad and Todd (long before Hanson & MMMBop)

Shelley and Mare no longer have normal conversations. Chris, Molly, Alex, and I have had several heart-to-heart conversations with our sister.

"You have to mellow out," we tell her. "You can't be so confrontational!" We beg her to lighten up with Mare and not get under her skin.

"She's the one that needs to mellow out," Shelley says insisting she's not the problem.

"Mare's a self-centered bitch who needs to put her kids first for a change."

She does have a point. Nevertheless, we know keeping the peace requires effort from Shelley. Chris even tries a comedic approach. When *Showdown* by *ELO* plays on the radio, Chris grabs anything remotely resembling a microphone and sings the words to Shelley. Although it's always a compelling performance, this too, has no effect and Shelley continues to spar with Mare about everything. During their next fight, just as Shelley is getting all worked up, Mare becomes eerily calm.

"Time out. Let's smoke a joint," she says.

"Is that your solution for everything?" Shelley hisses.

"Maybe," Mare says quietly before sitting down with her papers and a bag of weed. After taking a couple of hits she looks at Shelley and says, "We're not going to fight anymore."

"Yea right," Shelley says crossing her arms.

"You're moving out to live with my sister in Idaho." Then she leans directly into Shelley's face. "Before school gets out and at least for the entire summer."

Shelley looks genuinely surprised for a second and then madder than I've ever seen her. Maybe she thinks Mare is bluffing.

"Buy me a one-way fucking ticket!" she yells, raising the volume of each word. She's had leather lungs since she was a kid. Mare had already bought the one-way Greyhound Bus ticket. She pulls the envelope from her backpack and slides it across the table. Shelley examines the ticket, crumples it up and throws it back at Mare. It bounces harmlessly off her mule-tooth necklace. Shelley gets up, red in the face, holding back tears, stomps her feet upstairs and slams the bedroom door behind her.

It was a quiet night after that.

Then, about a week and a half before school is out for the summer, my sister just disappears. We didn't get to see her off or say goodbye. Her trip left us wondering how long she'd be gone.

"How long will Shelley be in Idaho?" I ask Mare.

"Until she gets her act together."

"We're talking about Shelley. That could take a while."

"Fine with me. Her being gone is better for all of us." She announces coldly. The next thing we know, she's packing up Shelley's clothes and art supplies. "I'll store her stuff at Charlie's, so you'll have a little more space and much better energy in the apartment."

The energy in the apartment becomes worse than ever.

Mare's act sends a loud and clear message to the rest of us. Mom can and will cast any one of us aside with the wave of her hand. No one is safe. We'd better go with her flow, or she'll find a way to flow us right out of her life. Best to be mindful and tiptoe around her. We start treating our mother delicately; like you would a spoiled child, careful to not spark a confrontation. She is a child—a wild child who also happens to be our mom—a mother capable of locking a door, throwing away the key and never looking back.

∞   ∞   ∞

Shane rolls over onto his back and starts to snore quietly. I look at him and his brother in the dark shadows of the shed realizing they're essentially doomed to experience a lot of the same unsettling anxiety I felt as a child. My God. They already have. Yes, Mare was an absentee parent, but at least she still existed. Their mother is gone forever. That's going to affect both of them for the rest of their lives. My heart is heavy and aches for them. Even the worst of the worst shit we experienced growing up, pales in comparison to what's happening now. I could easily cry, but I don't want to wake them up. I try side-stepping my sorrow by thinking more about other times but can no longer focus for more than a moment. My brain has become a broken record stuck in an endless loop of grief.

I beg for sleep, but it never happens. It's too hot, cramped, and uncomfortable on the floor. As I'm finally nodding off, it gets light outside. I cover my eyes with yesterday's socks, but it's no use. Within minutes, the shed is filled with light and another day without my sister has already begun.

Seventh

July 7th, 1996

Just pulling myself up off the floor to stand requires an epic battle with gravity. My back is killing me. So are my neck, hips, and shoulders—not enough padding on the shed floor. It's not just the muscles; my bones and tendons ache too, like I've aged fifty years overnight. Knowing that I'll be sore all day affects my mood. It's going to be a long day. I reach over the kids for my shoes and hobble to the outhouse to pee. Shane and Skyler are still asleep when I get back and Not the cat is laying comfortably in my space on the floor. I politely shoo her back outside. It's too early to go inside, so I dawdle away an hour sitting in the van listening to the radio and checking on the kids every fifteen minutes until Skyler wakes up. He reaches up wanting to be picked up, and when I do I'm not thinking about my back at all.

Skyler relaxes into my arms and slumps his head against my neck. I grab what I need to change his diaper dancing around the shed and over Shane like a ballerina. We go to the washer and dryer shed to take care of business and I'm shocked and amazed by the sheer weight and mass of his diaper. This number two is one for the record books! One more like this and I could do some curls, some squats—get a little work out. Once he's all cleaned up and I apologize to the environment, we go back outside. I try setting him on the ground, but he still wants to be held so I carry him along the trails below the red, knuckle-twisting, branches of the madrone trees.

"Tree tunnel," I say, in the dense sections where the limbs and leaves blot out the sky. He looks up at the canopy of trees overhead like a stargazer. As he does, I see them bending towards us in the reflection of his eyes. Eventually we hear the first voices of morning and follow them into the house.

Mare brings a fat joint to my lips so I can take a hit. Wake and bake again. What else would I expect at Blue Moon Ranch? A hauntingly familiar breakfast consisting of brown rice, tofu, chips and salsa, hard-boiled eggs, raw zucchini, and monster-sized Kit-Kat bars is laid out again. Mare hovers about, watering plants, eating, toking, and tidying up, all at the same time. Just like Chris, she's a multitasker.

"Journey and I would love to watch the boys today while you pick up Ali and Shelley. I bet you could use a little break." Mare is such a sweetheart when she wants to be. A break from the kids and poop-patrol sounds really good. Molly tells her boys that they're coming with us.

"I'll show you where I was working when I met your father. And I can show you our house, too." I think she wants to keep her boys from taking any drugs Mare and Journey are sure to offer. Al elects to stay behind.

"I'm going to scare me some hippies!" he says, looking up from his plate, dressed to kill in his Army gear.

"We're putting the word out to our friends that we're having a wake in honor of Christina today," Mare says. "So, when you get back, expect a party." I imagine spreading news to people living in remote, off-the-grid, untold, locations would be difficult. *Smoke signals?* Mare hands me a twenty and a list of things to pick up at the grocery store. I give her the bill back. She hands me a joint. I take it. She hands me another joint. I take it. This could go on forever.

"Three for the road should do it," I say.

We bid our farewells and set off. Journey opens and then locks the gate behind us and we're on our way. It feels weird *not* to have Shane and Skyler with me. We turn left on 101 heading north. Soon we're passing Wavy Gravy's Hog Farm, Camp Winnarainbow. I tell Molly what little I know about the man.

"His commune handled security for Woodstock. Instead of policemen, they were 'please-men' and 'please-women' who kindly asked people to do this and not do that. When all the vendors ran out of food the nearby towns all pitched in. Wavy Gravy and his people cooked for thousands of people. Remember the album? He's the one who says, 'What I have in mind is breakfast for four hundred-thousand… this must be heaven!'"

"I do remember that," says Molly quietly, staring ahead down the road through the windshield that's equally become her window into the past.

I turn onto Branscomb Road, which is a county-maintained, unpaved narrow path used only by locals—and only in dry weather. Most maps don't show this road at all. At the crest of the coastal range, you round what appears to be just another bend in the road lined with dusty evergreens, when suddenly a spectacular view of the ocean is revealed. It's like having the entire Pacific Ocean sneak up and surprise you. This game of peek-a-boo continues as you descend toward the sea, coasting along, letting gravity and the massive pull of the sea itself carry you along.

It's one of those roads that's longer than you remember. It finally spits us onto the Pacific Coast Highway a few miles north of Westport. This section of the coastline is spectacular. We cling to hairpin turns etched into rocky cliffs hovering a thousand feet above the ocean. Everything here is in a constant state of change. No wonder Mare loves the coast. Giant kelp forests sway lazily in the swells. Long masses of burgundy-colored seaweed vines line the beach like the tangled hair of sea monsters. Contrasting the rocky cliffs are areas of soft grassy meadows with breathtaking views of the ocean. Cows, sheep, goats, and a growing number of llamas meander in the picturesque clearings, unimpressed by the incredible vistas before them. They seem like some the luckiest grazers on this green earth.

We reach the tiny town of Westport, which reminds me of a base camp. The post office is adjoined to the general store that has a single gas pump out front. Inside, there's also a deli-restaurant, a butcher shop with an old-fashioned pickle barrel.

"This is where I met your father," Molly says, pointing at the deli. I'm expecting a reaction from her kids, but their expressions don't change. Maybe this just makes them miss their father. Maybe they just need time to let it sink in.

Highway 1, depending on your direction, pretty much starts and ends right here. But it has always been the end of the road to me—the final outpost of civilization. Journey took Mare as far away as possible, and would have gone further, but ran out of road. Shelley lived in a tiny trailer perched on the bluff just south of town for years. Molly's miniature trailer sat in a dry creek bed near here until she moved in with Kurt. It's interesting that so much of my family gravitated to this end-of-the-line destination.

Molly points the way to the house Kurt built up a gravel road and through a steep narrow gulch. I have to use the van's lowest gear to make the grade. You could walk faster. At the top there's a clearing and a funky wooden house that looks like it's been added on to over the years.

"Kurt and I lived here for two years. Ali was born here." Molly says.

"You want to get out and look around? It looks deserted."

"No. Not really. I just wanted them to see it."

"I remember visiting when Ali was just a baby."

"Eleven years ago…" Molly says, a swell of memories carrying her away.

"Before this I lived just down the road in the tiniest trailer in a dry creek bed with no running water or electricity," she says. "I'd burn the propane stove to keep warm and light candles to see at night. It's a miracle I never blew that tin can up! I was seventeen years old, a waitress at the Westport Deli, who didn't know how to count change when I met Kurt. He was thirty-three and extremely grungy. He looked misplaced in time—like a California prospector during the gold rush. But I saw through all that facial hair and grime because he had a house with electricity, heat, and an honest-to-God toilet. I wasn't attracted to him at first. I was in love with the idea of living in a house. It didn't matter that he was so much older than me because love is ageless, especially when it's a matter of life, death and running water. I saw what Kurt could provide and promptly moved in and then we got married. A year later, one day before my nineteenth birthday, Ali was born. By that time, I definitely loved him. He was a really good man, and I knew he'd be a great father." She pauses, perhaps remembering some things not worth mentioning. "Now let's go get my little girl."

We make our way back to the highway and continue south. When we reach Sapphire's house, it looks empty, not a car, pet, or person in sight. Still, we go through the motion of getting out, looking around and knocking on doors. Molly is anxious but not for long. We hear the hum of a motorcycle purring its way towards us and my little sister's eyes light up.

"There they are!"

"Sapphire has a motorcycle?" I ask.

"Not a motorcycle—a 'gnarly Harley.'" And what a sight they are cruising towards us; pristine landscape, wind in their face, dust flying up behind them like a scene from Easy Rider.

Sapphire's long red hair cannot be contained by her helmet. She brings the beast to a stop in front of us and swings the kickstand into place. Ali jumps off the bike, removes her helmet, sets it on the seat, shakes her head, spits hair from her mouth and hugs her mother in one fluid motion.

Next, she hugs the rest of us and proceeds to tell us all about her strange road trip with Shelley, Mare and Journey.

Ali turns twelve next month. She's capable of breaking the speed barriers of speech with perfect enunciation. It runs in our family—mainly with the girls.

"Oh my God, it was so bizarre. We smoked joint after joint the entire way. By the time we got to the coast, it was completely fogged in—like a *Prince* video! But then we noticed it was only foggy in the car, so we rolled down the windows and realized it was actually pretty clear outside. Clambake! That's how much pot we smoked!"

She's talking about as fast as a human possibly can. "We stopped about a million times along the way, because Mare and Journey have to get stoned next to every lake, river, bridge and pretty rock they see, if you know what I mean and I think you do. Shelley and I were like, right on! Let's party! But then it took forever to get anywhere. Anyway, everything was fine until we got about a mile from Shelley's house, and then she started fah-reaking out. She said I couldn't spend the night with her. I was like, what the fuck? Why not? She said she was in shock from Chris's death, needed to be alone, and that she wasn't ready to drive herself or me anywhere in a car yet. Total meltdown—never saw it coming. I don't know why, but I didn't want to stay with Mare and Journey alone. Strange vibes. From Journey. You know. Trust your gut. So we dropped Shelley off at her 'cat-ranch' while she called Sapphire. Oh my god. Wait until you see Shelley's place. The whole thing was so bizarre! Who is this Sapphire chick named after a gemstone? Whatever."

"The next thing I know, Mare and Journey pretty much kick me out of the car at Sapphire's house after an awkward four-second introduction and drive away. Once I met Sapphire, everything was totally fine. It was way better than staying with Mare and Journey. It was actually a blast. And it was nice of Mare to give me a fistful of joints. That was sweet. Thanks, grandma! This has been so beyond weird. Believe me, it's been a wild ride."

"Why didn't you call me?" Molly says.

"I was too baked to call, plus it was late, plus Mare said she'd call the next day anyway. She didn't? Big surprise. I didn't call yesterday because I knew you'd be on the road. I knew you'd call Sapphire when you got to Mare's place. It all worked out. I like Sapphire. She's great! It was just hell getting here."

Molly gives Sapphire a big thank you hug.

"Sapphire knew you way before Dad did," Ali says. "And I learned some very interesting things about you…"

"I'm sure you did," says Molly, shooting Sapphire a look.

"It's okay that you went through a nympho stage, Mom. And just because *you* did, doesn't mean *I* will."

"Don't believe everything you hear," Molly says, shooting Sapphire a much different look.

Ali responds quickly, "Whatever! Everyone in our family is insane! But that's why I love 'em so much."

"Actually, our family does have a long, colorful history of mental illness, I say. "Physically? No problem. We're good specimens—blessed with good genes. I mean, just look at us, right? But from a mental perspective… Well, let's just say there's some coo-coo-birds nesting in our family tree."

"We make crazy look good," says Ali.

"Exactly. That's our niche, our contribution to society and certainly something to instill into our children. Of course, I tend to forget this tidbit of information when filling out medical papers or consulting with doctors and nurses."

"Yea. Best to keep that on the down-low," Molly says.

"Oh, hi Doctor. Things are good…" I say pretending to be at a clinic. "Umm, but do you have anything for anxiety, bipolar disorder, insomnia, psychosis, ODD, hysteria, schizophrenia, ADD, trauma, ADHD, agoraphobia, delusions, claustrophobia, OCD, denial, addiction, post-traumatic stress disorder, depression, manic episodes, sleep paralysis, hallucinations and paranoia? You do? Great! Prescription please."

"Oh, that's funny, brother."

"Only because it's true. Anyway, we should hit the road."

Back on the highway, in the distance, we see a familiar flume of billowing steam coming from the lumber mill in Fort Bragg. The pillar of white cloud grows larger as we get closer to town. I don't think about this part of my past often but only because it was the worst year and a half of my life. I'd love to forget about it entirely, but it has a way of invading my subconscious, the cornerstone of my reoccurring stress dream. Fort Bragg, or "Fart Bag" as we called it, never felt like home. Nothing good happened here. It's where we sort of semi-reunited after Mare disbanded the family. What should have been a good thing, became more bad craziness. A marine layer is blanketing the town. Driving through town stirs up long lost feelings that materialize out of the fog. Just bits and pieces, sharp and loud, fast, and slow from all directions. My head begins to spin.

∞   ∞   ∞

West TV. It's still there on the corner only now it's a furniture store. My work-study job in high school. Jim West worked at the mill and made a life-changing decision to better himself. Through a correspondence class, he learned how to fix television sets. He made enough money to buy the Cliff House, Fort Bragg's fanciest restaurant overlooking the Noyo Bridge and beyond. Jim loved to demonstrate his strength by doing one arm push-ups. He also smoked like a chimney. Every workbench had dark brown edges from years of burning butts. Terrible job, but his gun-barrel blue Mercedes Benz 450SLC was a joy to drive. Wiping brown nicotine dots off the windows and making bank deposits was part of my job. In these moments, the car was essentially mine and I think it spoiled me for life.

Wheezy Rider. I'm the only one who rides a bike to school even after they add a bike rack for me out front. It's almost always a wet ride. My first class is English, and we spend most of the time silently writing in our journals but I'm unable to breathe quietly because of my chronic asthma. I'm sure the entire room can hear me wheezing. I have to constantly cough to clear my lungs and have no choice but to swallow the phlegm, which leads to even more wheezing.

Bus Station. Alex is thirteen. Him and Journey start butting heads. Mare snips the situation in the bud by sending Alex to live with his father in Morro Bay. My brother acts tough until it's time to go to the bus station. He cries up a storm begging Mom for mercy.

"Don't make me go. I'll be good. I promise to get along with Journey! Please. Please. Please!" Mare would have none of it. She literally drags him onto the bus kicking and screaming. I can see my brother crying through the window as the bus leaves the station. Our cold-hearted mother just waves to him like he's off to summer camp for a week. It's a scene right out of a sad, disturbing and, depressing movie, only it isn't a movie—this shit is real.

Poor Molly. Molly is the only one who moves to Fort Bragg with Mare and Journey during the summer of 1978. They camp in the bus at Dolphin Cove in the Noyo Harbor. Molly is just shy of sixteen and living in a twenty-foot bus with Mare and her new partner, Journey. She's six miles from school and not on a bus route. She walks there and back five days a week until the real rain hits, and then, with Mare's approval, she drops out. It gets worse.

Journey wants to form a love triangle with Mare and Molly. Mare approves of the idea, Molly does not and runs off to live with Chris and Allen in Davis. Molly explains her predicament and is welcomed into their home. But, a few days later, Allen begins pressuring Molly to join him and Chris in bed. Molly's refusal to comply creates awkward tensions between all three of them. In order to escape that situation, she has no choice but to return to the nightmare Mare and Journey had created. What a completely fucked up situation she had to endure. My poor little sister! And shame on Mare for not looking out for her children.

The bile-green apartment building. After nine months of bus-camping, Mare and Journey finally rent a one-room apartment in town. I was living in Sonora with Brad, Susie and Todd before moving back in with my family. A couple of weeks later, Chris and Allen drove Alex up from Davis to join us. The five of us were all crammed into the place like a crisis center. It never stops raining. Alex and I share the room next to the only bathroom. Mare and Journey sleep on a pad in the living room. As soon as I start working at West TV to save money for college, Journey starts charging me for rent.

Bag of Shrooms. Just two months shy of graduating high school, Mare and Journey ditch the apartment and move into the bus again—this time up in Westport. Poor Molly has to move back in with them until she can save enough money to buy her dangerous, dry-creek-bed trailer. My best option is to move in with my ex-girlfriend's dad until I graduate. Mare and Journey inform me that they will NOT be attending my graduation. However, they do give me a large grocery bag of killer "shrooms" the week before. "Eat up," Mare says encouragingly. "It will make the end of school and your graduation ceremony way more interesting."

My reoccurring stress dream. I'm back at Fart Bag high school, at my current age, desperately waiting to graduate so I can get the fuck out. In the dream, I count down the months on my fingers. I'm a man and it's highly embarrassing to be in high school with all these kids. I have another life to tend to, but cannot leave until finishing my senior year, which never ends.

∞   ∞   ∞

All these negative feelings come rushing back like a punch in the face. Being here is like scuba diving too deep and realizing you don't have enough air to get back up. Molly and I look at each other, trying to make sense of it all. She shakes her head as we pass our old apartment building. Neither one of us speaks but so much is exchanged. Just the look on each other's faces says it all.

We travel over the Noyo Bridge, past the Casper exit and into the beautiful and touristy town of Mendocino. We cross the Big River Bridge, take a left on Comptche Ukiah road, heading away from the coast. The landscape changes rapidly. We go from towering redwoods and damp green ferns to dry grass, shrubs, and a sparse pygmy forest. The temperature is climbing. Somehow, I'm able to identify the correct dirt road that leads to Shelley's house.

"This is it?" asks Molly, hoping this is a cruel joke.

"Yup. This is it," says Ali.

"Oh man," says Joey.

"Holy shit," says Will.

Molly has every right to be shell-shocked. Shelley has never been one to be tidy and organized. Disorder is in her DNA. This affects everything around her like rings in a pond. The closer you get to my sister, the more you appreciate chaos theory and the concept of entropy. I've seen it progress over the years, so I've had time to adjust. But this is Molly's first visit to Shelley's place and she's astonished, wondering how her sister can possibly live this way. Molly must be wondering if there was a natural disaster earlier in the day, or if the county garbage trucks mistakenly dumped everyone's trash here instead of the local landfill.

I drive between walls of stacked garbage and debris and park next to a rusty washing machine and a lopsided pile of tires. Shelley's house is a crooked mess of rotting wood and moss. Molly looks like she doesn't want to get out of the van.

"Have your kids had tetanus shots lately?" I ask to lighten her mood. We open the doors and tentatively set foot into Shelley's world.

Eighth
July 7th, 1996

My sister is the *Willard* of cats.

That's an exaggeration, but still. As we're getting out of the van, we're immediately confronted with a bona fide kitty stampede. The felines are everywhere and in all the shapes, sizes, and colors they come in. Several of them follow us to the deck. Step-by-well-placed-step, we make our way up the broken stairs, over the protruding nails, past the shattered glass to Shelley's front door. This is part of my sister's security system. It helps her feel safe having a semi-dangerous and noisy entry that could potentially piss off a barefoot intruder.

"How many cats do you think Shelley has?" asks Willie, sweeping one up into his arms.

"Lots!" Snaps Ali.

We knock and knock some more but no one answers the door. "I guess I'll go get her," Molly says, opening the door cautiously.

"Yeah. I'll wait… heh-chooooooo! …out here," I say.

"Bless you," says Joey.

"Thank you."

Several cats are rubbing into my legs lovingly. My nose tickles. My eyes are starting to itch. Suddenly, Shelley stomps through the door, past me with no eye contact and disappears around the corner—maybe to pee? It wouldn't surprise me if her toilet was broken. Molly appears in the doorway for a moment shaking her head. Shelley marches back inside, past her little sister slamming the door shut behind her. A moment later Molly cracks the door open.

"She's a little miffed that I woke her up," she says.

"It's two-thirty."

"I know, Bro."

I take a deep breath in search of patience. "We should cut her some slack. Losing Chris is hard on everyone. It's obviously hard on Shelley too. Yes, she looks like a carnie on a bender—but I don't look any better. I feel sorry for her," I say.

Thanks to my level-three, code-red allergic reaction, I have no choice but to blow colossal strings of albumin-like goo, one clogged nasal passage at a time, from the deck into the weeds below.

"I feel sorry for *you*," Molly says.

"Go back inside and try to get her going. I'm getting hungry."

"She'll warm up," Molly says. "Then we'll eat somewhere on the way back to M & J's."

Just as Molly is about to close the door, Shelley pokes her head out.

"I'm so glad you guys are here," she says. She's looking down, her voice is weak and lacks conviction but it's still a nice gesture. Besides, she's never been much of a morning person, even in the middle of the afternoon. She gives Molly a quick hug and they disappear inside.

"Heh-chooooooo!!!"

"Bless you," Ali says.

"Thank you."

"Are you okay, Uncle Tom?" Joey asks.

"Can you say neuter?" I say, trying to sound like Robin Williams doing Mr. Rogers. No one laughs except Joey even though I doubt he knows either of those people or what neuter means. But he is a seven-year-old boy—which is my ideal audience. I'm not making fun of Shelley as much as I'm mocking myself. Of course, I do make fun of Shelley, and I'm sure she makes fun of me. We all poke fun of each other, that's what brothers and sisters do. Most of the time it's directly to their face because we know all the right buttons to push. Sometimes, we aim our dig about a sibling or parent behind their back—a practice we call, 'conscientious backstabbing.' Even then, it's never terribly malicious. Our family battles are more psychologically based; we use verbal digs meant to humiliate. We're like verbal sharp-shooting snipers armed with stun guns and for the most part, our verbal assaults are compliant with the Geneva Convention protocols.

Of course, there were some physical bouts growing up to determine and redetermine the pecking order. Shelley was fourteen when she threw me to the ground. But when I got up and pinned her down, she realized I was stronger than her now. Knowing was enough. There was no need to throw any punches, we'd established mutual respect.

About fifty-seven sneezes later, Shelley reappears on the deck, all decked out—a whole new person. She went from hobo to hottie. She cleans up well. She looks pretty with the sun on her face in her summer dress with cat hair floating all around her.

"If you guys are hungry, we can eat here. I have lots of nutritious foods in the house."

Wait. Did she just say, 'lots of nutritious foods?' Who talks like that? And what is she referring to? Purina Cat Chow?

"Oh, that's sweet of you. But we're thinking about going out to eat on the way to Blue Moon Ranch. It will be easier," Molly suggests.

"I can't eat here anyway…" I say, turning away, preparing to hawk another loogie. "…for obvious reasons."

"Okay, but before we go, you guys have to see my studio!"

"Make it fast. I'll wait in the van. It only hurts when I breathe." Nothing. Not even from Joey. Tough crowd. They follow Shelley as she weaves through the clutter in the yard, followed once again by some four-legged fur balls. I've seen her studio many times, so I sit in the van and look at it from the outside. It reminds me of an illustration you'd see in an Old Mother Goose book—like a quilt sewn with patches of plywood, the structure is busy, asymmetrical, and intricate. The original angles have warped and bow toward the ground lowering its profile. It has two windows. One is set about knee-high, which provides a lovely view of the weeds. The other is at a cockeyed angle and caked with too much dirt to see through.

The door is on the backside. Getting there requires traversing a series of broken wood pallets with giant thistles growing through them. The cartoonish door is unusually small and narrow, which makes you feel oversized and out of place as you enter. It's dim and dank inside and the unique aroma is an earthy mix of mold and cat piss. The floor is a choppy sea of colors comprised of layers upon layers of carpet samples.

Her artwork is everywhere, ink drawings on paper, half-finished paintings, doodles, charcoal sketches, illustrations and photographs from books and magazines. There's lots of found items for inspiration like seashells, dried flowers, a rusting teapot, driftwood, and interesting rocks. It's a mess and it stinks, but she's creative and I'm glad she has her own space to feed her wonderfully talented and tortured artistic soul.

While I'm visualizing my sister's art in my head, I realize something awesome. In addition to rainbows, unicorns, dragons, sunsets, clouds, stars, polka-dot mushrooms, seashells, pot leaves, castles, mermaids, waterfalls, nymphs, feathers, and kitty cats, Shelley's art often includes hummingbirds. Hummingbirds!

Shelley's art is another way to stay connected to Chris!

Then, out of nowhere, something incredible happens. A hummingbird zips right past the windshield, directly in front of me and lands on a nearby branch to my left. The van window is already down, and I can see it perfectly. *Is this real? I was just thinking about hummingbirds and then one appears out of the blue?* I want the moment to last, and deliberately slow down my breathing to stretch out time. The sleek little bird cocks its head and starts chirping. That calming sensation I felt before returns. And then I feel the delicate thread that links me to Chris, to the kids, to this moment, to nature, life, death, the universe… everything. It's deep—so deep I feel it in every atom of my body.

The hummingbird lifts and hovers in place momentarily. I can hear the steady hum of its wings before it rockets away over the meadow at warp speed. Even after it disappears into the bright sky, I'm still smiling. Chris had moved about with the electricity of life; a radiant gold smear of sun burned into the light of her eyes. She glittered with the joy found in simply being alive. Seeing the bird was no miracle, but it's more than a coincidence. I can't stop smiling. Thanks to that silly bird, I feel renewed optimism. Chris is in a better place. Shane and Skyler will adapt to their new life—whatever that might be. We will survive. Life will go on. For the first time since she died, I'm willing to face the future. I'll have to share this experience with everyone later. Right now, I'm perfectly content just letting it sink in.

Molly, Ali, Willie, Joey, and Shelley make their way back to the van walking single file. Everyone takes a spot and starts buckling up when Shelley says, "Wait! I almost forgot!" She slides the van door open and jumps out. Inside the washing machine in her front yard is a bag of cat food. The sound of the squeaking lid arouses a battalion of converging cats.

"Oh my God!" Molly gasps, realizing her sister is, in fact, the cat-lady of Mendocino. She didn't mean for her shocked reaction to be so loud. Shelley looks hurt.

"Don't make fun of my cats," she says, pouring the food into bowls. "They're my babies. I only have like five of them. Snoodles, Scabby, Shadow, Ranger, Pus-Pus, Won-Ton, Velvet and Vicious are mine. All the rest, like Psycho, Prancer, Mr. Boo, Mitzy, Scar Face, Thunder, and Vegas—are just visitors." She sounds defensive. Molly jabs Ali in the ribs, who gets the point and stops snickering. Molly's right. We'll laugh about this later—during one of our nice conscientious backstabbing sessions.

The road from Fort Bragg to Willits is only twenty-seven miles, but it takes more than an hour to drive it. From start to finish, it's just as beautiful as it is grueling. The road twists through groves of towering redwoods. Lush green ferns, some ludicrously large, conceal the russet-colored forest floor and hidden streams. Just when you think the hairpin turns cannot possibly get any tighter, they do.

By the time we reach Willits, everyone is starving. We detect the comforting smell of greasy food before we see Inez's Restaurant and park. Craving regular food, we order cheeseburgers, meatloaf, mashed potatoes, gravy, French fries, coleslaw, French Dips, onion rings, chocolate shakes, sides of meatballs, and breadsticks. We eat like bears preparing for hibernation. We have multiple jaw-gasms. I unbutton my jeans to make room for dessert, which is so good I buy a whole pie to bring with us. We waddle back to the van, stop at the grocery store, fuel up and hit the road for the final leg of our tour. We reach a section of road that feels like a tree tunnel and suddenly I find myself missing Shane and Skyler.

We cross through the creek near Mare and Journey's place as the sun is setting. Wild shades of orange and red reflect off the surface, turning it into molten lava. When we get closer, the road is lined with beat-up cars, weathered trucks, all-terrain vehicles, and sketchy meth-lab looking vans. We park and start the long walk in. The music gets louder, but I can't tell if the lyrics are French, Spanish, or Portuguese. Who knows? Mare and Journey could be going through a Basque phase. Walking in pairs, carrying our goods, the six of us make our way, following the beat step-by-step, under the spell of the strange music.

As we get closer the sounds of a raging party can be heard; beer cans popping, people laughing, the cacophony of overlapping conversations pierced by swear words. Through the trees, I can see several figures standing around a fire, most of them holding the glow of a cigarette—or joint. It's a big party. I'm worried about the boys. Hopefully, someone is watching Shane and Skyler. Anxiety swan dives into my chest. I'm in no mood to party. I don't know these people and they don't know Chris. I remind myself to be considerate. Mare and Journey are entitled to deal with Chris's death however they see fit. After all, there's nothing like being with your friends and getting wasted to forget your troubles and lift your spirits.

I find Shane and Skyler playing by the creek. They're fine, but this is deep water with a current strong enough to sweep them away. A minute later, Mare appears out of nowhere. After spotting me, she reassures me that she was watching the boys the whole time—though she clearly wasn't. With the party in full swing outside, I move Shane and Skyler inside and turn on the TV. We have no intention of joining the party, but that doesn't keep the party from finding us. Just as we settle in, an odd couple saunters through the door.

He's a tall, gaunt man joined by a frumpy Asian woman. In the dim light, he appears to have no eyebrows. They come over to where we're sitting. I was correct. No eyebrows. I try to imagine the moment in which he thought removing them was a nifty idea. His creamy complexion contrasts his curly jet-black hair. The plump woman is shaped like a "V" with lunging breasts. She is a female Tasmanian devil. I smile. They smile. I feel somewhat relieved. *Funny looking creatures, but friendly.*

She has many tattoos in many colors. I can't make out the one on her shoulder. It looks like Mr. Peanut with his cane. But that would be silly. Our eyes sort of meet, not entirely because hers are moving completely independent of each other, like the Cookie Monster on Sesame Street.

"My name is Kohoutek, like da disappointing comet. But everyone calls me Kotex," she says, in a thick Asian accent. *Kotex?* I cannot believe what I'm hearing. She bends down and says, 'hi' to Shane and Skyler. Her breasts hang so low they nearly touch the ground. I was right. She does have a Mr. Peanut tattoo.

"Kotex?" I ask.

"Yeah, but it not mean I on da rag all da time!" She laughs aggressively, then punches my shoulder. "Dis here, he my old man," she says, backhanding her partner squarely in the chest. "I say old man, but he forr-teen years younger den me. Dat right. Look out, Kotex got it going O-O-O-ON!" She lifts her arms and gyrates her hips in what is normally a seductive motion. Skyler gets up and starts dancing with her. It looks like they're hula hooping in slow motion. We start laughing. It feels amazing to laugh. It's a blessing, a miracle—delivered by two of creations oddest characters, which makes it all the more special.

Her old man tells a couple of stories that are hard to follow, mainly because as he speaks, his fingers pluck away annoyingly upon an invisible lute. His top teeth are straight, but the bottom looks like the Manhattan skyline. He gets up and returns with two coffee mugs of wine. They settle down and watch the tube with us. One of those Hollywood gossip shows is on, and I'm stunned that they know more about pop culture than I do because I can only picture them living in an underground cave or high in a tree house. Skyler is crawling all over Kotex examining her tattoos. He stops at a Chinese symbol on her thigh and looks up at her.

"Dat one means *Be Curious.* Just like you being right now!"

They finish their drinks and prepare to go back outside. As she gives the boys hugs goodbye, she catches me looking down her shirt. It was just a reflex—an accident, an unfortunate mistake. I'm certainly not attracted to her. Nevertheless, she looks back at me with her crazy, spinning eyes and smiles sensually. It's gross, but what can I do?

I smile back and say, "Kotex got it going o-o-o-on!"

"You know dat's da truth!" She says on her way out.

"They were nice," Shane says.

"Very nice," I say.

My brother Al is the next to visit. He stumbles in looking full of energy in his Army fatigues, and plops down next me. "I got this one hippie soooo good today..." and proceeds to tell me in great detail how it played out. "The poor guy thought it was a C.A.M.P. bust and almost shit a brick."

"Mission accomplished. Congratulations. I can't believe Mare lets you freak out her friends."

"Oh, he's okay. We laughed. No harm. No foul. He told me that he really thought I was the fuzz. The 'fuzz'—who uses that word anymore?"

"People who are generally out of touch with the rest of the world," I say. "The kind of people you find here."

"I'll introduce you to him. He's got a mole on this side of his face shaped like New Hampshire and a mullet. He smells like feet. You'll like him," he says, laughing out loud. Al is a hoot when he's buzzed.

"Gosh, I can't wait. He sounds great." My brother devours half the pie I bought before wandering back to the party.

Mare pops inside twice without hardly acknowledging us. There's something strange about the way she's carrying herself. Normally, she's light on her feet, agile and fluid. Tonight, she's cautious, moving very deliberately, as if the floor is either incredibly sticky or slippery. And then it suddenly hits me; she's on drugs. I feel like I'm the parent and she's the teen trying not to act fucked-up around me. For the very first time in my life, my mother appears old.

The next time she comes in, I get up and make my way to her so I can look into her fully dilated pupils. She's on more than just booze and buds. It's hard to guess what is flowing through her system: mushrooms, ecstasy, peyote, uppers, downers, or a combination of drugs? With this group, it wouldn't surprise me if they were scraping toad skins for psychedelic chemicals. She blows kisses at the kids that she can apparently see floating across the room. Then, while she's struggling to open her own front door, a mostly naked guy with a guitar walks in and closes it behind her.

Who's this caveman wearing Adidas?

The last man I saw wearing a pelt loincloth in public was Ted Nugent at A Day on the Green concert at the Oakland Coliseum. This guy is much chubbier, but he does have a guitar slung over his back like a freshly killed animal. He begins sniffing the air like a wolf. We look at each other but don't introduce ourselves. He begins examining the knick-knacks and collage work on the walls. I can relate to that. I hear him singing softly and glance over my shoulder. It's David Bowie's *Space Oddity:* I was expecting something from *Double Live Gonzo*. I don't hear him leave. He either went back to the party or rejoined his clan who are on the verge of harnessing fire.

There are other visitors, some with hippie names like Unity and Luna, some with semi-hippie nicknames like Stash and Sticky-Ricky, and some with perfectly boring normal names like Steve and Nancy. Nothing on TV can compete with the real-life characters that stumble into our space. Shane and Skyler pass out on the floor around ten. I want to just throw a blanket over us and call it a night, but this space is already reserved for Molly and her kids who look ready to crash themselves. I really need to sleep, but the shed is right next to where the jam session is taking place. I go outside to assess the situation, mentally reminding myself to keep an open mind.

A mellow rhythm can be relaxing. A simple repetitive beat can slow down your mind and put you in a trance-like state. Unfortunately, this racket is anything but soothing. There are a dozen people sitting around the fire making noise. Lady Di is on the flute. Journey and loincloth-man are strumming guitars. Mole-mullet-man, who I cannot *wait* to meet, is playing spoons. People without instruments improvise by clapping, yelping, or banging rocks together. One girl is shaking a jar of coins very seriously like a virtuoso musician. She stops and thoughtfully pours out some of the change to fine-tune her instrument. This is the kind of noise you need if you're casting people for a headache commercial. Sleeping alongside this ruckus will be impossible. I'll have to wait it out and go back inside.

When the eleven o'clock news starts, I gently wake up Shane and lift Skyler off the floor and make our way to the tool shed. Skyler is startled by the noise and starts to cry, which is fine with me. *Here's your reason to quit.* But even with him wailing, it takes a while before anyone notices us standing in front of the shed. Then, one-by-one, they all stop, and the noise comes to a tangled halt, like a marching band falling down a flight of stairs. Suddenly the only sound is that of the crackling fire. I'm surrounded by a montage of dark faces that are glazed, dazed, and confused.

"We need to sleep. This is where we sleep," I say, tipping my head towards the shed. "So, the music… can you please stop? Thank you."

"Fuck you!" Someone yells, followed by laughter.

"You could jam up at Skull Point." The words sound silly even as they're leaving my mouth. Gauging by the looks on their faces, I might as well have spoken in Swahili. Now would be an opportune time for Mare to speak up on my behalf, but who knows where she is—in search of more toad skins?

Journey clears his throat and says, "We jus' gonna finish a cuppa more songs. Den we quit. Five—ten minutes most."

"You can join us," someone says handing me a tambourine. I give her my best, 'Don't-you-fucking-hand-me-a-tambourine' expression.

"Ten minutes is cool. But please, no longer. It's late and the kids need sleep. I need to sleep too."

We climb the shed stairs and as I'm closing the door, someone barks, "Don't let the bedbugs bite!" This is less of a cliché and more of a genuine warning considering where we're bedding down. Then someone says, "One, two, one-two-three…" while someone else counts, "…a-two, and a-four, and a-six." *Oh, they're jamming now.*

Ten minutes, I say to myself. *I can tolerate anything for ten minutes.* I think of the suffering Jews in German concentration camps. After another entire hour of jam-torture, I'm ready to join them on the train to Dachau. I try yelling from the shed and pounding on the wall, but it does no good. I finally get up and make another plea for them to stop or move to another place. This time they set down their instruments, their rocks, spoons, sticks, and jars of coins. Someone calls me an asshole; another calls me a turd-taster, which gets a chuckle. It's a small price to pay for getting them to finally stop.

Ninth

July 7th, 1996

The jam session may be over, but the party is still raging. I'm beyond spent, in desperate need of sleep but the sounds of car doors slamming, people swearing, and bursts of laughter are still going strong. Maybe I can't sleep but I can pretend to be somewhere else. I let my mind wander back to the Avocado Apartments and think about my sister Shelley.

∞   ∞   ∞

I read in a psychology book that first-born children are much more likely to develop into well-adjusted, happy, affluent, and generally successful people. In the book, this is because the first child receives the lion's share of attention as compared to the following siblings. It's essentially a sliding scale; greater parental participation, especially with both parents, equates to greater development in the child and ultimately in the adult they become. A large proportion of Presidents, astronauts, doctors, scientists, CEO's, artists, philosophers, writers, architects, and even game show hosts are first born children. Shelley is the first-born baby in our family, and she'll have nothing to do with this silly-sliding-scale-of-success nonsense.

Nothing really motivates Shelley. Some things just keep her awake longer. She was born to hang out, lounge, coast, kick back, crash, nap, loll, drift, doze, and sleep. Of course, sometimes she can shine with the best of them and when she does her boundless energy is contagious. Art may be her primary passion, but she also loves music, all forms of dance, gardening, organic food, yoga, nature, and all kinds of animals—particularly cats. She's always been an incredible artist who the rest of us looked up to. Even the thoughtless doodles she scribbles mindlessly while speaking on the phone are miniature works of art.

She's always had a set of Rapidograph drafting pens, endless tin trays of colorful felt-tip pens, compasses, stencils, colored pencils, all kinds and sizes of paper and other art supplies. She draws on anything within reach, including the bottom of her shoes. Her distinctive, intricate style could be described as groovy pop art. She creates highly detailed, bright, and playful scenes that can hold your attention for hours. She often uses bold outlines which are perfect for tattoos, street art and adult coloring books. Some of the pens render a line finer than a strand of hair. When she's creating, her patience and attention to detail are phenomenal. Her go-to images include flowers, nymphs with gossamer wings, star-eyed unicorns, interlocking vines, plump cherubs, rainbows, night skies, twinkling stars, crescent moons, and ringed planets. You can count the scales on her fire-breathing dragons. Her mermaids, adorned with seashell jewelry, make you smile. When she's in the mood, she draws on us. We take turns letting her decorate our little arms and legs with her designs. Her drafting pens hurt—but it's worth it. We wore our homemade tattoos with pride and kept them dry, so they'd last as long as possible before they cracked and faded away.

Shelley's art is way better in color.

We all look up to Shelley because she's the oldest—so she's cool by default. Shelley's job is to test the limits and push the boundaries. She's our mentor of manipulation, our guru of mischief and our director of deviance. She isn't as carefree as Chris or as wild as Molly. She seems to sway between periods of struggle and self-doubt with joyful enthusiasm and confidence. She knows lots of people but spends time with a select few. Her best friends tend to have something to keep them occupied while she draws, reading, making jewelry, braiding hair, or practicing or listening to music.

It's hard to say who Shelley resembles more. Her mix of parental genes is as messy as the life she lives. She's such a blend of both parents that she really doesn't resemble either one. She has light brown eyes with a halo of green glowing near the pupil. Her hair is neither light nor dark, it's right in the middle. She hates it when people say she's a dishwater blonde. Sometimes she gets them back by saying, "Well, you're a skid-mark brunette."

Shelley makes it clear that Mare is incapable of enforcing any rules. Our mother gave up on that kind of parenting long ago. Now she's more interested in teaching us about Karma and recycling and 'being a good traveler on this spaceship we call earth.' We don't have a curfew. She believes we should, 'Just come home when the party's over.' Her parenting speech varies from month to month, but the general message is the same.

"Every action you take, every decision you make in this world is a pebble that ripples on the surface of this water we call reality. Positive actions create beautiful waves; you can even surf on them. Negative actions create destructive swells that can sink a ship. Moving water produces negative ions, which happen to be anything *but* negative. Respect each other's property and personal space. Don't piss people off unnecessarily. Like get off the phone when you know someone else wants to use it. If you see a plant that needs watering, water it. If you see something that needs to be cleaned—clean it—even if it's not your mess. I'm not your fucking maid. Speak kindly and be patient. Remember that love is the highest vibration in the universe. Abide by this code or you'll lose your privileges. I'll take your pot for the day—or even longer if I think it's necessary."

She also had some advice specifically tailored for me on my twelfth birthday:

"If you help a girl mess up her bed during sex, you better help her make that bed afterwards. And never forget that men and women are wired differently. You'll want to cum within the first few minutes of penetration—but don't you dare! Women take longer and they won't keep you around unless you learn to slow down."

What do you even say in this situation? I wasn't close to having sex with anyone including myself at this age. Of course, this is appalling coming from my own mother, but it was also enlightening, and it becomes one of the rare pieces of advice that I actually take to heart, can't forget, and put into practice later in life.

Toward the end of that first summer in the apartment complex, Mare slams on the breaks with Charlie. But instead of moving back in with us, she moves into a converted water tower perched up high on stilts out in the country with her new man, Larry Glickstein. *Here we go again.* The structure looks like the nest of the Fluffy Back Tit-Babbler, only much larger. This might have been Mare's 'hair' stage because against all odds, Larry is even hairier than Charlie. We don't see much of her now. His place is too far out of town for Mare's bike, and she doesn't drive.

My mother is literally land locked in a water tower with Hairy Larry.

One day, she announces that Larry will be driving us to Idaho to pick up our sister—and that we, 'get to go.' *Are we really picking up Shelley? Or does she plan to ditch the rest of us there and go home free from all her children?* We know Charlie would refuse to take part of such an evil plan, but we aren't sure about our mom. She seems capable of abandoning us. Maybe she broke up with Charlie and hooked up with Larry and his reliable transportation just to get the job done.

Larry's personality is the complete opposite of Charlie's. Actually, Larry lacks any personality whatsoever. He does have a genuine New York accent; he does have the Bob Dylan look going for him—under all that hair, of course. And fortunately for me, he has a tic, a weakness I can target. He's an asymmetrical blinker that's easy to imitate and exaggerate, which I know will piss him and my mother off. I need someone I can take my anger, fear, and anxiety out on and Larry lands the part. I turn the littlest twitch of his left eye into a virtuoso performance of a man having a drawn out, progressively worse and eventually deadly seizure that ends with him shitting his pants. I start slow and then all out sprint with it. It takes a lot of self-control for Larry not to lash out at me. He's very good at ignoring me even though I know he hates my guts. Larry's another one of those guys who has no interest in any of us kids. He puts up with us to get down with our mother. Mare's no dummy. She knows we dislike Larry so she tells us it will be a short trip.

"Plus, it's a chance for us all to get out of town, take a road trip and visit family."

I love road trips. But not this kind. I want to feel excited about seeing Shelley again. I want to see and experience new things along the way. I want to enjoy the company of Chris, Molly and Alex. I want to see my aunt, uncle and my cousins, Amy and Michelle. I want to have fun but I'm not. It's a miserably long drive in the back of Hairy Larry's pick-up truck. Most of the time, we huddle in the shade under a canvas tarp. As we get further north the temperature alternates between hot and freezing cold. When we cross the Idaho border near Fruitland, I see my mother lean in and kiss Larry. My stomach turns left, the truck goes straight, and I don't feel right. *Why couldn't this trip take place in the bus with Charlie?* My hands became fists. I pound them aggressively on the window ruining their moment. Larry slams on the brakes. My head bounces off the glass in the back of the cab. My mother's eyes are locked on me like laser beams. Larry skids to a stop and flies out of the truck. I'm pretty sure he's about to kick my ass. I've been frantically thinking of what to say that will calm him down.

"We want to get stoned in Idaho!" I say smiling and hoping for the best.

"Getting stoned was actually *my* idea," Chris says, right on cue, knowing this will help my cause.

"We *all* want to get high," adds Molly.

"Can we smoke a joint here? Stretch our legs?" Chris asks Mare.

Our mother peers at each of us, one-by-one, with a long questionable look. Eventually, she reaches for her backpack, digs into her stash, and hands us a couple joints. Like I've said before, when it comes to drugs, we're incredibly, gracious, kind and generous. We plunge from the truck, stretch, snack, and pass the joints around. While I'm getting high, I decide not to be mad at Larry anymore. Hating him isn't going to make the trip any better. I'm more mad at my mother anyway.

Growing up, I had taught myself a trick. When our mother made liver and onions, I developed a method to get it down without barfing. I simply did my best to not allow the food to touch my tongue, take the minimum number of bites and quickly wash it down with whatever we had. Now I'll apply the same concept to my eyes. I'll avoid looking in Larry's direction. I'm sure it will work, and it does. I stare at other things to keep him out of the picture. I watch the painted line on the side of the road like an endless movie. At night, I focus on the red glow of our taillights, where things flash in and out of existence, trees, guard rails, headlights, and fence posts. They wink at me and then disappear quickly into the darkness of the past. It should be noted that I've been stoned for the majority of this ride. Just when I think, *Seriously. We'll never get there*, we finally arrive.

"Where's Charlie?" Is the first thing Shelley asks Mare.

"This is my new old man, Larry," Mare says.

Larry reaches out his hand. Shelley just looks at it for a moment and then offers hers. You could see her thinking, *if I want a ride home, I better shake this hairy mother fuckers hand.* I love my sister's ability to instantly read fucked up situations so well.

Chris, Molly, Alex with cousins Amy & Michelle.

We figure our mom will want to hang out with her little sister, Lynn, and give us time to bond with our cousins Amy and her little sister, Michelle. Michelle was just a baby when I met Amy for the first time in Cincinnati. We waste no time getting down to the important issues. Issues we need to get off our chests. Issues that can only be discussed fully between family members.

"I don't like Dana," Amy says, getting down to business.

"We don't like Larry" Chris says right back at her.

"Who's this Larry guy?" Amy asks.

"Larry's our mother's new boyfriend-of-the-month. We love her real boyfriend, Charlie." Chris says.

"Where's Charlie?" Amy asks.

"He's back in Davis. They'll probably get back together when we get home," Molly says.

"I hope so," I say, joining the conversation.

"Why do you love Charlie?" Amy asks.

"Because Charlie is the only one of her boyfriends who loves us kids," Molly says.

"Who's this Dana guy?" Chris asks.

"Dana was a carpenter working on our house in Cincinnati when mom was married to my dad, Jim." Amy says. "They fell in love and tried to run away with me and Michelle."

"They ditched the scene?" I ask.

"Yup. In the name of love."

"Oh, wow," says Molly.

"But Jim is mean and smart. He's, my dad. Michelle's dad is also named Jim, but he's a different Jim. Apparently, my mother was in a Jim phase when she had an affair with him. Anyway, my dad tracked us down and dragged us home with the help of the police. If we didn't go back, he was somehow going to have us *both* put in foster homes. He managed to control the divorce lawyers and even the judge. So, they stayed married a little longer until he finally gave up and agreed to getting divorced. I didn't want to be separated from my sister and I couldn't live with my real dad either. That wasn't an option. Anyway, Michelle went and lived with her dad, and I had no choice but to go with mom and Dana. We all lived in the same area for the next few years and then we moved here. Michelle still lives in Ohio. She's just visiting us for part of the summer."

"I can't believe how young your mother looks. How old was she when she had you?" Chris asks.

"Fifteen," Amy says.

"I'm fifteen," Chris says.

"Are you ready to have a kid?"

"Mmm—maybe next year," Chris says joking. We all laugh.

"Why don't you like Dana?" Molly asks.

"Actually, Dana isn't all that bad. It's just that we live out here in the sticks and I only get to see my sister like once or twice a year if we're lucky. We had a real house in Ohio. You know. Running water, electricity. A bath."

"Your house is still being built. Once it's done, you'll have all that," I say, hoping to cheer her up.

"We've been here *three* years. That building over there is still our bathroom. And that pump over there; we still have to use that to bring water into the house," Amy says.

"Do you have a TV?" Molly asks.

"Nope," Amy replies sharply.

"You don't have a bathtub or shower? Chris asks.

"Nope. Well, sort of. We have to pump shitloads of water, heat it up with propane and pour it into a trough on the back deck. It's such a chore that we only do it once a week. And the worst part is we all take baths together!"

"Jesus, Amy. We're definitely related. Your situation is just as fucked up as ours," Chris says with empathy.

"You might be even *more* hippied out than we are," I say.

"I bet we are, and it sucks," Amy says.

"At least it's really beautiful here. You're like a nature girl living all off the land out in the middle of a forest some place in the where-the-fuck-are-we part of Idaho!" Chris says.

We laugh. Amy does too. "You city slickers think you know everything but you don't know shit. I bet you can't even milk a goat."

"Goats?" Alex says, suddenly interested in the conversation now that animals have been mentioned.

"We got two goats, six chickens, a dog, two cats and a pack of scary raccoons stirring shit up at night."

"Then what are we waiting for?" Alex says. "Show 'em to us!"

"I don't do goats, but they sure try and do me," I say, though it's a joke mostly for myself.

Our cousins take us on a grand tour of the place, and we love every minute of it. I know we'd feel more connected to Amy and Michelle if we could just see them more. Shelley and Lynn set the outside table and prepare food while Dana starts a cooking fire. A little later, he begins carving from a massive carcass and announces, "Elk meat for feast," which sounded so caveman-barbaric it cracks us all up. Apparently, Elk is a large deer-like animal he hunts with a bow or spear or with his bare hands at a nearby location when they're migrating. Dana is a strapping specimen. He's a lanky man comprised mostly of long blonde hair, braided into a horse tail and bulging muscles. He'd be the perfect model for a sculptor working on a Thor statue.

My aunt Lynn is beautiful. She's a younger version of my mother only she inherited even more of the infamous Johnson hair gene. They're a good-looking couple and seem completely and forever in love, something I doubt I'll ever see happen with my mother. Dana and Lynn are young, wide-eyed hippies. Lynn wears a lot of make-up so she's kind of a glamorous hippie—like Cher.

After dinner, I see them sharing a joint with Larry, Mare, Chris, and Shelley. They're all laughing and having a great time. Dana says, 'far out' a lot and Lynn likes to ask, 'can you dig it?' My aunt and uncle are adorable and they're family and the familiar sense of chaos in the way they live makes me feel right at home. I'm sure they'll let the rest of us get high later and we'll talk about what we'll do during our visit. After such a long drive, I'm guessing we'll be here for a week or more.

Wrong.

We leave the next day.

Does our mother not miss her sister?

The ride home always goes faster than the ride there. Almost always. It's a long, hot, sweaty, crowded, uncomfortable trip back to California. Traveling in the truck bed is so loud and windy we can't really talk or catch up with Shelley. When we finally get home, Mare promptly breaks it off with Larry and we never see him again—which is fine with us.

"Why did you and Larry break up?" I ask.

"There's no running water in his water tower. Isn't that weird?"

"Not really."

"Well, I just couldn't handle *that*."

I will never understand my mother.

Then, right on cue, she's back with Charlie—at least for the time being. Nothing with our mother is permanent. She's shifts like ice in arctic waters. We're at the mercy of her whims. It feels like I exist on a fault line, next to an active volcano in a tornado zone during tsunami season. I believe there's no point in ever getting comfortable in life because life is full of surprises—especially life with Mare. I've had to learn the hard way that not all surprises are good.

It's great to get home, back to our tiny apartment, all together again. I also missed my new best friend, Brad. On one typical blazing hot afternoon, Brad and I go inside for a drink and hear music playing softly upstairs.

"Shhhhh," he whispers holding his finger on *my* mouth smooshing it out place. "Let's sneak upstairs to see who it is."

Brad is hoping to see one of my sisters, or even my mom partially dressed. I roll my eyes. He doesn't have to speak— we're way past that stage of communication in our friendship. He does something with his eye and then I do something with my eyebrow, and he knows I'll follow him silently up the stairs. A song from the new *Wings* album is playing on the portable radio that's been moved into the bathroom. Brad crouches low and slithers up the first few stairs like a snake. He likes snakes. They call the left-handed quarterback of the Oakland Raiders, Kenny Stabler, The Snake. Brad's obsessed with the team. I'm directly beside him. When we get to the top, it sounds like there might be two people in the bathroom, but we can't see in without being seen ourselves, so we sit against the wall on the green shag carpet and listen. Then someone starts to sing— very badly. Brad and I have to immediately cover our mouths with both hands to keep from cracking up.

It's my little brother, Alex. He has no idea we're listening because he begins to sing with blustering bravado. Brad and I exchange looks and then he slowly peeks around the corner and comes back quickly holding his mouth again and pointing his thumb over his shoulder as if I need to be reminded of where to look. We trade places and I ease my way to the door jam and look inside. Alex isn't singing to himself. He's singing to Charlie's dog, Blue. Alex loves animals wholeheartedly, but this display is beyond ridiculous. I clinch my jaw to keep from laughing. Brad and I look at each other and make our eyes as big as dinner plates. We're able to low-crawl to the other side of the door and get front row floor space so we can enjoy the entire show. He has the dog sitting atop the toilet. As he sings, he's swaying his butt and cocking his head like a real rock star. The best worst part is when he starts miming the chorus to the dog; when the song says, "I" he puts his thumb to his chest, on "love" he cups both hands over his heart, and on "you" he points lovingly at the dog. Blue sits tall, wagging her tail the whole time loving the attention. When the song ends, Brad and I sit up and applaud.

The look on my brother's face is priceless. He'd been caught. His skin changes color faster than a cuttlefish and for a moment he appears to be on the brink of tears—tears of shame. But then he smiles, bows gracefully and thanks us for coming to his show. Smart kid. Nevertheless, Brad and I pull him to the ground and torture him with insults and tickles. We so busted him, and he knows it. Blue barks twice and joins the ruckus. I can still torture my brother to this day just by quickly miming those three words, *I love you.*

Alex is reaching the next level of self-awareness. Maybe staying with Theo and his family when we suddenly moved back to Davis and the trip to Idaho was helping him see his own life in a new light. Mom and Charlie had drained the waterbed and moved it out of the apartment. A few days later they dragged in our old brown crush velvet couch. This thing belongs in a Marx Brothers movie; like where they'd hide the loot in a cushion and run around it in a chase scene. A little at a time, they bring over the rest of our furniture that had been in storage and set up the living room. Even though Christmas is a few months away, Mare also sets up her Nativity Scene. It no longer looks much like Jesus's birth scene. She'd painted all the characters into hippies. The camel's blanket now appears to be tie-dyed, and she painted peace signs and hearts on the walls of the manger. The ox lost one of his horns years ago. Mare used green paint for the pot leaves she painted on both sides of the blanket under his saddle. She painted the baby Jesus a lovely shade of brown telling us it's more historically accurate this way. The usual knick-knacks find their way back to us as well, records, candles, astrology books. Soon the living room looks and feels much more like the kind of room we're familiar with.

But Alex has a hard time readjusting. We're all home one evening watching television when a Levitz furniture commercial comes on. Levitz TV commercials are annoying. They're on all the time. The announcer has a deep, ominous voice like Satan. He describes the two-piece love seats and sofas, the five-piece bedroom sets and the twelve-piece matching dinette sets that you have to have now, and it won't cost you a penny because your first payment isn't due for years! We tune out these commercials, but not Alex. He's glued to the TV sucking up every second. When the commercial ends, he gets up, turns down the volume, looks around the room and then directs a simple question to our mother in a very serious tone.

"How come we don't shop at Levitz?" His voice has never been more concerned. The innocence in his question combined with the look on his face is priceless. We witnessed his epiphany live—a quintessential moment of self-awareness.

"Oh my God!" yells Chris.

"That was *so* cute!" said Molly.

Mare is laughing, Charlie is on the floor wiping the tears from his eyes. I'm busting up and Alex shoots us a serious expression expecting an answer.

"That kind of furniture is ugly, expensive and made of shit," Mare says.

"Is it because we're hippies?" asks Alex.

"Correct-a-mundo" says Charlie.

"I thought so," my little brother says, nodding his head, catching on.

Alex had just reached a new level of awareness. His innocent question would of course become another one of our family's catch phrases. All you have to do to surface all the emotion and feelings that come with the sudden realization that your family is living outside of the norm, is to utter his innocently pure and simple question, *How come we don't shop at Levitz?*

Molly, Alex, and I on a couch you can't buy at Levitz.

The following year is America's Bicentennial, and a lot of weird, patriotic-inspired shit is going on; *Bicentennial Minutes*, are interrupting our favorite TV shows, bicentennial quarters, half dollars and one-dollar coins are circulating, mail arrives with bicentennial stamps and *Schoolhouse Rock!* releases several educational cartoon shorts on ABC with annoying songs like, "I'm Just a Bill" that will haunt me for the rest of my life. Johnny Cash is the Grand Marshall at the U.S. Bicentennial parade. The king and queen of England come over on a royal yacht and hang out with President Ford and his wife, Betty.

I'm in the eighth grade. Brad's in the ninth. I go to Holmes. He goes to the other junior high, Emerson. Shelley is a senior and Chris is a sophomore at Davis high school. Molly's a seventh grader one grade behind me at Holmes. Alex is one grade behind Todd who's in the sixth grade at North Davis Elementary school.

"Pick a spot, any spot," Brad says, pointing to various locations on his face. We're in his upstairs bedroom at the apartment complex.

"Right there," I say pointing to the tip of his nose.

"Okay. Now watch."

Using his index fingers, Brad squeezes out a platoon of tiny white puss worms from the pores on his nose. This is a grotesque display of human mucus and yet I cannot pull my eyes away. I pick another spot and then another and no matter where I point, he's able to produce the same effect. He really doesn't have bad skin or any big pimples or zits. There just seems to be an aquifer of puss somewhere below his skin. This may have had something to do with the fact that we're always hungry and consume massive quantities of junk food.

We used to go to Albertsons and buy a tray of Danishes with lemon goo or raspberry jelly in the middle and a quart of milk. Then we'd plop down right in front of the automatic doors, so we'd get the occasional blast of cool air as people entered. In plain view, we'd unapologetically stuff our faces full of sweet rolls and share the milk. At least we drink from different corners of the carton. Still, we still must have looked like barbarians. We also stuff our faces at Taco Bell devouring tacos in two bites and bean burritos in three. We like to order giant plates of fries from the college burger joint, a place called The Graduate, and drown them in ketchup to make them even more filling. We raid each other's cabinets at home consuming the oddest combinations of food. Hour after hour, we eat whatever we can find; cereal, saltines, peanut butter, Aunt Jemima coffee cake kits—the kind you add an egg to and squish about in a baggy before cooking. We eat cold corn right out of the can, pickles, olives, barbecue sauce, cabbage, salsa, liverwurst, onions, pizza rolls, brown sugar, black beans, spoonfuls of white Alfredo sauce and anything else we can find. Teenage boys don't eat for quality or taste. We eat because our stomach hurts if we don't. We'd split a loaf of bread and eat it dry just to avoid the nausea that comes with severe hunger. And yet despite all this eating, I'm still a skinny wimp waiting for a growth spurt so I can move on with life.

It's a common sight at the Avocado Townhouse Apartments to see me carrying a pillow and a sleeping bag over to Brad's apartment to spend the night. His mother lets them run the air conditioner at night, a luxury we couldn't afford. But there's fucked up shit going on at his house too, like the time we hear Susie stumble home late at night with a man. Within minutes of the bedroom door slamming, we hear them having sex—very loud sex with lots of grunting, moaning and screams of pleasure. I know Brad and Todd are embarrassed, but I reassure them that this is in no way shocking to me. I tell them about the partition drapes my mother used to create her bedroom and how they did nothing when it came to blocking sound. What's shocking was discovering who Susie was with that night.

The next morning, while we're eating cereal, Susie comes down the stairs with her date and we know him. It's our friend, Grant Keeney's older brother, Myles, who's a senior in high school. This obviously makes things uncomfortable for Brad. He doesn't want news of his mother's Mrs. Robinson encounter reaching our friends. I know how Brad feels and even more importantly, I know how to make him feel better. I tell him the story about my mother and the low-flying plane that buzzed us while we were on a naked nature hike. I describe how all the man's parts were somehow outside the plane flapping violently in the wind. Brad's essentially one of us—a survivor. Yes, we are powerless when it comes to our mother's behavior, but we don't have to try and hide it as much anymore. Having an understanding, non-judgmental pal like Brad, goes a long way on the road to survival. We both have fucked up family situations but at least we can laugh about them with each other.

Susie's encounter with one of our classmates is a one-night stand. Unfortunately, the next guy she gets involved with is worse. Teddy is a bear—the kind that doesn't think twice about ripping your face off with a quick swat of his paw. Teddy is also a genuine asshole; a tattooed-up redneck, with a blonde mustache pointing down the sides of his face to his pointed cowboy boots. Teddy is also an angry, short-tempered alcoholic, with endless attitude. Brad's mom is hot. She must have always had her pick of men, yet she goes for guys who are no good for her at all. Who knows what she sees in this divorced, hardened, train-wreck of a man? He happens to be one of the three managers overseeing the operations and maintenance of the apartment complex. At first, Susie is able to soften Teddy's rusty edges enough that he's semi-tolerable—as long as they're both sober. The problem is, they're rarely sober at the same time. He's mostly a day drinker. Susie mostly drinks at night, and they don't both have to be drunk for bad shit to happen. When they're both drunk, especially at night, things would get scary at Brad's house. One time Brad wakes up in the middle of the night thinking he's having a bad dream only to find Teddy towering over him. He's holding Brad's portable TV high above his head about to throw it down. Brad manages to roll onto the floor just in time to miss it. The TV bounces off the mattress and smashes into the wall. The sound wakes Susie who stumbles into the room drunk, semi-dressed and reeking of liquor. Todd starts crying. Susie is able to get the dangerous Teddy bear out of her kid's room. That night, both Brad and Todd grab their pillows and sleeping bags and walk over to our apartment to spend the night.

Susie would never listen to her kids, or me—but she might listen to my mother. Someone has to inform her that Brad and Todd no longer feel safe sleeping at home. She needs to know how destructive and abusive the situation is and how it's affecting her children. Brad and I sit down with Mare and after hearing us out, she agrees to help. Mare's solution is simple. She attempts to convert Susie from loving booze to loving pot, but it doesn't work. Then Teddy starts getting even more pissy and tells Susie not to hang out with 'those crazy hippies' too much. He threatens to call the cops on us because he knows we're using and dealing illegal drugs and have too many people stuffed into one unit. I know Teddy will follow through and rat us out, but Susie threatens to leave him forever if he does. They're drinkers. It's their poison of choice and there's no stopping them.

To avoid the chaos at his house and mine, we spend many nights sleeping on the lounge chairs from the pool in the cabana. Brad and Todd share some of the raunchy playground jokes, poems, and parodies they've heard, and Alex and I do the same. We're an easy to please audience; four boys between the age of ten and fifteen who still laugh out loud at anything associated with diarrhea. We're able to recall a ton of material. There are several themes of one-liners. Book titles for example, *Under the Bleachers* by Seymore Butts, *Things That Itch* by Mike Rotch and *Twenty Yards to the Outhouse* by Willie Makit, illustrated by Betty Wont and published by Andy Dint. We made up our own words to popular jingles. Alex sings, *We're American Airlines, Hoping You DIE On Our Jets!* Todd comes up with a twist for the Sominex jungle, *Take Terminix tonight and sleep. Restful sleep, sleep, sleeeeep…* Brad brings up an oldie but a goodie; *N-E-S-T-L-E-S, what comes out of you A-S-S? Cho-co-late!!!* This reminds my brother of another classic; *Milk, Milk, Lemonade, 'Round the Corner Chocolate's Made!* I follow that one with; *Fat, thick, wide or thin, Vaseline will get it in!!!*

Another popular theme among us are the 'Confucius Say' jokes;

Woman who cook carrots and peas in same pot very unsanitary and, Man with hand in pocket feel pretty cocky.

We'd parody popular songs. "Have you heard the song called *Morning Wood*? It goes like this: It's getting near dawn, and I've got a hard on. It's from *Cream*."

"Cream your jeans."

We laugh at the lamest jokes; "What are tires made of?"

"Rubber."

"What are rain boots made of?"

"Rubber."

"If you saw Farrah Fawcett in the shower, what would you do?

And the cruder the material the better.

"What goes in long and hard and comes out short, wet and sticky?" (Pause.)

"Bubble gum. What were YOU thinking of?"

"What starts with F and ends with U-C-K?" (Pause)

"Fire truck. What were YOU thinking of?"

It was bound to happen. Sooner or later, I had to show Brad the Blue Flame trick I learned from Charlie. And when I do it quickly evolves into a competition we refer to as, *Olympic Farting*. We give new meaning to the term 'Olympic Flame.' We each choose a country to represent. I'm Pierre Pee-ew from Paris, Brad is Helmut von Hinny from Germany, Alex is Re-Fried Rico from Mexico and Todd is Beni-Farta from Japan. We stay in character during the entire competition. It's a very serious event with intricate international rules.

The festivities actually began earlier in the day with a special trip on our bikes to Albertsons to buy our own particular fart-enhancing foods. I liked to eat PayDay bars and Raisin Bran while Brad favors a combination of sunflower seeds and apple juice. To move the gas into the proper place, sometimes I'll do a headstand or walk on my hands as part of my warm-up routine. We'd take turns introducing ourselves and then roll up on our back to see who could create the biggest, most pungent, and powerful blue flame. Then we'd judge each other's efforts in the different categories like color, duration, pressure, presentation, artistry, choreography, etc. on a scale of one to ten. These are the magical days of youth—when just being with your friends waiting for your body to be able to fart again is more than ample entertainment. Yes, those nights were a gas, and they were helpful too. We had our challenges and they had theirs. And knowing that we weren't alone, made all our lives just a little more tolerable.

One day, Brad hears me talking to my father on the phone. When the call ends, he stands there staring at me shaking his head like a schoolteacher.

"You're a phony! You're like Sybil!"

I had never thought about it before but he's absolutely right. Every time I speak with my Dad on the phone it's as if an entirely new personality comes over me. I think I do it to cover up what's really going on. I know my father can't handle the truth so instead of saying Chris isn't home right now, she's scoring some buds for Mom I'd say, 'Golly gee Dad, you just missed her, she went to study at the library with a group of highly intelligent friends.' Instead of telling him that Molly's taking birth control and that she's been suspended from school for drinking on campus, I'd say, 'Molly has her pick of the boys and thoroughly enjoys her popularity.' Whenever he asks how I'm doing I'd use adjectives I assumed he once used as a teen; like swell, keen, neato and bees knees.

Brad proceeds to perform an excellent imitation of me.

"Golly father, how delightfully wonderful for you to call. Academically, things are going swell. I'm rather confident that my next report card will exceed your expectations. This stage of puberty is simply splendid. And how might I ask are you fairing, my dear father?"

This is embarrassing to hear because he *does* sound like me and it's so true. I feel as if I have to talk to my Dad the way I do. In my mind I'm not lying. I'm just telling him the things he wants to hear—things he can handle. He has no idea how we actually live. His little God-fearing Midwestern children have evolved into a band of gypsies, tramps, and thieves. We only see Dad once or twice a year and some years we don't see him at all. When we do, we get all dressed up, act straight and pretend to be proper. There's no smoking or cussing around our father! No one talks about the peyote buttons in the fridge, or the people Mare takes acid with or how she disappears from our lives for days on end. No one mentions the yelling matches between Mare and Shelley. We don't discuss the drug deals we make for our mother. Instead, we make-believe we're the wholesome, milk-drinking, clean-cut kids of his dreams. I love my Dad and I know he loves me but we live three thousand miles apart. Truth is power that comes with pros and cons. If my father *were* to find out and somehow understand how we actually live, it might kill him—none of us want that.

Even if it doesn't kill him, he'd be in for one hell of a shock.

Tenth

July 8th, 1996

Before I know it, the first laser beams of morning light are burning their way into the shed.

I'm severely sleep-deprived. Every muscle, tendon, and bone in my body is pissed off at the world. My taste buds have been replaced with reptilian scales. I have a cramp that goes from the arch of my right foot all the way to the nape of my neck. My knife-jabbing headache is a broken record pounding *Whoom-Bah! Whoom-Bah! Whoom-Bah!* Inside my head. I'm in a super-grumpy-pissed-off-at-the-world-bad-attitude mood.

Do not fuck with me. I woke up on the wrong side of the shed.

I'm tired of the hippie-freaksters. Why can't our family have some private time? We could look at Mare's pictures of Chris. We could listen to some of her favorite music. What's Mare's favorite Chris story? I want Shane to know how special his mother is and see how she's still loved by her family. But as the sun rises, so does the party. People gradually emerge from truck beds, cars, tents, the woods, from under rocks and out of thin air. I can't take it anymore. Enough is enough. I'm going home today. *Enough numbing myself with drugs. I'm done!* That morning, I corner my mother near the kitchen sink.

"How long is this party going to last?" I ask more sharply than intended. She smiles, as if I'd given her a compliment.

"Oh, I don't want this party to *ever* end."

"One of the best things you taught me was moderation. Well, I need to exercise moderation when it comes to hanging out with your friends. This is supposed to be about us. This is supposed to be about Chris. I'm tired. I can't sleep here. I'm sore. I'm done with this party-like-there's-no-tomorrow thing we're doing. My sister just died. Your daughter is gone. Let's deal with it. You said we'd have a wake here. I don't see a wake. If it ain't happening, I might as well take the boys home."

"Really? That's how you feel?" Mare asks, looking and sounded wounded.

"Our family needs to deal with what happened."

"We *are* dealing with what happened. This is how I grieve. It's a process. Don't take my grandsons away right now. Give us a little more time. You're not that selfish, are you?" She's balancing on the very edge of crying and suddenly I've lost my momentum.

"No. It's just…"

"—Then let's not talk about it. Not right now anyway. Hey Sweetie, let me make you one of my famous Mendocino mimosas. Doesn't that sound good?"

Inside, I'm screaming with frustration but on the outside, I'm actually nodding in agreement. That's all it takes for her to get her way. Just like that, I've committed to staying another day. The party goes on like a living thing, steadily growing as it feeds off different groups of people who continue to arrive. Shane, Skyler, and I hide out in the van for the rest of the morning just to avoid the party scene.

"Want some raisins?" I ask the kids. Shane offers his hand and I pour some into his palm. "These are good for you. They have iron in them." A few minutes pass, then he offers his hand for more.

"I can taste the iron," he says.

"You can?"

"Yea. Some of them have little hard parts inside. That must be the iron," he explains.

I know he's talking about the occasional stem that raisins conceal and consider correcting him but it's pretty cute, so I let it go for now.

"Yes. Iron makes you strong," I say, and we nibble on some more. "Do you guys want to go home tomorrow?"

"Sure," says Shane.

"Fee-fo glish," says Skyler.

"Let's go find Molly and tell her the plan."

I find my sister sitting in front of the Buddha Garden braiding Ali's hair.

"I'm definitely driving home tomorrow morning. I can't stand it here much longer," I say.

"Oh, we're *so* going with you." She says. "Nothing feels right about this anymore."

"I'm ready to get back to reality," adds Ali.

"Need anything washed?" I ask. "I'm gonna do a load of laundry to pass the time."

"Actually, I do. Let me finish Ali's hair then I'll meet you at the laundry shack."

"I'll watch the kids for a while," offers Ali.

"Awesome. Thanks Ali," I say.

Journey built what is essentially an outside closet just big enough for a side-by-side washer and dryer. Molly adds some clothes to the load and starts the machine. We each take a seat atop the mismatched appliances.

"For a cheap thrill, wait for the spin cycle," I say.

"Funny. Hey, do you remember how we had to do our own laundry when we were kids? It was no big deal. Just another chore Mare made us do for ourselves in the name of independence."

"It was no big deal as long as we had a washer and dryer at home, but then that changed. They just disappeared from our garage on "L" Street one day. I'm sure Mare sold them when money was tight."

"Money was always tight."

"True. Don't get me started on the letters she told us to write to our dad, begging for more money," I say.

"Dear Dad. I'm hungry. Please send ten dollars so I can buy a loaf of bread, milk, cereal and some Oompa-Loompas. Love, Molly."

Dear DAD,   Feb. 27, 1977
    We have a problem here. What I understand is that we are short a soport check. And you don't pay them on time. I know we are short cause I can tell by the things we eat for dinner and my mom can't even afford to by me a new pair of pants. My mom dosn't and wont read your letters, all she wants, is for you to pay the check, on time, cause when you dont, it makes me feel like you dont care about what I eat, and how I live. I want no hosseb and no problems all's we want is for the check to arrive on time, so we can have a decent meal and some

money to live on. I'm sorry I'm putting this so bluntly, but it's a problem and I want it to stop cause I'm sick of hosseling it all the time. I've got other things, more important to worry about.

Love,
Molly Mary

Molly's letter sounds more like Mare.

"Yep. Lots of 'dear dad' letters. So, back to the we had no washing or dryer at home and had to fend for ourselves subject. You, Chris, and Shelley had friends you could take your laundry to. So did Mare. And she must have done Alex's clothes too. You lucky fucks. When it first happened, I was ten years old. Image is everything when your ten, right? Your body is just starting to show the first signs of adolescence. You're suddenly hyper aware of who you are and how you present yourself to the world. Well, I was showing the world my circus-like sense of balance, peddling down the street, steering with one hand, while supporting the oversized box of dirty clothes with the other. That was the longest ride in the world to me; from our "L" Street house to the laundromat next to

Albertsons. I was constantly worried I'd be spotted by someone I know. Why? Because it's kind of hard to look cool—like you really have your shit together, while taking a box of dirty clothes on a bike ride."

"I can relate," Molly says.

"No matter what time you decide to sneak out, you run into the people you're trying the hardest to hide from. Like the cool kids you can't eat lunch with at school. They'd make me stop to see what's in the box.

"Oh... is Tommy going to get his poopy-woopy stains out of his undies today?"

"Gosh, I sure hope so."

"Funny," Molly says, smiling but not laughing.

"Bike Laundry scarred me for life."

"Get it out brother," she says, lighting up a cigarette.

"I'd put it off for as long as possible—until my socks and underwear were so crusty and moldable that you could shape them into foul smelling sculptures. I was always about two days shy from infection when I'd finally accept that it had to be done."

"In the beginning, I was scrawny, and it was hard to balance the box on my lap. The hamper fit perfectly on the back with the spring clamp. But then everyone would be able to see what I was doing. I found a cardboard box to hide the hamper in. I could rest it on the handlebars and ride totally blind, which I did, and ran into a parked car. It was one of those wet foggy days. As I was gathering my clothes, I saw a bumper sticker that read, *Have You Hugged Your Kid Today?*"

"Oh, my poor brother," Molly says, blowing smoke from one side of her smile.

"Once it was in the wash, I'd hide behind a magazine, ideally facing away from the window so no one could look in and see me. Inevitably, the machine I chose would start rocking, only a little at first and then violently—enough so that it would vibrate forward like a giant wind-up toy. People are looking around to identify the asshole who broke the machine by setting it on the spin-out-of-control-cycle. You start thinking, I don't really need those clothes. I'll just leave now."

"Oh dear!"

"I bet there's bike laundry in hell. I don't know why it felt so degrading. Maybe it was the neighbors pretending not to see me even though I know they were staring. You imagine hearing laughter every time a car, bike or pedestrian crosses your path. It didn't get any easier over time. It got worse."

"How so?" Molly says.

"Girls. The thought of running into a girl I liked while doing bike laundry freaked me out. You know that first love feeling, right? For guys it's the *first lust* feeling. I was lusting for Cecelia Goldberg. You know her. This was seventh grade. She was basically the equivalent of Phoebe Cates in, *Fast Times at Ridgemont High*; perfect. Of course, she didn't know I existed, but I knew she had the 'it' factor. And 'it' sucked when she saw me through the window folding clothes. For some reason, probably because we weren't at school, she suddenly knows me and comes walking in as if we have a lot to talk about."

"No way!"

"Yes way!"

"Then what?"

"I was at the folding stage, so I began praying; Please let there be no shit stains on my tighty-whities in her line of vision. I'm too tongue tied and shell shocked to speak. I'm thinking, *why now?* Cecelia was so nice and wasn't judgmental at all. I was the one freaking out. But in my defense, all my whites, including my jock strap had turned pink from a pillowcase Mare had just tie-dyed red. I couldn't just relax and enjoy the moment. Instead, I projected my own pity, which bounced off her and landed back on me. I didn't want her feeling sorry for me. I figured a woman of this caliber deserves a man with working appliances. I can't provide that for her. I'm not worthy."

"At least you're a man who can do his own laundry. That's something."

"She did say I was an excellent folder."

"That was nice."

"There's nothing like discussing the mysteries of static cling with the woman of your dreams."

"Nothing."

"I didn't like standing out. Mare forced us to stand out too much."

"I felt that way a lot growing up too," my sister says. "I was self-conscious about my thrift store clothes, hand-me-downs and our yellow bus."

"Drop us off here, we'd yell at Charlie."

"But we're still a mile away from school!" he'd say.

"Duh! We know! We'd yell. And Charlie, wanting to be our friend, would insist on driving us all the way there." I say.

"And then he'd honk the horn and wave as we were sprinting off, so everyone at school would see us," Molly adds.

"Coming out of the short bus."

"Yep. Good times."

"Best of times," I say.

"And now the worst of times—because Chris is gone," Molly says, suddenly sad, as if a dark cloud just erased the sun.

"She's gone *and* she left her poor kids behind."

"This is a tragedy. Those boys need a miracle," Molly says.

"Don't look at me. There's no way I can give them what they need."

"Tom, you're going to have the hardest time if you *don't* get the boys."

"Well, I don't see that happening. We'll figure something out. We have to."

Although we end on a sad note, her company does wonders for my mood. Knowing I'll be back in Sacramento tomorrow means I only have to tolerate one more miserable night in the shed. I've never missed my own bed as much as I do now.

The last night in the shed is even worse than ever because I'm already 'floor-sore' from the prior two nights. Plus, carrying Skyler so much has made me use muscles I never knew existed. Just as I'm drifting off around midnight, Skyler wakes up. He must have had a bad dream. He begins crying so hard that he can't catch his breath and is gasping for air in between every painful scream. Even I know this is not normal crying. Shane wakes up, looks at his brother and me through swollen eyes and then rolls back over and covers his ears. I strain just to stand and lift Skyler into my weary arms. I set him in the car seat I'd left outside and tiptoe towards the house in search of a fresh bottle. Molly hears me coming through the door and whispers,

"What's wrong?"

"I have no idea," I say whispering back. "Bad dreams?"

Molly kindly gets up and offers to help. Skyler clearly does not want his bottle, chucks it on to the ground and continues wailing like a banshee.

"This happened on the first night. He wants his mother—it's as simple as that," I explain to Molly.

"Well, that breaks what's left of my heart," she says.

"Yours and mine both."

Molly and I take turns holding Skyler and walking around outside in the dark. His painful cries echo into the long black shadows of night. Carrying him under the tree-tunnels while speaking to him softly starts to calm him down. Molly and I continue taking turns, trading him back and forth, until he falls asleep. We can't believe how hard he was crying. It's just so sad and hauntingly familiar.

We get him back into the shed while he's knocked out, exhausted by his own trauma. At some point during all the commotion, I pull a muscle in the back of my neck. A sharp pain slices its way to my shoulder, down my arm and to the tips of my fingers. There's no position I can find on the floor that doesn't hurt.

Shane begins to nose-whistle quietly in his sleep. I roll to the side and watch both kids sleep for a few minutes. Skyler's breath is oddly sweet. When do we lose that baby-breath smell and why? Does life make us sour over time? Has that process already begun with these kids? Have they been mentally damaged by the loss of their mother at such a young age? I know I experienced my share of childhood trauma, but nothing so early or so dramatic as losing a mother. Will their loss surface one day and in what form? Death is a form of abandonment. How will Shane and Skyler ever process this heavy load? I'd like to help but have no idea how. Worthless. That's how I feel about the whole thing. I have no idea what the healing process is for kids their age. I'm not a parent. I know jack shit about kids. I'm caught in whirlwind of worry and need to change the subject, so I let my mind drift back to Davis, back to those days that were at the beginning of the end. The end being the last time we all lived together under the same roof.

∞   ∞   ∞

My mother has a 'catch-all' approach to the healing process growing up. Her cure for any illness, discomfort and injury is always the same; "Sit on the pot." I'm surprised it wasn't, "Sit on the pot and smoke some pot." Anyway, this motherly advice is worthless unless your ailment was stomach related. You could get stung by a bee. "Sit on the pot." You could sprain your ankle and show her the swelling. "Sit on the pot." You could be bleeding out your ears. "Sit on the pot." You could have a femur bone sticking out of your thigh. "Sit on the pot." The only other medical advice she ever offers is equally worthless; "When you go to bed tonight, right before you fall asleep, tell your body to heal itself. Your body's ability to heal itself is *amazing.* Tell yourself you're going to feel all better when you wake up the next day and guess what? You will!" If you woke up the next day and that bone is still sticking out of your thigh, it was your own fault for not discussing it properly with yourself. Her teachings in the wellness department is something I filed in the, 'Worthless Advice' folder I had created in my brain.

Here's another file from the same folder titled: Reading. My mother doesn't read books sequentially. Growing up, I loved that she had a constant stream of library books rotating through our house at any given time. There were always about a dozen books, maybe that was the limit set by the library, scattered about at any given time. I assumed she read each book cover-to-cover every three weeks, fully absorbing the content—and, because she's Mare, had bended the content to suit her needs before returning them and picking up a new set. Then one day I happen to watch her read. She selects a book, opens it randomly, reads for a moment, and then sets the book down and opens another. She does this several times with several books before I can't stand it any longer.

"What are you doing?"

"I'm reading." She says, stating the obvious, not bothering to look up.

"Are you? Or are you reading random pages from a bunch of books all at once?"

"Yes. That's how I read."

"That's not how books are meant to be read."

"It works for me. I let the universe offer me the tidbits of information I need to feed the intellectual aspects of my soul," she says, as if this should be obvious to me.

"Well, they're sequential. Books have a beginning, a middle and an end. The parts at the beginning have to be read before the middle and later parts for the story to make sense."

"Well, that's western-style learning and logic."

"We live in the western world, right?"

"We do, but we don't have to follow all the western rules."

"Oh really?"

"What I do is just another way of learning. It's non-sequential. I'm acquiring knowledge intuitively."

"Working out. That. How's. For you?"

"Ha, ha. Funny. Just. Thanks. Fine."

This was only mildly annoying, so I let it go and didn't think about it again until I see my little brother doing the same thing one day.

"You learn that from Mom?" I ask.

"Yep," he says.

"Wouldn't you learn more if you read books from beginning to end like everyone else does?"

"Maybe. But this is ten times faster and more fun."

"You never know if you've read the whole book."

"Yes, I do."

"You can't remember every little part you read."

"Yes, I can."

"If she read her books upside down would you, too?"

"I'd probably try it."

"If she set fire to a book to force herself to read it fast, would you do the same."

"Hell yes! Got a match?"

"My ass and your face."

"You need some new material."

"Maybe I'll get a book full of jokes."

"You should."

"I'll tell the punch lines first and the set up last and see if anyone laughs."

"People laugh at you all the time. Behind your back."

"Good one."

"Thanks."

Mom and Shelley are going at it one evening really hard when suddenly we hear it, SLAP! I jump up and see them glaring at each other in the kitchen. Shelley's mouth is an "O" like she's blowing smoke rings. I can see the impression of my mother's hand coming into view on Shelley's cheek like a photograph developing in a darkroom. Their eyes are locked. Shelley's are welling up with tears. Her sadness suddenly becomes rage, and she slaps Mare back. SLAP!—just as loud. Mare's hands rise and then fall to her side like robotic limbs with bad circuits. Shelley runs upstairs stomping her feet and crying. Mare steadies herself on the wall. Her expression is a mix of shock and anger. Then her face completely changes, and she appears surprisingly relaxed—void of all emotion, a robot with a pretty face. She takes four calm steps into the living room and announces, "Your sister Shelley will be moving out."

Shelley is only sixteen years old. No one questions the legality of this news. Mare has drawn a line. Shelley will have to figure something out fast. She happens to have a friend who is also in dire straits at home; Patty DalPorto. Patty is unforgettable. Her voice is gift wrapped in Zig Zag rolling papers. She speaks slowly in a deep tone, droning through words she randomly lengthens. She chews on vowels and spits out consonants sounding like she's completely stoned out of her mind. Her larynx is submerged in cannabis oil. When Patty actually is stoned, she might as well be playing a character in a Cheech and Chong movie. Patty has the hands down, best stoner, hippie-chick voice in the entire universe. Shelley moves in with Patty. This lasts a month. Then Shelley and Patty, move into a shack on Olive Drive that Patty's parents rent just to help the girls get started. They would have to start paying their own rent after three months.

I ride my bike over to visit. The grime, the smell, the noise, the number of slow-moving sickly cats, rusting cars, trash, the waist-high weeds overwhelm me to the point of tears. It's like being slapped in the face with poverty. We go into the tiny space and smoke a joint, but it isn't enough to drown the smell of mold and mold-killing chemicals. Their tiny home feels crowded, and when the train goes by, we feel it in our bones.

"You don't want to be here when it rains," Shelley says, trying to make light of the situation, pointing to the moldy water stains on the ceiling.

"We've got a tin roof man," adds Patty.

"I don't want to be here at all. I feel sorry for you," I say, smiling and taking another hit. Shelley drops out of school and starts working at Kentucky Fried Chicken. She's also studying for the GED and has no free time for art, and she looks like she's carrying the weight of the world on her shoulders. Her living situation isn't something we can talk about with our mother. When Mare mentions Shelley, she makes it sound like forcing her from the nest was just the ticket.

"Shelley's growing up. She's taking care of herself now. Do you know how proud that makes me feel?"

Charlie takes us to Kentucky Fried Chicken one evening to pick up dinner and perhaps enjoy a brief visit with Shelley. We get fully loaded on the way and we're full of excitement to see our long, lost older sister. Seeing Shelley in her uniform for the first time is like seeing a cat in a life jacket swimming. Her bright, polyester uniform is an appaloosa of grease. She's sweaty. Her jaw is clenched, and she's obviously stressed out.

"You look pretty," says Molly looking at her sister's attire.

"Pretty greasy," Shelley says. "Only here they don't call it grease they call it *juice*."

"How late do you work?" asks Chris.

"Late. We don't close until ten. Then I have to help clean up. I head home around eleven—unless we have to clean one of the fryers."

"We miss you," Chris says, speaking for all of us.

"I miss you guys too. All I do is study and work. I never see my friends. I miss just hanging out and listening to music and having time to draw. I miss my family."

"Come see me when I'm not working. It's like I don't even know you guys anymore."

She hears a machine go, ping! wipes her brow, smiles bravely, and goes back to work. She's right, I think. *It is like I don't know her anymore.* She disappears in the back.

We take our food and head towards the bus. Shelley sneaks out the back door and is waiting there for us to say goodbye. Shelley climbs on board and gives each of us a hug. It starts out okay then quickly becomes incredibly sad and we do our best not to cry. Mare's on the pad up front watching. Shelley turns and faces her last. They lock eyes and I don't know if they're going to laugh, cry, slap or throw punches at each other. Shelley leans into Mare and they slowly embrace. We hear her weeping into our mother's shoulder. Mare strokes her daughter's head gently. It's sad and I'm unable to swallow. I know Shelley regrets slapping Mare back. She's not happy. She wants to come home with us right now and end this nightmare. Our mother lets go and gently pushes Shelley aside as if she's repositioning a mannequin. Shelley's head droops as she climbs down the stairs. Charlie's brown eyes are pools of tears. He closes the door and turns the bus around. The loose gravel in the parking lot sounds like dried bones crushing beneath our wheels. No one says a word all the way home.

Our giant bag of food is placed on the table, and we take our seats. Charlie lifts the lid of our family bucket and begins sorting things about. God bless you, Colonel Sanders. You thought of everything. Not only did we get our chicken, but also six shortening-bread rolls, Cole slaw in a cup made of Styrofoam and mashed potato with gravy in another. Also, a bag of salt and pepper to suit any possible taste, a foil-bag each of ketchup and mustard, plus plastic knives and forks wrapped in paper napkins and the story of Colonel Sanders printed on two sides of the bucket, so we have something to read while dining.

The only thing missing is Shelley.

Our sister's absence remains an off-limit topic with our mother but not among ourselves. We know Shelley is too young to be out on her own. We put our heads together trying to come up with a solution and fail. Yes, we knew this day would come but now that it's here, we're miserably unprepared so I tell myself it's only temporary, that she'll be allowed to move back in once Mare feels she's made her point. At first, it's impossible to think about anything else but Shelley. There's a giant hole in our family but we manage to talk about other things instead. Sadly, as time goes on, I start to accept it.

Maybe it's my age, or the era—maybe I was in survival mode. Thinking about her makes me wonder which one of us will be next... Chris? Me, Molly? Alex? Maybe all of us at once? It's too painful to think about so I try not to. And in the process, I think less about Shelley, too. I'm ashamed for not missing her more. My oldest sister disappears along with her art supplies. Once I'm no longer seeing her wonderful art on a regular basis, Shelley's presence fades away about as fast as one of her hand-drawn tattoos.

"We're moving at the end of this month," Mare says handing me a freshly rolled joint.

"Okay." I almost expected this to happen sooner or later.

"Where are we moving to?" I ask.

"A big old house on D Street. Downtown. It's amazing."

"But we have a pool here," I say, knowing it's a moot point to Mare.

"Well, this place is bigger and the rent's lower, so I already got it all lined up."

"What's the address? I'll ride by and check it out."

Mare flips open her note book, turns a couple pages, and gives it to me. "I've been living there a while," Mare mentions like old news. Suddenly Molly looks up from the Peter Frampton Live album in her lap and gives our mother a jaw dropping look.

"Wait. You've been 'living there a while?' How long?" Molly asks, trying to tame her voice into a tolerable tone.

"You kids need space. I need space. I told you I was moving out to give you guys more room. At first, I was at Charlie's but then I needed some space from him too, and one of my friends was renting a room in this big house downtown with a bunch of other far out people, so I took it. It's only been a few months."

Mare just shrugs her shoulders and starts to roll a joint. This news barely affects me, though I wonder who's paying her rent since she doesn't work. This news does, however, bother my sister a lot. Molly's eyes pool up with water. Her neck and cheeks turn red, like she's just sprinted a mile. Mare must be feeling Molly's eyes on her. She continues rolling joint after joint, never looking up from her task until she feels enough time has passed for Molly to cool off. When Mare reaches for Molly to hand her the joint, Molly stands up and steps back. She shakes her head and looks at Mare with an expression studded with questions marks and exclamation points.

"You don't even want to live with your own children???!!! Shame on you. That's fucked up, Mare!! You're the only mother I know who would do such a thing!" Then she leaves the room. Our mother takes a quick hit off the joint and watches Molly go.

"Wow!" Mare says, laughing. "Guess I'm not getting the mother of year award from that one today."

Brad and I ride by the house the next day after school. It's directly across the street from the Rexall Pharmacy and next door to the Pence Gallery, which is a new structure, small and modern, completely out of place like a sailboat in a cornfield. The house itself is also out of place, too because everything around it is commercial property and I feel oddly out of place living there from day one. In addition to giving up the pool and cabana, we also lost the convenience of the apartments' laundry room. There are, however two laundromats within easy walking distance so at lease I can do my laundry without having to peddle it anywhere.

"You're going to be living right downtown," Brad says.

"Is that good or bad?" I ask.

"You better lock up your bike." He says chuckling.

At this stage in my life, moving my stuff from one location to another is a no-brainer task. I have four plastic milk cartons that I'm able to fit all my books and knick-knacks in, one big cardboard box of clothes and shoes, a small cardboard box with sporting goods, a foam mat that unrolls into a bed, one pillow, one backpack for school stuff and a bike. Charlie is happy to help with the move. The house is big but not in a practical manner. It has a large entryway with no closets that's simply wasted space. There's a long porch wrapping around two sides of the structure with lots of screens and some bamboo shades. It has a large enough living room, but the kitchen-dining room and the bedrooms are small. There's a strange deep and narrow pantry in the kitchen. We clean the shit out of it only to achieve a shabby state of being. There's bigger issues than just dirt; peeling paint, missing molding, warped floors, moldy smells, water stains, mystery stains… chalk outlines of people who have died here and there… No, it's not that bad, but close.

Alex and I share the screened in, wrap-around porch and we can hear every imaginable noise you can think of at night. We'll worry about how cold it gets when winter rolls around. Chris and Molly cram into one room; Mare and Charlie cram into the other. About a week after moving in, Shelley comes over to visit. While we're showing her around, she takes an extra-long look at the pantry. And during dinner, after mustering considerable bravery she looks up, reaches out her hand and rests it on her mother's.

"Mare, I have a favor to ask. If you need to think about it before answering, that's cool. I understand," Shelley says nervously losing momentum with each word. Mare doesn't look up from her chile relleno at first, she just keeps eating away at it like a caterpillar mowing through a delicious leaf.

Shelley squeezes her mother's hand a little tighter. Mare finally stops moving and looks directly at her oldest daughter.

"It sure would be nice to be with everyone again. I miss everyone and I hope you miss me back. I'm all alone. You guys still have each other. I want to get out of my shit shack on Olive Drive and rent out the pantry."

Mare smiles. She cocks her head ever so slightly and looks like she's about to say something very important but then looks down at her food, saws off another bite and lifts it to her mouth. "Mmmmm," she says leaving Shelley wondering if she's thinking about her request or just enjoying her food.

"What do you think? Do you guys want me to move back in with you?" Shelley asks looking around the room at each of us.

"I do," says Chris.

"I do too," Molly says.

"Yes! Come back!" yells Alex raising his hand to vote his opinion.

"That's a big 10-4," I say because I'm going through a CB radio phase.

Mare's cheeks are swollen with chile relleno. She takes her time so that everyone's eyes get stuck on and around her like summer flies in the windowsill waiting for her to say something.

"That would be illegal. It's not a bedroom."

When has that ever mattered? You turned our family room into your bedroom in the L street house. You broke the Alvarado lease when we all moved in there. My mother LOVES to bend and break rules. We could turn the living room into Shelley's room, or she'd fit on the porch with Alex and I. Why is she suddenly being so proper? I wonder.

"You can charge me rent. I'll chip in. Let's be a family again," Shelley offers.

"Oh honey, you'll always be a huge part of this family. That never changes."

"Then let's find a way. We can work something out, right?"

Shelley looks hopeful for a moment. Then Mare's smile collapses away from her eyes and Shelley can sense that she has not penetrated the fortress. Chris looks like she's about to jump in and petition for Shelley, but Mare beats her to the punch.

"You don't want to move backwards in life. I'm too proud of you to allow that to happen."

"But Mare—" Shelley starts to say.

"But nothing. We're keeping things the way they are. At least for now."

Shelley sighs heavily struggling to accept defeat. She looks at Chris. Chris tells her she's sorry with her eyes. Then Molly does the same. I lift my shoulders and hands to express my sorrow.

Chris and I look at each other searching one last time for something that might change our mother's mind. We come up blank. Nothing. When Shelley goes back home that night, we're forced to accept that Shelley is *never* moving back in with us. First there were five, now there are four. The countdown has begun.

The D Street house immediately becomes a party destination. Because it's downtown, it's the place people meet up at to get buzzed before going out and also the place people return to when the bars close down. We had already experienced our share of weird shit, but we would take weird shit to a whole new level in this house. It was so darn "D": Downtown. Drugs. Dirty. Decrepit. Drama. Disgraceful. Degrading. Dysfunction. Dangerous. Detestable. Decay. Demise. Demonic. Demoralizing. Depressing and Devastating. The D Street house is ground zero for Disaster with a capitol "D". I don't even know where to start…

∞   ∞   ∞

I chase, but never catch sleep. And then the sun is already too high and it's light enough in the shed to count the spider bites on my arms and legs. It's just another day that insists on starting despite my dread. But it's also the day I get to leave this place and go home and that motivates me enough to get up and get going.

Eleventh

July 9th, 1996

People are already up, drinking, smoking, and talking shit. It's early. The party's on simmer, but it's not going away. It fuels my conviction to get the hell out of here. When Mare sees me packing the van, she catches my gaze, throws me a fake smile, and saunters my way.

"So, what's your rush?" She asks.

"No rush. I'm just packing. What time is Chris's wake happening today?" I ask, with malicious sarcasm, knowing Chris's wake will never happen.

"It's happening now. This party is a celebration of Christina's life. Our closest friends and family are all here. Loosen up, my son. Enjoy yourself."

"I thought Journey was going to do some kind of ceremony for Chris."

"He his—it's in the works. Are your eyes open? Can you NOT SEE how much pain I'm in? Why are you being so selfish?"

Main course: Guilt.

"Here," she says, handing me one of the thickest joints she's ever rolled.

Side dish: Drugs.

"Light it up. Take a hit. You'll feel better. Maybe you can stay another day or two in honor of Chris and support your family—be a good son."

I wave off the joint. Mare flinches. "We need to get back. I called my answering machine there were tons of messages. Things need to get done. We can't check out and hide forever."

"I'm not doing either of those things," she says calmly.

"I mean to find out what really happened to Chris. We owe it to her to do that, right?"

"What's happened has happened. We'll find out. Waiting another twenty-four hours isn't going to change anything. We have time."

"Well, I respectfully disagree."

"Look at me," she says. "The word *giving* is in the word *grieving*." Did you know that? Today is not about what's best for Tom. Give a little. Adjust your schedule."

"Well, there's a *fun* in *funeral*, so sometimes your little word game is pure bullshit."

"Why can't a funeral be fun? And fuck you if my healing process is different than yours. Yes, you lost your sister, but I lost my daughter. Give me time to adjust to that, will you? Think about how your egocentric, selfish decisions affect others."

She's on the verge of crying, but I don't feel like coming to her rescue this time. An extremely tense minute passes. *Maybe I am being selfish,* I think to myself. But the thought of staying repulses me.

"I'm sorry. I love you. But we really need to go."

She looks at me with her big sad eyes. "You can leave Shane and Skyler here."

"Thanks, but no thanks. They're coming with me." Like an Oscar winner, she makes her eyes even sadder. "I love you Mare; and I understand you need to deal with this in your own way. I respect that. So, you've got to let me deal with this my own way, too. I need to get home. That's how I feel."

"It would be one thing if it was just you. But you're taking Shane and Skyler and Molly and her kids, too. Right? You're their ride, right?"

"Yea. They're leaving too. Maybe Al can stay."

"I'll stay," my brother says, joining us—not missing a beat. His timing is impeccable. "I just have to call work and request more time off due to this family crisis."

It's enough to diffuse the situation. She gives Al a warm hug and me the cold shoulder. I breathe a sigh of relief. Mare goes back inside, sits at the table, and writes a eulogy for Chris while Molly and I finish packing. We say our goodbyes to people we know, and people we don't.

"We didn't get a chance to meet," I say to a man in his late forties, who's been growing his hair since his early twenties.

"My name is Leap," he says extending his hand.

"I'm Tom. Mare's son."

"Nice to meet you."

"You, too. I like your name. Were you born in a leap year?"

"No," he snorts, shaking his head in disgust and briskly walking away.

"Nice to meet you," I say to the empty space he left behind. *What is it with people's names around here? Leap of Faith? Leap Frog? Giant Leap for Mankind?*

"Leap is short for Phillippe. He gots some webbed toes on his left foot," Journey tells me, which on one hand makes perfect sense and has the other scratching my head. Mare gradually accepts we're leaving and starts talking to me just before we leave.

"I'll call you tomorrow and let you know our plans. Drive safe. You have lots of precious cargo onboard." She blows kisses to the faces in the van.

I watch her disappear in the mirror as we drive away. The farther we drive from Blue Moon Ranch, the more I feel my version of reality returning. We go through a town that's nothing but an outline of a dot on the map and I'm so relieved knowing I'm headed home.

It's weird knowing exactly where you are yet feeling completely lost. I may have moved past denial but I'm still nowhere near acceptance on this altered-state highway of life.

The landscape rushing by the windows is like the last five days: one big blur. When Chris died, everything went from right, to wrong so incredibly fast. So much has happened since getting that horrible call at work, but it feels like we've done nothing. We're just swirling in the chaos like those Fourth of July Black Snakes, the harmless looking flammable pills that emit an impossibly large snake-like ash. Our sorrow and our despair never ends—it just keeps pouring out because Chris is gone.

Forever.

Who's going to take care of Shane and Skyler? How are we going to keep her precious boys in the family? Maybe I should step up. They could do worse. They already stick to me like glue. Can I give up my life for theirs? I don't think so. No way. Mare and Journey obviously don't want to raise them—and what if they did? They're not exactly ideal candidates. My mother took an early retirement from motherhood. We were forced from the nest when she moved into the bus. It's safe to say that at least some of our issues can be traced back to childhood trauma. Mare is sixty years old. She and Journey live a simple, isolated life centered on the cultivation of ever stronger cannabis. What kind of role model would Mare and Journey make for Shane and Skyler? Blue Moon Ranch is in the middle of nowhere. There's no one around for miles, no kids to play with, no group sports. Learning to grow killer buds is great but what about other important life skills? If they did want the boys, would I let that happen? Could I live with myself? Time-sharing the kids makes no sense. They need stability, security, and love—the sooner the better.

It feels good to drive. Holding the wheel gives me a sense of control, in an out-of-control world. Everything feels so pointless. My hopelessness stretches far beyond the road ahead of me.

In the rearview mirror, I see my sister Molly and consider the harsh fact that she lost her husband. I look at Ali, Willie, and Joey—they have no father. Next to them are Shane and

Skyler—they have no mother. The gravity of it all is both pulling us together and tearing us apart. Who knows what will happen next? Molly is completely drained. I've never seen her wear the same blank expression for so long. Shane and Skyler are sleeping, their bodies positioned similarly, heads slumped to the right, rosy cheeks, hair damp with sweat. At three and a half years apart, they certainly look different, yet they share plenty of the same handsome features making it obvious that they're brothers.

Shane has been like a rock. My only worry is that he isn't expressing enough emotion. Shouldn't he have a fit, a meltdown, or a temper tantrum? If anyone is entitled to a good cry, it's him. He's been a five-year-old pillar of strength. In fact, it's Shane who's making the rest of us feel better, just by continuing to be himself. Amazing.

In contrast, Skyler is pure emotion. When he's sad, he cries. When he's frustrated, he flails. When he's happy, he laughs. When he's tired, he whines. It's all very simple and absolutely foreign. One cry from Skyler triggers a painful chemical reaction inside my body. When I'm able to comfort him and he falls asleep in my arms—nothing feels better. I can console Shane with words, but comforting Skyler requires pure emotion in return.

It's been a quiet trip. Even as I pull into the driveway, no one says a word. We spill out of the van in slow motion, on road-weary legs and shuffle into the house. Home is good. Air conditioning is good. The thought of sleeping in my own bed is good. Blue Moon Ranch was exhausting. We want nothing more than to relax and readjust to civilization.

My thoughtful roommate, Monica, penned a note and taped it on a suitcase of beer in the fridge. FOR YOU! I think to myself, how nice. But when I look inside the cardboard box, there's only two beers left. Her note could have been clearer; SUCK MY SCRAPS, LOSERS! I check my phone messages. Dad called from the hotel. I call him back and make plans for dinner. Just as we're starting to relax, my roommate, bursts through the door.

She's loud and doesn't care that we're tired. She wants to party. I take her into the backyard to minimize her rowdy presence. She hands me a cigarette. I'm mad at myself for having no discipline, but not disgusted enough to stop. After all, if you can't smoke in the middle of a crisis, when can you? I take it from her thick fingers and light it up. It's good. I get the half-second dizzy shift of consciousness I experienced before. I keep her occupied out back while we smoke one after another.

I barely have time to brush my teeth, scrub my hands and splash water on my face before Dad arrives. I reek of smoke and shame. The thought of Dad, Mister-Health-Nut-Jogger, finding out that I've been smoking Marlboro reds sickens me. Lucky for me, Dad's not much of a hugger, even in this situation. We shake hands and sort of lean into each other. I hold my breath for a moment then blow a sigh of relief over his shoulder.

I admire, respect, and love my father but unfortunately, we don't have a deep relationship. This can happen when you live on opposite sides of the country. But it's not just the distance. He always wanted the freedom to live the life of a freelance travel writer and not be bogged down by family obligations. Dad's great with people—but is more comfortable with temporary relationships. Our visits and phone calls were always great, even to this day—but looking back, they were also quite few and so far between. Dad really has no idea of the lives we live. Growing up, we only told him the good things he wanted to hear. Any one of us can tell when another one of us is talking on the phone with our father. We suddenly become much more wholesome. Our dialogue takes on the artificial tone of TV characters. He likes to be alone. He's a wordsmith and a wonderfully gifted writer—he's seen and experienced so much of the world. But when it comes to family relationships, he's like a lifeboat lost at sea.

I watch him unzip and reach into his travel bag of crap—I mean goodies. He presents various knick-knacks to the kids. My father is not a thief, he's just really good at getting free stuff. Year after year, Dad stuck us with plenty of worthless horse hockey. When we were little, it was great. As we got older, we caught on that it was crap. We didn't want to hurt his feelings, so we'd maintain enough fake enthusiasm while accepting his worthless offerings.

Dad snatches mugs, maps, badges, toothbrushes, soaps, airline blankets, candles, spoons, patches, postcards, wet-naps, lapel-pins and more—souvenirs from all over the world. He nabs them from travel offices, off airplanes and from maid carts. No matter where he travels, if it's not screwed down and will fit in his suitcase, then it's probably on its way to one of us. Now it's the next generation's turn to receive and we get to stand by and watch.

Despite the excitement he's created with the kids, he looks tired. There's a hint of sadness shadowing his expression. I know he'll rally and give us his best. He'll be the steady, thoughtful, considerate father we need him to be right now. I try to remember when I saw him last. Our trip to the hospital to visit Chris comes to mind. That was a painful visit. This is a million times worse. I wonder what's going through his mind? Does he think Mare is partially at fault for what has happened to Chris? Is he feeling any sense of responsibility like I am?

Before I can jump in and save us, I hear him talking with Monica. "Would you like to join us for dinner. My treat."

"Fu… or sure!" She was about to say fuck yea, so it was a good save. "I'm always working out and always starving." She reaches up with the palm of her hand so Dad can give her a high five. Then she laughs. Her voice is unusually deep. It wasn't always this way.

When she first moved in, Monica was a petite girl with big blue eyes and long blond hair. During the last year she's added considerably to her girth. Rigorous exercise and illegal Mexican 'enhancers' have caused drastic changes, including the tone of her voice. She had her hair cropped short except for a tuft of spiked platinum bangs. Picture Tweety Bird on steroids. Her breasts have all but evaporated, but there is a good chance she's growing some sort of a hybrid male genitalia downstairs—I don't think about it. Lately, she's been over-tanning and is the color of a well-oiled saddle. Although Monica was married to a man for a short period a long time ago, everyone accepts that she's gay—everyone except Monica, that is. I've seen the way she looks at my dates. She's practically a dude. Even when a girl spends the night with her, she plays it off like they simply drank too much and happened to pass out in the same bed.

Monica is a low-budget living chemistry experiment in progress, and I'm curious to see what happens next. She's loud, messy, has a breathalyzer affixed to her Jeep's ignition and has been late with the rent before. But she's also loyal, generous, and very entertaining. She dressed as the SNL character, Pat— It's Time for Androgyny—for Halloween last year. We have the picture of her on our fridge in costume looking confused in front of the men's and women's restrooms. That alone makes her pretty awesome.

All eight of us pile into the rental van with the dented cargo box and drive to the nearest Denny's, Carrow's, Eppie's, Lyon's, or Baker's Square. In my state of mind, it doesn't matter. These restaurants all look, sound, taste and smell the same, from the size of the menus down to the sanitizers in the urinals. These places serve the same combinations of food, furnished from the same suppliers, prepared by the same semi-skilled, mostly Hispanic cooks. Waitresses' adept at feigning happiness, wearing heavily stained uniforms, serve humongous portions of mediocre food on over-sized plates, garnished with wilted parsley. Welcome to America. In Sacramento, these restaurants are always packed, mostly with crowds of preppy-looking people brainwashed into believing they're enjoying gourmet cuisine. I'm not a food snob; it's just how Sacramento is. People here eat out more than they eat in.

It takes a while for the host to seat a group as large as ours. We finally get a set of pushed-together tables, and everyone disappears behind a wall of menus.

"The reason these menus are so large is because of the staggering high illiteracy rate in America," Dad says from somewhere. "This way people can just point to what they want."

"Really?" asks Molly, from somewhere else at the table. All I can see are glossy pictures of food everywhere.

"Really," he says. "I read an article about it on the plane on my way here."

"I bet Shane can read the menu," I add.

"Dinner is on me, so order whatever looks good," Dad says, politely from behind his laminated billboard of food.

We don't notice that our waitress is standing next to our table until she says, in the happiest high-pitched voice you've ever heard, "Hi! My name is Tracie. That's Tracie with an 'I' and a happy face instead of a dot, and an E not a Y. Don't ask me why!" She's chomping fluorescent green gum while she speaks and is suddenly the most annoying person in the world. "It's my sincere pleasure to be serving you tonight. Would you like to order something to drink first, or maybe an appetizer— or maybe both?"

She was born and raised in Sacramento. I can tell by her accent. Sacramento is full of cute, young girls just like her. A surprisingly large number of them have moved back in with their parents to help them raise the kid they had a few years ago with a guy they refer to as 'my mistake.' Give her a few months and she'll be more disenfranchised and will have a harder time feigning happiness.

"I'll have the surf and turf," says Monica with authority, "and a Coke with no ice!" It is the most expensive and silliest thing on the menu. We're in Sacramento. What is she getting, Delta lobster?

Dad is pretending to be illiterate and points to a plate of pot roast on his menu, "I'll have this," he starts, "but instead of this," he points to the corn, "can I get this instead?"—pointing to the vegetable medley on another plate in a different photo. He flips the menu over and points to the glass of milk in yet another photograph. "And non-fat this to drink."

Our food arrives, looking much less glorious than the highly stylized photos had suggested. Dad keeps the conversation going by asking everyone questions and sharing interesting tidbits from his recent travels. When Tracie brings the bill, my father tells her to stay put while he examines it for errors. She can tell he's only teasing and rests her hand on his shoulder.

"You're in luck Tracie, it appears to be correct." He slides his credit card into her hand. She winks and sashays away towards the cash register. Ali and I catch him looking at her ass.

"God Grandpa! You're such a flirt!" Ali says.

"You think?" I say.

"What are you talking about? I didn't do a thing," he says, defensively.

"She totally rubbed your shoulder and winked at you," Ali says.

"No, no, no. She just wants a big tip. I'm totally innocent."

We know he's not innocent because he's done this all his life. I'm guilty of doing the same thing. I blame him because I, too, find it almost impossible not to flirt with attractive women. It's embarrassing—and it often goes very wrong and yet it doesn't stop me from doing it the next time. I got it from him. Genetics are crazy.

Once Shane, Skyler, Willie, and Joey are down for the night, Molly, Ali, and I begin the inevitable heavy conversation we need to have with Dad. Monica, who has no sense of family privacy, sits right down at the table, and joins us. Dad does his best to put into words what can't really be expressed: how sad he feels, how the news triggered his memory of meeting Jeff for the first time and how happy his daughter was. I remember that day, too. Unlike my father, I knew Jeff back in high school when he was a big, tough punk with a bad reputation. He was trouble and I avoided him. There was a remote possibility that he'd changed over the years, but it didn't take long to see that he was the same fucked-up conniving asshole he'd always been. Chris didn't see him for who he was. Her biological clock was ticking at the speed of now-or-never. All she saw were babies.

Dad removes his glasses and rubs his eyes. "Shane and Skyler are left motherless, those poor, unfortunate boys. What's their fate? You read about these things; domestic violence, the O.J. Simpson case... But you never imagine it actually happening in your own family. This is overwhelming. It's an honest-to-God catastrophe."

His voice begins to tremble. It's clear he's been hurt to his core. I underestimated the depth of his sadness until tonight. Ali wraps her arms around his shoulders and hugs him gently.

"Have you talked about where Shane and Skyler are going to live?" Dad asks.

"Nothing has been decided yet, other than we have to keep the boys together," I say.

"I wish I could take Shane and Skyler home with us. But with Kurt gone, it's more than I can handle." Molly says.

"Mom. You can't," adds Ali.

"Absolutely," Dad agrees. "You have your own family obligations. That's totally understandable. What about Mare and Journey? Have they expressed an interest in adopting them?"

"Not really," I begin. "Mare proposed a time-sharing plan where we would all take turns raising them. In my opinion, the kids shouldn't be moved around too much. They need something long-term and stable. But honestly, I don't think Mare wants to raise kids at this stage in her life. Instead of coming out and saying so, Mare and Journey are quietly waiting on the sidelines to see what happens."

"They're hoping you'll raise them," Molly says, looking at me.

"No duh. I think everyone's hoping for that. If we want to keep the boys in the family, then I'm the logical choice. I have a house. I'm dependable. I have a good job… I can juggle… They're getting more and more attached. The list goes on…"

"You're not a viable choice," Dad says cutting me off. "You're a single man. It would ruin your life," he's clearly distressed and concerned. "You taking them on would be a *huge* mistake. Think about what's best for Shane and Skyler, not what's best for the family. Don't get me wrong. I'd like to keep them in the family too, but only if that's the best place for them to be. Otherwise, it would be better having them adopted into a family, a nearby family, so you can still be part of their lives. There are wonderful couples out there who desperately want to raise children but can't conceive; I'm talking about really good people who are fully prepared for parenthood—emotionally, financially. Keeping them in the family might make everyone feel better in the short run, but is that better for anyone in the long run? Am I wrong?"

"No, that makes sense," I say. "First of all, these kids could never ruin my life. Secondly, I'm certain that I don't want to raise them. The reason everyone wants to hang on to Shane and Skyler is because they're our link to Chris. Look at them. Can you not totally see Chris in their faces, especially Shane's? If we lose them, we lose a major connection to Chris. Of course, we feel this way."

"I don't want to see my son's life drastically altered because of my daughter's death. Enough damage has already been done."

"Well, as long as we're being honest, then you should know how selfish I really am. I don't want the responsibility of raising children, let alone ones I didn't bring into the world—even if they are my sister's. Am I capable of raising the boys? Yes. But no thank you. I don't want to give up my lifestyle or my freedom. I love being a bachelor and conversing with beautiful women. I met this one girl at The Paradise Beach Club who had nice high cheeks and a great jaw line. I told her she had really great, 'I'd-like-to-bone-you-structure.' Another time at another place, I started talking with a beautiful girl and mentioned that 'My mother is a seamstress, which means I could take you home tonight, rip that pretty little dress right off your body and mend it for you in the morning on my Pfaff.' After that, she was putty in my hands. I love the hunt—sometimes even more than the catch. It's a rush. And I have a hot tub. Why would I want to give all this up? Life is good. I love women. End of story."

Ali and Monica are fascinated with the unfolding drama and are hanging on every word. "Well, that's pretty darn honest," Molly, says.

Our conversation winds down quickly. I shrug my shoulders. It feels like there's nothing else to say, but I couldn't be more wrong. Just as I'm about to get up and announce that I'm going to bed, Monica taps the edge of the table and clears her throat.

"That's one thing Tom and I have in common," says Monica, muscling her way into the conversation. "We BOTH love women!" Her proclamation is followed by total silence. I think the fish stopped swimming. Monica studies each of us one at a time with her big blue eyes then laughs hysterically before looking at us again one-by-one for a reaction.

We're in a mild state of shock. She couldn't have picked a more peculiar moment to come waltzing out of the closet to finally and unnecessarily go public in regard to her sexual preference. My father is staring straight ahead as expressionless as a poker player. I can't imagine what he's thinking. Molly's eyes are wide open. Her eyebrows are like Lucy's when Ricky catches her on stage at the cabana. Ali is a marble statue with an unhinged jaw. I can easily see the fillings on her back molars.

"Well, isn't that special?" I say, in my Dana Carvey Church Chat voice.

We all laugh. Monica's chortle is, by far, the loudest. We awkwardly congratulate Monica for being so grounded and comfortable in regard to her sexuality. Dad drives back to his hotel, the rest of us crawl off to bed, leaving Monica perfectly happy at the table sucking down another beer.

I'm beyond grateful to be sleeping in my own bed and it's never felt better in my life. Still, it takes a while for my mind to slow down enough to fall asleep. But when I do, I sleep so hard I don't think I moved all night. The night passes in a flash and another day begins.

Twelfth

July 10th, 1996

"Eee-see-rah! Eee-see-rah! Eee-see-rah!"

This strange song seeps into my dream where I'm marching along with a throng of munchkins toward the Emerald City. The movie ends. The curtain closes. I suddenly realize the sound is real and open my eyes. Skyler's gap-toothed grin is in my face, and I know exactly what he's saying. *Eat cereal! Eat cereal!* Normally no one likes to be woken up, but he's so damn cute, all I can do is smile back and kiss his chubby cheeks.

"Good morning, Sky-man. Sleep well?"

We get up carefully, so we don't wake Shane, who moved from the floor to my bed at some point during the night. Skyler follows me into the bathroom. First, I go, then without saying a word, I pull down his diaper, hold him over the potty and he goes. I follow his little bowed legs into the living room and change his diaper. While I'm getting breakfast ready, I see Shane coming down the hall. He plops down, pours himself a bowl of cereal and drowns it in milk. Skyler's rambling about the weather or the stock market in his own jabber-talk that sounds perfectly natural. Shane proceeds to read every word on the box of cereal including 'pyridoxine hydrochloride,' which he pronounces remarkably well for a five-year-old. We have the first part of the morning to ourselves and it's rather nice.

Monica gets up, showers, blows her nose, blow-dries her hair, blows into her breathalyzer and is off to work. Molly and her kids are up next, and another round of cereal and toast is served. While the kids are eating, Molly and I figure the best way to tackle the day is a tag-team approach. She's going to take everyone, including Dad, to Water World for the first part of the day—before it gets too hot. This will free me up to get my things done. When they get back, I'll watch all the kids so she can work on her list. Molly and lists go hand-in-hand ever since she was a kid.

"Dad will love Water World," she says, demonstrating, sarcasm quite well. I know what she means. My father despises hot weather. His ideal climate was depicted in The *Empire Strikes Back* on the ice planet, Hoth. By nine-thirty, they're off and I have the entire house all to myself. It's suddenly so quiet and void. It feels strange. I busy myself with some domestics and then sort the backlog of mail. Along with all the junk flyers and bills is a package from Peggy. Inside, there's a letter and two black-and-white photos of Chris. One of the pictures is only two inches square but it has a huge impact on me. I read the letter quickly and linger on the precious image of my sister. It's impossibly beautiful and sad. I'm overcome with sorrow knowing that this sweet, innocent little girl no longer exists. Standing motionless, my eyes well under a veil of water, the kitchen lights blossom into dozens of tiny stars, and I let myself cry. Not wanting to stain the photographs, I lean away from the counter and see my tears fall to the floor. This is an unexpected wave of emotion, equal parts love, and loss. I look up Peggy's number in my address book. I get her machine, leave a message and go back to moving stuff around and cleaning up the house. About fifteen minutes later, the phone rings and I know it's Peggy.

Christina at three.

"Hello."

"Hi Tommy. It's me and Clare. How sweet of you to call. It's pretty far out actually. Clare and I both took the day off work to be together because we're having such a hard time with Christina's death. And then you call."

"Oh Peggy. Oh Clare. I just got your letter and pictures. That one of her when she's about three. Priceless. Thank you so much. I'm looking at it right now."

"Those pictures belong to you. How are you holding up, Tommy? I know this is incredibly hard for you and your family."

"I'm doing okay. When I start to feel sorry for myself, I think about Shane and Skyler and how much worse their loss is compared to mine. We just got back from spending three days with Mare and Journey up at their place in Laytonville. Two days too many for me. It really wasn't a great scene; lots of people I didn't know, people Chris certainly didn't know, all partying away. We were supposed to have a wake of some kind, complete with Journey's Indian compliant eagle feathers, but it never happened. I drove Shane and Skyler, Molly, and her kids back here to my house yesterday. We'd had enough. Today we're attempting to take care of business. We're taking turns with the kids. My Dad is also here. Alex and Shelley are still with Mare and Journey. It's been crazy. How did you find out about Chris?"

"Shelley called Clare and Clare called me at work. I went straight home and called the rest of my kids and told them the sad news. Our hearts go out to you. We're all very shaken up. Especially Clare. Those two were tight. Everyone in your family, Tommy is part of ours. So, this tragedy affects all of us. And we just want to help you get through it. Christina is one of the kindest souls I've ever known. She's one of a kind."

"So true…"

"Life can be harsh, Tommy. You have to take care of yourself in order to stay strong. Clare and I just want to take care of you so much right now."

"We do, Tommy. We love you so much," Clare says.

"You guys are so sweet. Thank you."

"I've been crying my eyes out," Clare says. "I can't believe what happened. I've been a mess since I found out and for the last few days, I've been wearing knee-high socks at half-mast in honor of Christina."

"Oh Clare."

Hearing Clare's voice sends a chain reaction of synapse activity in my brain. She used to slur her words when she was young and excited. She grew into her tongue in her teens. The tone and cadence of her voice is the same. I miss her. We don't talk nearly enough. Not her fault or mine, just side-tracked by separate lives.

"Listen Tommy," Peggy says. "We want to see you guys. We want to help. We can babysit the kids, do some cooking, cleaning, whatever it takes to make your lives a tad more tolerable. What do you think?"

"Oh Peggy, I wish you were here right now, but Mare and Journey have shut down. They're being very seclusive and private with what's happened. They don't want anyone except immediate family to be at Chris's funeral, which supposedly is happening this Saturday in Davis. I've had to tell Chris's best friend, Myrna that she can't attend—and her other friends too. I don't understand it but I'm trying to respect Mare's wishes. She's says we'll have a memorial service *after* the funeral but I don't know when that is yet. And you know Mare. Despite your generosity she won't acknowledge your existence—even now. And now with Journey in the picture, we're not allowed to bring up the past, including you guys, which really sucks. We're so fucked up and it's all coming out right now."

"It's okay. Give Mare the space she needs. Let her call the shots for now. Just know that Clare and I are on standby ready to help—just call. Anytime. We're three hours away—two and a half if Clare drives."

"We really want to see you and the boys, Tommy," Clare says. "We're ready when you are. I'm serious, God damn it!"

"I know you are. Thank you, Clare. Thank you, Peggy. Love you so much. It bums me out that we can't see each other when we need to the most."

"Well, you only have one mother, so you do your best to love her no matter what. Especially now. Right?"

"Right. Still, I wish things were different. Mare and Journey are just so weird. They live in their own little cocooned universe lost in time and space."

"Think of them as *different* instead of weird, Tommy. It's less offensive and just as accurate."

"Okay."

"Listen, I know you have a lot to do, but give us a quick update on Shane and Skyler," Peggy says.

"Okay. Let's see… I got some advice from a psychologist before talking to Shane and I broke the news to him as gently as I could. He took it like a little man. I think I was more shook up than him. He's really amazing. I know he's got the world on his shoulders but he's keeping it together. Skyler is definitely going through withdraws and separation anxiety missing his mom. He's too young to understand what's happening. He's running on pure emotion. I'm doing my best, despite not knowing what the fuck I'm doing. Sometimes he cries so hard I know he's crying for Chris, and he gets hyperventilated and can't catch his breath. It's scary. Molly's been a huge help. She gives him some much needed motherly love."

"Don't you be so hard on yourself. I know you, Tommy, and you're a good person. I'm sure you're giving those kids exactly what they need right now—they're lucky to have you."

"Thanks."

"Remember, we're just a phone call away."

We say, 'I love you' several more times before ending the call. The baby pictures of Chris, talking with Peggy and Clare; it stirs up a lot of emotions, and it feels good to let them out. The call was an unexpected treat that sparked a sense of connection. Somehow, in the middle of a crisis, I'm able to feel a speck of gratitude. Knowing other people understand the situation makes it just a little better to face the challenges ahead.

I pour myself another cup of coffee and prepare myself for the next call. This time to the Davis Enterprise Record where I'm transferred to someone in "deaths, obituaries, and funeral notices." *I'll take careers no child has ever wished for, for one hundred please.* To my surprise, the woman who takes my call is genuinely sincere, kind and patient. I dictate the letter my mother wrote until she's able to read it back word for word.

Christina Marie Bross, 36, of Davis, CA was born into the spirit on July 3rd, 1996. Private family services will be held. Christina, or Chris, as family and friends knew her, was born in Cincinnati, Ohio, on March 30th, 1960. The family moved to California in 1964 and Chris lived in Davis since the age of 11. She graduated from Davis High School in 1978. Chris's love of home and family was the most important thing in her life, and she included many friends from far and wide in that family. She is survived by her sons, Shane Bross, age 5, and Skyler Bross, age 16 months, her father, Thomas Bross of Boston, MA, Mare Leader, mother, and Journey Leader of Laytonville, CA, two brothers, Tom Bross of Rancho Cordova, and Al Smith of Morro Bay, her sisters, Shelley Bross, of Mendocino and Molly Dodson, and her children, Ali, Willie and Joey of Careywood, Idaho. A trust fund will be set up in Shane and Skyler's name at First Northern Bank in Davis to accept donations for the benefit of the children. A memorial service will be held in Davis later this month in which all of Chris's friends, family and acquaintances will be welcome. A notice will appear in this paper once the date and location have been set.

This call goes better than anticipated. *Might as well ride the momentum. I need to call the coroner's office sooner or later.* I dial the number hoping to get some good news for a change—like they have enough evidence to convict Jeff. The results of the autopsy should be ready by now. I know the criminal charges Jeff faces depend on the cause of death. Halfway through the numbers, I hang up. *They had so much time to tamper with the scene.* Now I'm worried about a lack of evidence and fear Jeff will get off scot-free. The momentum is gone, and I pace about venting my nervous energy before mustering up the courage to call again. After being transferred three times, I reach the deputy coroner, a man named Robert A. Labrash, who performed the autopsy. This alone is creepy. I tell him who I am and why I'm calling. He sounds cold, buttoned down, and by the book. But I doubt you could have this kind of job and be any other way. He puts me on hold for several minutes. When he comes back, he says he has a copy of the report in front of him. I hear him shuffling papers.

"The cause of death is undetermined."

"What?"

"I'll read it right off the report: The decedent's blood was negative for cocaine but positive for benzoylecgonine, a cocaine metabolite. Cause of death is listed as acute subarachnoid and intracerebral hemorrhage due to a ruptured aneurysm of the middle cerebral artery. Other significant conditions include a cocaine metabolite detected and chronic physical abuse."

"Slow down," I say. "I don't know what half those words mean. Wasn't there evidence that she was beaten up?"

"Yes. There were multiple abrasions, lacerations, swelling and bruising."

"So, she was beaten to death. She was murdered."

"No. Please listen carefully. The cause of death is a brain aneurysm. There was no deathblow. A cocaine-like substance was present in her blood. There is a correlation between cocaine use and brain aneurysms. Therefore, the primary cause of death is the brain aneurysm, not the bodily trauma."

This is even worse than I expected. Jeff killed my sister. I was just preparing myself to hear exactly how. I'm completely taken aback. My mind is racing but I can't seem to speak.

Yes, Chris did have a drug problem, I'm not denying that, but she didn't overdose. Why is the chronic physical abuse secondary to the cocaine metabolite? My sister died suddenly, but Jeff had been killing her for years.

"Mr. Bross. Are you still there?"

"Yes… What a lucky break for Jeff, wouldn't you say?"

"What do you mean?"

"Here's a guy with a criminal record of spousal abuse. One night, while he's beating my sister to the brink of death, she just happens to die of a brain aneurysm. Give me a break! Never mind that he didn't call 911 in time to save her life." My voice is shaking.

This is bullshit! Jeff killed her and he must pay for what he's done. He made her suffer again and again and eventually, he killed her. First, he beat her up mentally—then physically he beat her to death.

"I know this is difficult. Please try and understand. The pathologist ruled that this death was due to an underlying cause, that being the ruptured brain aneurysm."

"How much of this cocaine-like substance did you find in her blood? Was it an overdose?"

"No. There was only a trace of the substance. However, people who use cocaine over time are more prone to suffer ruptured aneurysms."

He sounds impatient, as if he can't be bothered any longer going over the details of my sister's worthless life. As far as he's concerned, Chris was just another junkie, and junkies die all the time. Case closed.

"A trace? That doesn't sound like much. Would you say she was on drugs the night she died?"

"Yes, I would."

"Can, you be sure?"

"No. It's possible the drug was introduced a few days, or even weeks, before her aneurysm. It could have been residual. The body stores it."

At the very least, he must be guilty of a wrongful death. Even if he didn't intentionally kill my sister, he let her die by not calling for help right away. I wish my brother was here. He'd know the right questions to ask. He knows all about anatomy, physiology, forensic pathology, and law enforcement. He'd get to the bottom of this. I hear Labrash breathing impatiently into the phone.

"Are people who get beat up over time, like boxers, more prone to suffer brain aneurysms?" I ask.

"That's not my area of expertise," he says curtly.

THINK!

"Were there any other drugs detected in her blood?"

"No other drugs were identified."

"No marijuana? No alcohol?"

"No." *That's strange. Jeff's dad said Chris was drunk, that she smelled like booze. And I know my sister. She would have definitely tested positive for marijuana. That's a fact.*

"What time did she die?"

Another pause, another turn of the page. "Just before ten in the morning."

Remember this. Write it down.

"If you don't mind, I really need to tend to other matters."

"Where's her body now?"

"Here."

Chills. "Where's here?" I ask.

"At the County Coroner's Office in Woodland. A family member can release the body to a funeral home or wherever you want it to go. All you need is the death certificate from the courthouse. I'm sorry, Mr. Bross, but I have other business to attend. We're done." He hangs up.

We're done?

I force myself to write down everything I can remember from the conversation. My shaking hand won't move fast enough. A death certificate seems rather pointless, and I have no idea how to go about getting one. Something isn't right. I remember Jeff's dad saying Chris spoke to him in the morning, that she was hung-over and slurring her words. She asked him to take Shane to school. But there was no alcohol in her blood. The aneurysm could have been affecting her speech. If that was the case, they let it go untreated for too long. By morning she might have been clinging to life; especially after the brutal attempts Jeff made to revive her.

Was Chris alive when she left the apartment? Was she alive when she got to the hospital? I need to see her medical files and reports. I want to talk to the doctor at the hospital and the paramedics, especially the one who arrived first. I need to look into their eyes and determine the truth.

I'm left cold with the sickening fact that Jeff and his father let my sister die. Maybe there was no deathblow, but letting someone die, who you could have saved by picking up the phone, must surely be a crime. Jeff obviously didn't want to call the police because he was guilty of beating her to death's door while likely under a restraining order. She could have been saved. They didn't call 911 when they should have. One or both of them is responsible for Chris's death and leaving her kids without a mother. *FUCK THEM BOTH!*

My head is spinning. The tornado returns. I can't fight back the tears. I call Mare with the news. She's just as stunned, dazed, angry, and confused as me.

"Call the coroner's office back, tell them this is unacceptable. You tell those fuckers we want a second opinion."

Journey is ranting something in the background about a conspiracy. "Jeff must have been a narc. 'Em fuckers fudged da lab reports," I hear him say. "To protect der own."

I make a spur of the moment decision and drive to the courthouse in Woodland so I can get a death certificate and arrange to have my sister's body moved to the funeral home in Davis. All I can think about during the drive is that justice must prevail. I'll make sure the police know the lies Jeff's dad told me. I'm sure there are more lies in the police report. I owe it to Chris to do everything I can. Jeff may have escaped a murder charge, but he's not out of the woods yet.

I take the back way to Woodland on Elkhorn Boulevard contemplating the conversation I had with the coroner the entire way. I navigate my way to the courthouse, go through the security screening and ask the uniformed security attendant where to go only to find out I'm in the wrong building. Once I find the right place, I stand in line for what seems to be forever before being called upon. I explain why I'm here to the vacant expression of the tired woman behind the counter. I get frustrated when I find out the fee is fifteen dollars per copy but learn that there's an ATM machine downstairs. I get back in line for what seems like forever again before finally getting the death certificates.

Before driving home, I make a couple of stops. First at the grocery store where I have to study the diaper packaging wondering how much Skyler weighs to pick the right size. Why are they so expensive? I figure as long as I'm here, I might as well pick up some more wipes and some back up pacifiers too. The next stop is at the corner liquor store to pick up the local newspapers. I grab a Sacramento Bee, a Davis

Enterprise, and the Woodland Daily Democrat. The moment I get home, I call Officer Cox but reach his machine. I try the other number and reach another recorded message. I thumb through the newspapers and find the story about my sister in two of them. Seeing the headline is nauseating. Once I clear my head, I sit down at the dining room table and read the articles methodically in search of new information. Unfortunately, there's nothing I don't already know. The Davis Police haven't determined the cause of death and while they do mention that 'the boyfriend' is being held for questioning, they skip all the details regarding his prior arrests and restraining orders. An hour later, while I'm organizing clothes, Officer Cox calls back. I get right to the point.

"There are some major inconsistencies in the story that Jeff's father concocted. It doesn't match up with the coroner's report. For example, he told me Chris was drunk the evening before her death, but there was no alcohol in her blood. According to the coroner's report, Chris died just before ten in the morning, but he said the para—"

"Mr. Bross," he says, cutting me off. "I can tell you're very upset, I understand that, but you've got to let us do our job."

"That's what worries me. Look at the job you've done so far. How long did it take for the police to arrive? Jeff and his father waited too long before calling 911. They had all the time in the world to tamper with evidence and the paramedics should have known instantly that this was a crime—"

"—Mr. Bross, the paramedics had their hands full trying to revive your sister. They were trying to save her life. That's their job. Had they detected anything suspicious, they would have contacted the police immediately."

"A nearly dead body with visible signs of trauma is suspicion enough. Everyone at the scene is considered a suspect, right?"

"Look, the Fowler's have done nothing but cooperate with our investigation. I'm hoping you'll do the same."

"Does that make them innocent?" He doesn't answer. "Is Jeff still in custody?"

"Not anymore. He posted bail yesterday. He's not considered a flight risk. He's probably at home now."

He's probably home now? What the fuck? If he's deliberately trying to upset me, it's working. I feel so frustrated I want to scream.

"That's great. And what if he comes after the kids? Did you even think about that? Is there a restraining order?" He doesn't answer. "Did you test Jeff for drugs?"

"I'm not at liberty to say."

"So, what happens next?"

"We're still building our case, but we need that statement from Shane we talked about. He's an eyewitness and his testimony could provide vital information. Considering his age, the sooner we interview him, the better. Tomorrow would be ideal. Can you bring him to the police station at one o'clock?"

"Why bother? If the cause of death is a brain aneurysm, what's the point?"

"His statement could clarify the degree of negligence exercised."

"Degree of negligence… seems obvious."

"Can I count on you to do that?"

"Won't it be hard on Shane? You're asking him to relive the worst night of his life all over again."

"Listen, I have kids. I know it won't be easy, but it's a necessary part of the investigation that needs to be done. The more information we have the better. We'll do our best to keep it short. What do you say?"

At this point, I'm so bewildered and baffled that I no longer know what to say or do. I just stand there like a life-sized bobble-head doll shaking.

"Tom?"

"We'll be there," I say weakly, thinking I can always change my mind.

"Great. Thank you for your cooperation. Davis police station, tomorrow, one o'clock. Ask for me." He hangs up abruptly, leaving me holding the dead line in my hand.

Once again, I feel that spinning sensation of being overwhelmed and out of control. It's like the car you can't control in a bad dream. The breaks don't work, and the steering is all wonky. I feel that sickening familiar, fast-rising tide again. It's me versus Earth's oceans. I start to shake uncontrollably.

What the hell am I doing?

Thirteenth

July 10th, 1996

I'm underwater—overwhelmed after talking to the coroner and the police. The details of her death are right in front of me, but I can't pull them into focus. There's no clear path to the truth, justice, or any sense of closure. Do I take Shane to the Davis Police Department, or should I back out? I'm not capable of making that decision now. I'm still a wreck when I hear Molly pull the van into the driveway.

I'll have to push my feelings aside, so they won't see the worry in my face. If I keep busy, they won't notice how I feel. Now isn't the time to share bad news or add to the drama or start a heavy conversation. I turn to the kids and smile. Their eyes are red. They smell like chlorine.

"You're all different shades of pink," I say as Molly hands me Skyler.

"We all used sunscreen. I swear," Molly says.

"It was God-awful hot out there." Dad groans, wiping his brow with a handkerchief. He looks like he just returned from the gates of hell, which is pretty much what Water World was for him.

"I'm not a hot weather guy and I'm not one to complain, but CHR-R-R-R-S-T it's hot!"

"Did you know that our father doesn't swim?" Molly asks, raising a brow.

"Yes. I remember that factoid from the past."

"He doesn't wear shorts either."

"Unless I'm jogging. What's wrong with that?" Dad says.

"You wore long pants to Water World?" I ask.

"When it's over one-hundred degrees, it doesn't matter what you wear."

"Dad, why don't you go to your hotel, crank up the air and take a cold shower?" I say.

"I'll take you up on that. You'll be okay, right?"

"We'll be fine. It's my turn to watch the kids so Molly can tackle her list. Come back this evening for dinner, around six or six-thirty. Sound like a plan?"

"Air conditioning. Cold shower. Come back for dinner. Yes. Good plan."

Molly and I change the kids into dry clothes, and I start yet another load of laundry, which has been non-stop ever since the kids arrived. We have a light lunch and then off goes Molly , in my car to take care of business. It's too hot to be outside so I turn on the TV and look through my collection for a movie the kids will like. I pick *Pee-Wee's Big Adventure*, sit down with Skyler in my arms, Shane by my side, and start the movie. The movie's a hit but they're so wiped out that Shane and Skyler fall asleep before Pee Wee figures out where his bike is. I watch the rest of the movie with Molly's kids, still wrestling with the pros and cons of keeping my appointment with Officer Cox. I don't want Shane and Skyler to nap too long, or they'll be up all night, so I gently nudge them awake. They've got beads of sweat on their brows and their hair is damp. Even with the air conditioner on, the house is warm.

"Let's all go to the Sunrise Mall."

"What for?" asks Willie.

"They have powerful air-conditioning and the life-preserving ice cream we need right now."

"Shotgun!" Ali says, beating her brothers to the punch.

I make sure everyone is buckled in correctly before starting the van. On our way to the mall, we pass a Toys R Us billboard.

"Wish we could go there," Willie says, longingly.

"We don't have stores like that where we live," says Joey, sadly.

"We hardly have any stores where we live," says Ali.

"It's always been my dream to go there," Willie adds almost pouting. I suddenly realize that this is a golden opportunity.

"Well, Uncle Tom is about to make your dreams come true."

They're delighted, excited and wide-eyed all at once. I figure it will be a welcome diversion from the shit show of negative circumstances we've all been dealing with. Just seeing the look in their eyes is already worth it. We walk through the doors. The kids stop and look around in awe. They're in a magic castle—heaven on Earth.

"You can each get one thing. Within reason," I add feeling the need to reel them in. As much as I'd like to give them the world, I do have limited finances.

"Really Uncle Tom?" Willie says.

"Yes really. Just don't break the bank."

They dash off in different directions on a treasure hunt strolling the aisles bubbling with energy and babbling excitedly. Willie brings me a Water Wiggle sprinkler, just like the one in we saw in the Pee Wee movie.

"You should get this," he says.

"I will get this! Good find! Thanks!"

Shane and Joey pick action figures, Willie gets a skateboard, Ali gets a kit for making bracelets and I buy Skyler the mini soccer ball he's been chasing around the store. They're all smiles. They thank me, and tell me how much they love me, which makes me wonder if sometimes money can buy love. We continue on to the Sunrise Mall, a mecca of retail riches all under one air-conditioned roof. Molly's kids have never experienced retail at this scale and wander in and out of all the shops stunned by the variety and volume of merchandise. I'm not a fan of malls but seeing their astonishment makes me happy.

"When we get home, I'll order a pizza and have it delivered," I say.

Ali raises a brow. "Delivered to your house?"

"Yes. And it better not be late or I get it for free."

"We don't have that where we live," she tells me.

"And we don't have moose, bald eagles and mountain goats. There are pros and cons to both places."

"I'm sick of living in the sticks. I'm gonna move to California after I graduate.

"*If* you graduate."

"You're that weird uncle every family has to deal with."

"The inappropriate one you try and hide from your friends?"

"Yes."

"You better watch your mouth."

"Make me!"

That's my cue. It's Pee-wee Herman time. "I don't make monkeys; I just train them!"

Everyone, including Skyler laughs. God, it feels good to laugh.

Back at home I order a large pizza. About thirty minutes later, Ali, Willie and Joey greet the delivery driver with the astonished eyes of a peasant witnessing the king and his royal carriage.

They're making me see things I take for granted in a whole new light. We sit around the table and tear into the slices. Skyler is a food painter, and his canvas is himself. Half his face is covered in pizza sauce. His trademark gap-toothed grin peering through the red mess.

Molly gets back home in time to join us for dinner, and we catch her up on our latest adventures. When we're done, we clean up the kids and the mess we created in the kitchen. Dad arrives looking much more comfortable and much less sweaty. He's not a fan of pizza so I make him a sandwich. When he asks for a glass of milk, I hand him Skyler's bottle.

"What am I supposed to do with this?"

"Come on Dad. You know what to do with a nipple."

"Very funny."

Molly kindly gives Shane and Skyler an early bath, so I won't have to do it later. I put a fresh diaper on Skyler, hand him a comb and tell him to ask Grandpa for help. He points his head toward the door and his body follows. He hands his grandfather the comb then climbs onto his lap. Dad begins combing his hair. They're both smiling as big as they can. I make a mad dash for my camera to capture this classic Kodak moment.

You press the button; we do the rest.

We spend the evening listening to music and thumbing through my photo albums. Molly helps me get all the kids down for the night. Once again, when the house is quiet, we have an opportunity to talk. We move into the dining room and settle around the table. I began telling them about my day; my horrible call with the coroner's office, telling Mare and Journey, and the pressure I'm getting from Officer Cox about interviewing Shane as a witness. Molly, Ali, and Dad listen sympathetically taking turns at shaking their heads in disbelief.

"So, as of now, the most they can charge Jeff with, is felony spousal abuse. I don't know what the maximum sentence for that is, but it's a lot less than murder or manslaughter," I say.

"That's if he is convicted. He could still get off scot-free," Molly says.

"Makes you feel all warm and fuzzy about our justice system, right?"

"Dear God, is this really happening?" moans Dad.

"This totally sucks," Ali adds.

"The police want to interview Shane tomorrow afternoon. Should I take him? Make Shane recall that awful night? It won't bring Chris back. I don't know what to do. What do you guys think?"

We begin another lengthy discussion, and when it's over they all agree.

"It's up to you, Tom."

Super.

"Mom and I talked. Then I spoke with the funeral home, too," Molly says. "Chris's funeral is on for this Saturday at eleven. Mare wants an open casket, so everyone has a chance to say goodbye to Chris. She also wants her body to be cremated. It's going to cost around three thousand dollars." She looks at our father. "Mare asked if you'd pay the bill and she'll pay you back for her half later."

"Of course I'll pay," Dad says, reaching for his wallet and handing me his American Express card as if I have the machine to process the transaction at the dining room table.

"They just need the deposit for now," Molly says. "If you meet with the police tomorrow, maybe you could drop it off. It's downtown at the end of D Street."

"I know where it is. As long as I'm in Davis, I can set-up the savings account for the kids, too."

"Don't forget to bring this." Molly says, handing me a brown grocery bag.

"What's this?"

"The dress I want Chris to wear." Her words fall like footsteps in the snow that come to a sudden and mysterious end. Chills of sorrow—another tidbit adding to the cold reality we face.

"She didn't have much. There wasn't anything nice enough in any of the bags you brought home from her apartment. We used to share clothes all the time. I'd like her to wear my dress. This makes it even more special—at least for me. I hope no one has a problem with this." Too choked up to speak, all we can do is nod our approval. Our eyes are brimming with tears.

That night, I lie awake trying to make up my mind. Taking Shane to testify against his own father is asking a lot of a five-year-old. But his testimony could be crucial. And what if it does lead to a stronger conviction against his father? How's Shane going to feel about that? Maybe purging to the police will help clear his system. *Wishful thinking.* The longer I lie awake, the more troubling tomorrow becomes. I try to divert my thoughts but I'm like a broken record. I keep spinning over the same questions, feeling the same fears and confusion over and over and over.

Fourteenth

July 11th, 1996

In the morning, while I'm helping Shane step into his pants, at point blank range, I pop a question, "How do you feel about talking to the police today?"

"I've talked to the police before," he says.

"Do you know what they want to talk to you about this time?"

"Yes."

"They want to talk about the last time you saw your mother."

"I know."

"Is that something you can talk about with them?" He shrugs his shoulders. "You don't have to if you don't want to. It's no big deal. It's your call." He nods. I pause and then ask, "So, was that a yes?"

"Okay. I'll talk to them."

"Then we'll take a ride in the Z to Davis and get it done. And if you change your mind on the way we can always turn around and come back home."

Honestly, it feels like I'm pushing Shane into doing this to ensure Jeff will have to be held accountable for his actions. I allow the trip to happen in part because I'm a victim of my need for revenge. I try and kid myself and think that Shane won't remember this in the long run, but my gut says it isn't so. I press on as determined and confused as I've ever been.

Shane, even atop his booster, looks small in the passenger seat. He's in good spirits as we drive, reading the road signs and asking odd questions about how the world works like; *Nobody's ever REALLY turned into a vegetable, right?* And, *Do fish fart?* He's also pointing out 'slug bugs' with amazing acuity. But when we reach the Yolo Causeway on the outer edge of town, he becomes quiet and gazes out the window.

"See those mountains?" I say pointing to the right. "That's the smallest mountain range in the entire world." Shane focuses on the spiny range in the distance and then faces me.

"Really?"

"It's true. The Sutter Buttes—they're only ten miles in diameter. You could easily walk around them in a day."

"Sutter Buttes," Shane whispers to himself.

"See that big old mountain out the other side?"

"Yea."

"That's Mount Diablo. Diablo means 'devil' in Spanish." He's not impressed. I don't want to force the conversation so I turn on the radio. We're being rocked gently in the car as we traverse the causeway. The familiar rhythm brings back all kinds of memories. Shane begins singing softly to the radio but I'm already drifting deeper into my own thoughts to give it much notice. I've crossed this section of road in all kinds of vehicles and then I get a feeling in my gut about each one that comes to mind; our blue Datsun station wagon, in Peggy's VW bus, in Brad's mother's Plymouth Volare, in one of Dad's rental cars, in the back of Larry Glickstien's truck, and in our yellow bus with the butterfly grill. Same pattern. Wildly different circumstances. Shane begins singing louder drawing me back into the car as we bounce down the road.

Of all the songs on the radio, I can't believe he knows all the words to, "Stayin' Alive" by the Bee Gees, from *Saturday Night Fever*. Shane's nailing it perfectly word-for-word. His angelic tone fits the falsetto singing style to a T. Chris must have played this song for Shane. I shake my head at the strangeness of it all. It's disco dance music and yet some of the lyrics bend to match our unfolding crisis perfectly. For the next few miles, it feels like Chris is singing through Shane to us both. Shane's best memories of his mom no doubt include music. She loved to sing. She knew all the words. He seems to have the same gift.

Was this album in my sister's collection?

That thought essentially ruins the moment. Now all I can think about is how I failed to retrieve my sister's things—her personal belongings with sentimental value like her photo albums and record collection. Chris's records belong with Shane—and Skyler. I failed the boys. I failed my sister. I failed my family and I doubt I'll get a second chance.

We reach the end of the causeway, and the freeway gradually descends back to ground level. The song ends, a commercial starts, so I turn off the radio. We take the first exit and bear right at the light at the top of the overpass. I'm taking the longer way into town so I can mentally prepare myself for the first task; setting up an account for the kids at First Northern Bank.

The moment we step inside, I see that one of the bankers is an old school friend of Chris's, Julie Peterson. Julie and Chris met in the seventh grade. My sister had close friends from every click at school. She was never a cheerleader like Julie was in high school, but this didn't change their friendship at all. Julie is the first person outside our family I'm confronted with who knows my sister. When Julie recognizes me, her expression changes. She's somehow able to smile while expressing sorrow at the same time. We walk toward each other. She glances at Shane. The emotional energy we're carrying becomes something heavier the closer we get. We fall into an awkward hug. She's so sad and speaks quietly into my ear.

"Oh, Tom. I'm so sorry about Chris. It's just awful."

I'm too close to losing it to say anything so I just gently pat her back. Julie's always been a genuine soul. Her grief brings mine to the surface. Tears fill my eyes. She leads me to her desk, reaches for a tissue then offers me the box. We sit. We chat about why I'm here. She slides a form towards me to fill out. Shane is quietly observing everything. I check the 'legal guardian' box on the paperwork. *That's a first.* Julie and I small talk about old times. It's not an easy situation for either of us, but seeing her pain is oddly helpful. Knowing there are others who miss, love and will remember Chris is comforting. When we're done, she stands so we can hug goodbye. Then she bends down and hugs Shane. As she stands back up, I follow a tear from the outside corner of her eye, down her cheek and all the way to the thinly carpeted floor.

"Thanks again, Julie. Not just for setting up the account but for everything else. For being Chris's friend, for remembering her. For being so understanding today. Thank you." I reach down taking Shane's hand into mine and nod goodbye.

With his little hand in mine, Shane and I walk from the bank, through the dry heat, to the Davis Funeral Home. It's only a few blocks away. The closer we get, the more I don't want to be there. Then we arrive. I pause at the bottom of the stairs. Shane squeezes my hand as if sensing I need some strength. As we climb, so does the sensation of dizziness. I get a head rush at the top. Shane reaches up and presses the doorbell button. We hear something like a stack of books falling over followed by footsteps. Then the door opens slowly. A teenage boy with evenly distributed smallpox-like pimples greets us. We take two steps inside. I won't allow myself to go any further. As I'm handing over the deposit and the clothes Molly gave me, it occurs to me that he lives here. *This is a family business.* I try to imagine living in a house where your daily chores include embalming cadavers, applying make-up, dressing lifeless bodies in clothes, and lifting them in and out of coffins. *My sister's body is here.* Instant creeps. We leave as soon as the receipt hits my hand. I start to feel better as we're walking away. By the time we get back to the car, I've recovered. We still have time for a bite before Shane's interview with the police.

"What's your favorite restaurant in the whole wide world?" I ask Shane.

Without pause, he shouts, "Dairy Queen!"

"Perfect. Let's go!"

I get him buckled up in his booster seat, drive across the railroad tracks and turn into the parking lot. I pull into the exact spot Charlie parked the bus in when we returned to Davis from San Anselmo on that dark, cold, foggy night so long ago. Shane orders chicken strips and a Coke, but I change it to Sprite because Molly told me it has no caffeine. We take our plastic number to our plastic table and sit on the plastic bench waiting for our plastic trays of food.

I choose the same table I sat at with my brother, my sisters and Mom's 'on-again-off-again' boyfriend, Charlie. This is where our mother revealed her plan, which was simply to drop us off at our friend's houses. Except in my case, it was into the garage of one of her ex-lovers. We were distributed like a litter of free puppies.

Shane is reading everything in sight. When he pronounces the 't' in *parfait*, I tell him that with French words, you almost never pronounce the last letter.

"Then why's it there?"

"That's a great question," I say wondering why I never asked any of my French teachers. For fun, I start teaching him how to count to eleven in French, which takes him all of three tries to master. Every sound is hilarious to him, especially eleven, 'onze', which we pronounce with extra nasal, 'oooonze'. Then he counts in Spanish to twenty and tells me he can keep going if I want him to. *He's practically trilingual! Is Shane selling himself to me right now? Maybe he thinks that by showing me how smart he is, I'll want to keep him. Or is that just something I'd do? Or am I just a clueless idiot when it comes to kids?*

We eat most of our food and Shane cleans up our table without me even asking. We get back in the car and buckle up.

"Okay, one last stop," I say reminding Shane. "Are you still up for this? We can easily back out. It's no big deal."

The expression in his eyes say 'no' and yet he says, "I'm ready." I want to believe him, so I ignore my gut. We get back in the Z, take a short drive to the police department and go inside.

Officer Cox is in his early forties and has almost no visible character lines, which means he doesn't use his face much to express himself. His papery skin is pulled tight across his wide cheekbones and long chin. His exaggerated bone structure gives him the appearance of a wood-carved marionette. He's dressed in his version of casual clothes; pleated taupe-colored khakis, a baboon-ass red polo shirt and leather loafers with those disturbing toe tassels. We shake hands tentatively—like one species to another. His are like wax. After some small talk about the weather, he tells us where the interview will take place, who will be there and how long he thinks it will last.

"You can wait in my office, Mr. Bross. Shane, please follow me."

"Wait a second. I thought I'd be in the room, too."

"I'm sorry you got that idea," he says. "We need a statement from Shane without a family member present. Standard procedure."

He glances at his watch. I look at Shane. I'm not sure what to do. "What if he needs me, you know, for some emotional support?"

"You'll be here when he's done."

"I meant in there, while he's answering questions."

"No can do."

You're a prick. I say inside my head

I kneel down to Shane's level.

"What do you think, Pal?"

He looks up at me with his big brown eyes and nods his head. I pat his back and stand. Officer Cox forces a quick smile and leads the little man away. Shane glances over his shoulder before disappearing. I'm left with nothing to do, trying to justify what's happening. After forty-five minutes, I get up to find them just as they're coming down the hall. Shane glances up and I catch the exhaustion in his sorrowful eyes.

At least it's over.

"It went well. Shane did great," Cox says, routinely as if someone else is controlling his strings.

I take this to mean that they got what they needed to make their case against Jeff. *You got your statement. Now do your job!* Officer Cox reaches out with his mannequin hand but I'm already pulling Shane to my side. My anger towards Jeff is convoluted by the guilt I feel for putting his son through this ordeal. I want nothing more than to get out of here as quickly as possible and go home.

"I'm so sorry you had to go through that," I say to Shane as we're walking to the car.

He looks at me, shrugs his shoulders, and remains silent. I don't push it. The poor kid has done enough talking today. I turn on the radio, but every song is inappropriate for our mood and nobody's singing any of the words. *I put Shane through hell because I want his father to pay for what he did to my sister. Jeff deserves to suffer. But all I've done is make Shane suffer instead.* I can practically feel the embodiment of shame sitting between Shane and me. We drive home without uttering another word.

Molly must have heard us pull into the garage and greets me at the kitchen door.

"Nadine called while you were gone," she says. "She wants to cook dinner for us tonight—here at your house. Is that okay?"

"Nadine. Yikes. Wow. I have to think about that one."

"I take it you guys aren't going out anymore?"

"No. Well, not exactly. We've had an off-and-on relationship for the last six months. Actually, it was more of an in-and-out relationship, if you know what I mean."

"Too much information."

"You know I affectionately refer to Nadine as my psycho ex-girlfriend. She's got issues, and we have a rocky past, but she's also a great person. My life is just so much easier without her playing a major role. She's all about the drama."

"You better call her right now because I told her yes and she sounded pretty excited."

"Don't you love her South Carolina accent? Actually, it's half Carolina, half So-Cal-Valley-Girl. I bet she said something like, *"Y'all have e-nuff on yer minds right now. Well dudes, don't worry about dinner. Take a breather and leave the cookin' to me!"*

"You sound *exactly* like her."

"I know. She's easy. In more ways than one."

Just then, there's a knocking on the door. Before anyone can even get up, the door opens. It's her.

"Hi everyone, I'm Nadine and I'm so happy to be meetin' y'all. I know who you are, because Tom has shown me pictures and told me all kinds of stories. Don't get up, jus' chill. You're Ali, and I must say you're even more beautiful in *purrson* than you are in pictures!" They hug as if they've been pals for years. "Willie, Joey, nice to meet you. I already know these guys," she says, smiling at Shane and Skyler. "How you guys doin'? Come give me some sugar… Where's Tom senior hiding?"

"Please let yourself in," I say, sarcastically.

"Don't act like that! I know you're happy to see me," she says, smiling from ear to ear.

She's right. I am happy to see her.

I have an equally big grin on my face. She looks great. In fact, she's so full of positive energy that I can practically see the aura radiating from her fake blond hair. We wrap our arms around each other. During the hug, she nibbles on my ear lobe and as we're letting go, she looks me in the eye and gives me her, 'I'm-gonna-fuck-your-brains-out,' expression.

I have to be strong. If I let Nadine get into my pants, I'll be letting her back into my life.

That would be disastrous—especially now.

"Dad will be here in about an hour. He'll be surprised to see you, though not as much as he was in New York," I say, as if she needs reminding.

I offer to help Nadine prepare the spaghetti and meatballs while Molly and Ali keep an eye on the kids. She pours two glasses of wine and continues dropping hints that she wants to make more than just dinner. At first, she's subtle; she leans into me from behind to grab a spoon, brushing her breasts gently against my back while I'm mincing garlic. Then, she's a bit more direct and rolls the raw Italian sausage into a hefty twelve-inch cock.

"There! Why, will you just look at that!"

I add two anatomically correct meatballs to the creation. We laugh out loud—so much for innuendo.

As soon as Dad arrives, Nadine showers him with the kind of affection normally reserved for soldiers returning from war. He loves every second of it. Dad likes Nadine. The last time they saw each other was just over a year ago when Nadine mysteriously materialized in Manhattan and shocked the shit out of us.

∞   ∞   ∞

At the time, I was working in-house in marketing for Merksamer Jewelers, a national chain headquartered in Sacramento. I volunteered to go to Buffalo to help close an underperforming store. Since I was flying to the East Coast on the company's dime, I extended the trip so I could visit with Dad in New York City. The plan was for us to meet at the Roosevelt Hotel. Nadine was a little jealous that I was going to New York and promised to do terrible things to me with her tongue when I got back. She told me to have a great time and gave me a passionate kiss goodbye.

Closing a store on unsuspecting employees is never fun. Because it's jewelry, it has to be a well-orchestrated procedure.

Although I personally didn't have to fire anyone, the depressing nature of the visit made time slow to a drip. My role was to ticket the inventory and get it sent back to corporate securely. With the mission accomplished, I caught a bus to The Big Apple and checked into the Roosevelt Hotel. Dad was taking the train down from Boston the next day. Our plan was to rendezvous in the lobby of the hotel in the morning. I chucked my bags into the room and went outside to take in the sights and ended up getting lost and loving every minute of it.

I found my way back to familiar territory and was near the Ed Sullivan Theater, when I stopped at a crowded intersection waiting for the light to change. It was the magic hour, late afternoon, the only time my skin appears remotely tan. I noticed a girl across the street who looked remarkably like Nadine and laughed it off. *Nadine is three thousand miles away.* I looked at the girl again. Her smile was as bright as the city lights. She couldn't stand still. Holy shit! It is Nadine! She starts flapping her arms like a baby bird. I stood there with my mouth wide open like a still-shot of an opera singer caught mid-note. I couldn't believe my eyes and started banging the side of my head to make sure it was real.

Nadine stood out from that sea of anonymity like a tide-washed jewel. Her smile was a beam of sunshine. When the signal changed to 'walk' we ran to each other and embraced in the middle of the street. After a long wet kiss and public display of groping, we shuffled to the sidewalk. Her surprise appearance was the most exciting thing that had ever happened to me. It was magical! Or was it insane? Either way, in that moment, I never felt more important, privileged, grateful or horny in my entire life.

"Comin' here's the craziest, most romantic thing I've ever done. But sheee-it, you only live once!" she said, like only she can.

I felt like the luckiest guy in the world. Imagine someone being that head-over-heels in love with little old me. Here's a woman who might just be fucked up enough in the head to be my soulmate. We could barely contain ourselves in the elevator up to my room. We made crazy, mad, passionate love for hours. When we woke up the city was still alive. We grabbed a spare blanket from the closet, a bottle of spiced rum from the corner liquor store and got on the open-air double-decker tour bus. We took the spiral stairway to heaven to the top and sat in the very back. Snuggling, sipping rum, gazing at the city lights, while getting frisky under the blanket—we were on the ride of a lifetime. I'd never felt so head-over-heels in love as I did that night.

The next morning, Nadine surprised the crap out of my father in the hotel lobby. We witnessed one of the all-time best double takes in history. Dad became our personal tour guide. For the next two days, he took us everywhere and we did everything. In my euphoric state, I began to have crazy-love-thoughts. I considered proposing to her at the top of the Empire State Building. But as fate would have it, the observatory was closed that day for maintenance. I took this as a sign to give it more thought. Thank God for guardian angels and union repair crews.

We left New York the same day on different flights; mine was several hours before hers. When I got home, I listened to my phone messages. Almost all of them were from Nadine and each was progressively worse. She kindly recorded her nervous breakdown for me. Why she didn't mention any of this before I got home is beyond me. About five messages in, she confessed her conviction that I was going back east to be with another woman. Her voice moaned at me through the machine, 'Well guess what? I'm going to be there and bust you on the spot!' I was crushed, embarrassed, hurt and a little frightened. Flying to New York at the last minute must have cost a fortune. I knew Nadine was insecure, volatile, distrustful, delusional, unstable, and unpredictable. But this was so *Basic Instinct* of her. This time she went too far. I didn't want anything to do with her anymore. It was the final straw.

She's always been crazy. It's part of her appeal. Nadine had a way of getting us into unusual situations, like the time she dragged me to one of her Sex and Love Addicts Anonymous meetings. I listened in shock as normal-looking people told their sad stories, which inevitably involved loving the wrong person, obsession over sex, chronic masturbation, or a combination of the three. This was extremely eye-opening to me. I had no idea this kind of addiction existed and wondered if I should give it a try. After the meeting, she led me down an alley and begged me to fuck her. There was very little privacy when she lifted her skirt and slipped out of her panties. Then I was deep inside of her, pounding against her from behind, trying to be quiet as we watched the other sex addicts leave the building. It was deranged, dangerous and delightful all at once.

Nadine was constantly trying to convince me that she was pregnant. She went through pee tests like toilet paper. She was and probably always will be, a hypochondriac. At one point or another, she claimed to have chronic yeast infections, Candida, irregular menstrual cycles, mysterious rashes, and unseen tumors. She convinced herself she had reflex sympathetic dystrophy, RSD for short. Then it was multiple sclerosis, tuberculosis, spastic bowel syndrome, and, of course, AIDS. She claimed to be suffering hair loss, bleeding gums, and swollen feet. It was all in her head, except for the anxiety attacks—those were real.

We were snowboarding at NorthStar when she just stopped and sat down in the middle of the run about thirty yards up the hill from me. I waited patiently for her to get up. She didn't appear hurt. After more waiting, I unclipped my bindings and started hiking up the hill. About halfway there, at the very top of her lungs, she screams, "Dew-eud, I'm having an ANX-I-E-TY ATTACK!" Her Cali-Carolina accent increased the shock value of her words. I heard laughter from the chair lift. Nadine was high maintenance, often embarrassing and always interesting.

Despite the constant drama, or maybe because of it, we fit together well. We had incredible sex. Somehow that justified all the insanity. Crazy I can take—but psycho, no way. After the New York incident, I built a wall to protect myself and vowed to never have feelings for her again. There are too many normal girls out there, girls who aren't repressing memories of childhood molestation—or whatever it is that's fucking with her brain. I made it clear that it was over between us and time to move on.

But not for long.

It was I who caved first. I craved her body and called her on the phone.

"I miss your body," I said.

"Well, you know what they say. Abstinence makes your dick grow harder."

Minutes later she was at my house again. We got together, not as boyfriend and girlfriend—I was very clear about that, but as consenting adults wanting sex—nothing more—as if that ever works. My penis had no problem penetrating the fortress I built. My wall was worthless when it came to her body. But when it came to blocking feelings, it performed flawlessly.

∞   ∞   ∞

Nadine's foot is slowly rubbing my crotch under the table, making it hard to participate in the dinner conversation. Naturally, Skyler is wearing his food. He grins ear-to-ear using both hands to stuff his mouth, smear his face with spaghetti providing us with some much-needed laughter. After dinner I put a movie on for the kids. Nadine pulls me aside whispers seductively in my ear.

"Dude, grab a blanket. Let's go to the river." Like a teen, I ask my little sister for permission to leave the house 'to go on a walk' with Nadine. She knows what we're up to because she rolls her eyes ever so slightly.

"Go," she says. "I'll put the kids to bed. We're fine."

I grab a spare sleeping bag from the garage on our way out. We cut through the elementary school behind my house and head for the river. The farther we get from the streetlights, the brighter the stars become. We follow the sound of moving water along a footpath near the river's edge to a soft spot in the grass and unroll the sleeping bag. Nadine, always brash and to the point, wastes no time giving it to me straight.

"Dude, I think you should adopt Shane and Skyler. Then you should marry me, and I'll help you raise them. The way I see it, it's best for everyone, including you. Shane and Skyler get a new set of parents who'll love 'em forever. You'll get two beautiful boys plus a fine young wife who loves to have sex with you. I get an instant family with no stretch marks! What could be better?"

My wall of defense is shaken by her generosity, but it's still standing. What she said was very direct, honest, and beautiful. But it didn't blind me, so I choose my words carefully.

"I promise to keep an open mind, but nothing's been decided yet. Mare and Journey might want to raise them," I say, even though it's not true.

"Oh, you wouldn't be able to live with yourself if you let that happen."

"Yea, why not?"

"Because Mare and Journey are a couple of old hippies. They don't want to raise any more kids. They want to raise killer crops of dope! I love Mare and Journey, but you know in your heart they'd mess Shane and Skyler up. Unintentionally, of course."

"I know, you're right, and Molly can't take them—"

"—Because she just lost Kurt and she has to get through that before taking on anymore."

"That's right."

"And your brother can't take 'em for a million reasons, and Shelley can't take 'em for a million more. So that leaves you."

"We could find a family who wants to adopt them."

"You could, but I'll tell you something you might not want to hear. Those boys have already bonded to you, and you're already bonded to them. Even before your sister died, there was a strong connection. Remember when we took Shane to Marine World and to San Francisco? He totally loves you, Tom, and so does Skyler! It *has* to be you. You have to keep those kids in your family. There's nothing in the world more precious than them two kids. And that's the truth. You understand that, right?"

"You sound just like Mare."

"Oh, fuck you!" she says, punching me in the arm.

"Ouch! Maybe they could stay with Mare and Journey until Molly's ready to adopt them. Like I said, nothing's been decided for sure just yet."

"Well then, just promise me you'll think about what I said. We'd make great parents. And as a bonus, Mr. Bross, you would have me, a super-fine foxy wife ten years younger than you who loves to suck your dick and make you feel really, really good like I'm about to do right now." *God, I love watching her mouth form words.*

I would never want to say anything that would stop a woman going down on me, so I shut up as she pulls off my underwear. She lifts off her shirt and unclasps her bra. She straddles my thighs and sits up gazing down at me. I look at her semi-silhouetted figure. She smiles alluringly, her teeth glowing white against the inky night sky. She leans forward and kisses me. Her mouth is wet and wonderful. She begins kissing her way down my body. It's even more wonderful.

"I'm going to clear your head," she says, giggling, taking me into her mouth. I look up at the stars. I have one of those intense, whole-body orgasms, leaving me brain-dead and blissful. For the next few minutes, we just listen to the sound of the river and the breeze blowing through the trees.

"I love you, dude."

I can't just get all sexed up without feeling some degree of emotion. "Nadine, I love you too, but not in the same way as you do. I'm not making any promises. Okay?"

"Just make one. That you'll think about it."

"Okay. I promise I'll think about it."

Walking hand-in-hand home, I really was thinking about it. She might just be crazy enough to make it work. We get home and she quietly puts me to bed without waking up Shane or Skyler. She's the perfect date. She comes over, cooks a scrumptious meal, is terrific company, offers to marry me so she can help raise my nephews, sucks me dry, tucks me in and then leaves so I can get a good night's sleep.

What a selfless offer.

Feeling relaxed from head to toe and with no excess brain activity keeping me awake, for the first time in what seems like forever, it only takes a minute to fall fast asleep.

Fifteenth

July 12th, 1996

The vibration I feel in my chest tells me there's a hummingbird nearby. Shane has the hose on the dried-out garden I've been ignoring in the backyard. Skyler's in my arms.

"Turn it off a second," I say softly, tapping Shane's shoulder. "Listen..." We listen for a few moments but don't hear anything. "Never mind."

Shane turns the sprayer back on. Then I feel it again, even stronger. It's got to be close. It's probably in the almond tree but with so many leaves, it's impossible to spot. We turn back to the garden.

"That's good for this part. Let's do the tomato plants."

Shane tugs on the hose as we move to a new spot, and he continues watering. Then we see it. The hummingbird appears out of nowhere, like magic, hovering near the mouth of the hose, just inches from Shane's hand.

"Look," Shane says.

"Hummer coming in to say 'hello'," I say quietly.

While Shane is studying the tiny bird, a smile of pure joy grows across his face. The nozzle is on a flat setting creating a fan-shaped spray. The hummingbird is floating in the air while cocking its head back and forth between us and the moving water. Suddenly, it flies directly through the water, hangs a mid-air U-turn, and does it again. That comforting vibration of its powerful wings fills my chest. It hovers towards the top of Shane's hand and looks like it's about to land but then suddenly jets away and we lose sight of it over the oleanders in the side yard. I'm smiling as big as the kids are.

"Well, that was amazing." I have a lump in my throat.

"It took a shower," Shane says, looking up at me.

"It sure did. Were you nervous having it so close to your hand?"

"Nah, I like the sound of its wings."

"Me too. I love that sound."

Skyler's still looking in the direction the bird's disappearance and whispers something nonsensical that sure sounds nice.

A few days ago, I could care less about hummingbirds; now they mean the world to me. Once again, it feels like something special just happened; like it was Chris who just stopped by for a quick visit. It's her way of checking in on her children—and me. I close my eyes and see my sister's face in my head. I tell her how much she's loved and missed. I thank her for the show and invite her to visit us again—anytime. Our time in the garden leaves me feeling both relaxed and revitalized.

We go back inside and tell Molly and her kids what happened. Molly and Ali look amazed. I didn't have to say much. They knew it was a big deal. They get it. Willie and Joey, however, look bored out of their minds. I catch them rolling their eyes.

"I guess you had to be there." Nothing. "I guess it's not as cool as Toys R Us." Still nothing. "Brad's cousin, Karl once cut a fart that went, PPPPBBBBBBT—pee-youuuuuu…" Blank stares. "I guess I'll cook breakfast now." They could care less.

Things go from being calm in the morning to chaotic in the afternoon when Mare, Journey, Shelley, and Al arrive in the Nova. They were going to make the drive yesterday but called and said they needed another day. It's good to see them. Shelley gives me a nice big, heartfelt hug, tells me she's 'droggy' and ducks into my room to take a nap. Al is on a mission. He charges into the house wanting to know if I have any plastic sprinkler parts on hand so he can construct a working prototype of a submarine he intends to build and test in my hot tub. Mare and Journey ask for rolling papers, which I know I have, but have to search to eventually find them. They roll one, smoke it, roll another, smoke it then roll a couple more.

"The funeral home in Davis felt very churchy. We don't go to church. You despise your catholic past. I can't imagine Chris wanting a traditional funeral," I say to my mother.

"Don't worry about it. I'll call them later today, so they get it right," Mare says. Then she changes the subject. I have more questions, but I know better than to ask. I've never been to a funeral before. All I have is the montage of TV funerals playing in my head. Chris would want us to sing, dance and share good vibes. *Will there be organ music? Does anyone actually like organ music? Has anyone actually danced to it? Do we dress up? Will we take turns to stand and talk about Chris?* These questions are stuck in my head like an annoying jingle. It sucked having to tell Kelly, Myrna, Lisa Thomas and others that the service is for immediate family only. Why are we turning away people who loved Chris? They just want to say goodbye to Chris and help us through this difficult time.

The one exception Mare makes is for my best friend, Brad, and at first, she didn't want him to come either. It took some gentle persuasion from Molly, Al, Shelley, and I to get her to change her mind. She knows Susie is my second Mom. She knows Brad is loved and accepted by everyone in our family. She knows he accepts and loves each of us for who we are. Brad's well aware of all our perfect imperfections; our weirdness, addictions, mania, and driving forces. I'm grateful we got Mare to see the light. Knowing he'll be there gives me a much needed boost.

Unlike me, Al took a direct approach; he simply invited his father to the funeral service and then broke the news to Mare. And much to my surprise, she's fine with him going.

John never forged strong ties with Shelley, Chris, me, or Molly. Al continued to have a relationship with his father, but the rest of us rarely saw him after he moved out. Why she's okay with John and not my dad is another interesting mystery. I guess it's like Peggy said, I only have one mother. I don't have to understand her, I just have to love her.

I call Dad at the hotel and tell him he really can't visit today with Mare and Journey being back in town. He's not upset, he might even be relieved. He tells me he has some work to do and that he'll see all of us tomorrow.

"Journey and I are gonna go find an urn for Christina's ashes," Mare informs me.

"It's easy to get lost in Sacramento. Want to borrow a map or my Thomas Guide?" I ask. Mare just smiles. I know what she's thinking; *we won't find the urn; the urn will find us.* And they're on their way.

As the day heats up, I set up the Water Wiggle in the backyard. Shelley, Molly, Al, Ali, and I sit outside with the kids watching them play. During the breaks they take to catch their breath, we teach the kids some of the things we did when we were little. We use our fingers on their back for 'Walking up the Trail.'

Walking up the trail… (two fingers taking steps along the lower spine)

X marks the spot… (use the index finger and draw a giant X)

Dot, dot, dash, dash, dot, dot… (make this as ticklish as possible)

Up comes a snake… (using the back of two fingers, follow the spine from bottom to top)

Bites you on the neck… (use the thumb and forefinger to gently squeeze the neck)

Blood runs down, blood runs down… (say this like a vampire, use both hands and jazz fingers to simulate blood running down the back)

Ocean breeze… (lift hair off the neck if necessary – blow on the neck)

Tight squeeze!… (gently squeeze the neck again)

Now you've got the chills!… (check arms for goose bumps and laugh)

We show the younger ones how to crack an imaginary egg on someone's head. We lay on our backs, balance them on our feet and lift them into the air like an airplane. When we do this, we always sing a few lines from an Arlo Guthrie song; Coming Into Los Angeleees… We do "Kneezels" too. You lie on your back with your knees up. The child lays on your shins and you take their hands, rocking them slowly forward and back while singing, 'Kneezels, kneezels, everyone loves the… (now, sing louder while lifting your knees high) KNEEZ-ZELS!' We thumb wrestle, give each other gentle rope burns and make fart noises by blowing on their precious little bellies.

We teach the kids some of the lame stuff we learned as kids. Al and I do this one:

"You remind me of a man."

"What kind of man?"

"A man of great power."

"What kind of power?"

"Power of Hoodoo."

"Hoodoo?"

"You do."

"Do what?"

"Remind me of a man…" And on and on it goes. Same with 'Life.'

"Whatcha reading?"

"Life magazine."

"How much is it?"

"Twenty-five cents."

"I don't have twenty-five cents."

"Well, that's life."

"What's life?

"A magazine." And around and around you go.

We show them an interactive playground poem.

Hi ya Jack, how's your back... (pat the person's back)

I haven't seen you in years... (tug the person's ear)

But I still knows you... (pinch the person's nose)

The kids are loving all the attention. My brother and sisters and I are loving all the memories we're recalling. I dash into the house and come back with a pencil and piece of paper.

"Check this out," I say as they gather around. "I learned this in junior high."

I write the word 'chump' in cursive writing. Then I flip the page over and it reads the same. "No matter how you look at it, you're still a chump!"

"Remember 'Bicycle'?" Shelley says.

"Mom showed us that one!" Ali says lowering herself to the ground, so her feet are facing Shelley's. They put their bare feet together and pedal slowly while singing "Bicycle Race" by Queen. Then they gradually pick up the pace and sing faster and faster until their feet can't keep up and slip apart.

Next, I show the kids how to use a blade of grass pressed firmly between your thumbs to make a dying duck call. Then, Molly remembers a song we used to sing while jumping rope. Shelley and I join in after the first couple of words.

"Not last night but the night before, twenty-four robbers came knocking on the door. Asked them what they wanted, and this is what they said: Chinese dancers do the splits, the kicks the turnaround, touch the ground out the back door!"

Next, Shelley remembers a clapping game we used to sing called 'Mary Mack' who had silver buttons down her back. She and Molly perform it for us. We entertain ourselves and the kids this way for several hours and it's amazing because it's fun and it provides the perfect distraction from tomorrow's funeral.

When Mare and Journey return, they present us with the long, rectangular, box they found. The dark wood is carved intricately and accented with colorful beads. On the top, which is also the lid, is a rendition of an elephant, head on.

Where the hell did they go, India?

"Look what we found," my mother says, proudly.

I like elephants, their depth of emotion, their acute memory, their social societies, and their mothering instincts. I'm fascinated by the fact that they grieve for their dead. In that regard, the box makes at least some sense. But personally, I don't believe this box matches my sister's essence at all. Yes, I was hoping for a bird—preferably a hummingbird because it suits her perfectly—light, sleek, agile, beautiful, darting here and there with precise strikes. Of course, it's irrational to think everyone else should make the same connection as me. My sister preferred simple, contemporary, and clean designs. This box is dark, ornate, and intricate. It doesn't matter. Mare thinks the elephant is perfect, so we all agree and that makes her feel good. I'm doing my best to go with the flow while wondering if Mare even chose the elephant box or if Journey did. *Or… did the elephant box choose Journey?*

Later Mare calls the funeral home from the privacy of the guest room. I imagine that she's blowing whoever's hair straight about the type of service she wants for Chris. She's probably ordering him to interject a bit of Buddhism, a dash of Hinduism blended with a pinch of Native American Peyote Religion. Knowing my mother, I'm sure she'll get her way.

My androgynous roommate, Monica, and another one of her female friends, join us for dinner. Monica is talking to my mother about the gym lunks she works with. Mare's laughing. It's great to see her happy. Afterwards, while we're smoking the post dinner joint, Monica gets cotton mouth so bad she looks like Fire Marshal Bill when she talks.

"Can I go to the funeral with you guys tomorrow?" Monica asks Mare, politely. Journey answers before my mother even has a chance.

"No. Dis funeral is fer da family only. We do a wake fer friends later. You welcome to dat," he says. "Fer sure."

Monica looks at Journey silently, but her big-eyed expression shouts, *who asked you?*

This is what I despise about Journey the most; that he doesn't let Mare speak, or practically think, for herself. This is what I hate most about our mother; that she lets Journey come between her and her kids. He may not be physically abusive, but he's just as controlling to Mare as Jeff was to Chris.

It gets late. I have a lot to think about and quietly leave the group for the sanctuary of my room. We made it through another day. I ease myself into bed and run directly into Skyler and another dirty diaper. I was SO wrong about childhood bowel movements! I get right back up and gently change him, which I'm getting pretty good at because he barely wakes up. Shane begins to snore quietly like a bear cub. My eyes are wide open. The impending dread of facing tomorrow makes it impossible to sleep. I'm still thinking about organ music, the origin of urns, the rituals we follow and what I'll say about Chris if called upon. What story should I tell about her? What's something she did that showcases her love of family and life? What are my three all-time favorite memories of my sister…?

Sixteenth

July 13th, 1996

I'm dreaming I'm nibbling on a cold ear of corn and wake up with Skyler's foot in my mouth. He senses I'm awake and spins around to face me. Just as my eyes are able to focus on his face, he spits out his wet pappy, which lands on my neck. He's got that crazy, cute, gap-tooth, ear-to-ear grin on his face again and he's ready to go. And so, must I.

Mare and I are cracking eggs and chopping up vegetables for breakfast. While we're standing side-by-side, I figure, *now's as good as time as any.*

"Dad is coming over this morning so he can follow us to the funeral," I say casually. She drops her spatula onto the counter and looks at me.

"Go call your father and tell him that he can meet us there. Right now! I don't want to see that man any more than necessary. Make sure he knows to steer clear of me." The edge in her voice is sharper than any of my kitchen knives.

"That's so nice considering he lost his daughter, too, and he's paying for half the funeral."

"It is nice of me. Your father hardly took the time to get to know any of his own children. He wasn't a big part of Chris's life, or yours for that matter. You know that."

I lock up and don't know what to say. *How can she still be so angry after all these years? And didn't you leave him to run off with our next-door neighbor, John? Wasn't it you who chose to*

move your children to another state? How much energy does it take
to carry a grudge for life?

"John's going to meet us there, too," says Al, butting into the
conversation. He reaches over my shoulder and grabs a piece
of bacon. "Funerals are a time to put aside our differences and
remember the person we all loved and lost." He takes a bite. It
was the perfect thing to say, the exact right words at the right
time. Mare smiles. She reaches down, picks up the spatula, sets
it in the sink and hugs my brother. Her arms can barely reach
all the way around him.

I disappear down the hall into my room, call Dad and
explain that he has to meet us there. I give him the address and
reassure him that finding us will be easy. "Davis is a small town.
Remember to keep a low profile from your ex-wife. Seriously.
She's being a little vicious today, if you know what I mean."

With this many people in the house, things happen in
shifts. Once one group finishes breakfast, another group
begins. We take turns with the shower and the full-length
closet door mirrors in the guest room. I put on some nicer
clothes, slacks, a button-down shirt and leather dress shoes.
Ali helps me dress Shane and Skyler in the best-looking clothes
we can find. When Ali's out of the shower, she blow dries her
hair and another line begins for those who want their turn.
Molly steers her boys into wearing the clothes she wants them
to wear and then works on their hair. When Shelley's ready to
use the shower, Al kindly let's her go before him. I'm sure the
hot water ran out a long time ago, but no one complains.

Mare and Journey have skipped the shower and are already
dressed in the same old garb ready to go at any time. I don't
know of any additions to their closet since the late 1970s. She's
wearing a black Bob Marley concert tour T-shirt accented with
her scarab-beetle necklace. Her jeans are so worn in, even
the second-generation patches are silky smooth. She's worn
a rotation of multicolored friendship bracelets on her wrists
and ankles for years. On her feet, as always, are Birkenstocks.

She's braless. Duh. I wasn't expecting anything different or special today. Seeing her in Gucci would be shocking. Journey is wearing jeans, a tie-dyed tee shirt and Birks. Mares behind him, pulling a brush through his hair. His legs are crossed, his back is straight, and his eyes are closed. They've already smoked several morning joints. I think he's purring.

Clothes are the canvas of Shelley's emotions. She cleans up very well but there will be none of that today. After her shower, she staggers back into the living room dragging her feet beneath a melancholy collection of gray and black layers. She looks homeless and sad, but we tell her she looks great. "I really don't give a shit how I look," she tells us. "Why look nice on such a depressing day?" She has a point.

When Brad arrives, he's greeted with a chain of hugs. He's a part of our family and we're excited to see him. After he's reintroduced to Molly's kids and has a chance to visit and catch up a little with most of the group, I take him into the backyard and fill him in on what we know and don't know about the circumstances of Chris's death. He feels it. Then Molly, Shelley and Ali join us as well and when they do, Brad begins telling old stories about Chris and our family.

"I remember the day we moved into the Alvarado apartments because there were good looking girls everywhere. I had no idea they were all from the same family. I didn't know Tom or Alex even existed at first because I was busy scoping out Shelley, Chris, and Molly. As I got to know Chris, I became really attracted to her and we started dating. Not dating but hanging out. Not really hanging out all that much either, we just made out. Only a few times over the course of a week or so. I was new to Davis, and she introduced me to her sisters and eventually her friends. One day, I went over to your apartment and knocked on the door to see if Chris was home and Tom opened the door. He said something like, 'which one are you here for?' meaning one of his sisters. Even after Tom and I became friends, I'd come over he'd tease me by saying, 'None of my sisters are home'."

"Chris had a babysitting job at the time for one of the apartment managers kids, a little girl named Twila or Tawny, I think it was Twila. She was four or five years old. Sometimes Tom helped Chris babysit. Well, one day Twila comes up to me and starts doing impressions, which was totally out of the blue and shocking. Tom taught her how to do Richard Nixon, John Wayne, Jimmy Stewart, Batman and more. Tom coached her in the cabana and when someone came by to check their mail or go to the pool or whatever, Twila could appear out of nowhere and say something weird like, 'I am not a criminal' in a Nixon voice, doing all the mannerisms or, 'Head 'em off at the pass,' like John Wayne or, 'You… you dirty rat' in a James Cagney voice. Seeing this little girl doing impressions was so random and hilarious. I saw Tom teaching her one day and finally figured it all out."

"I also did a lot of cussing cartoon characters back then.

"You did a lot of cartoon characters having orgasms, too," Brad adds.

"That's right. I almost forgot."

"Chris was a year ahead of me in high school, but we were in the same world history class. She was friends with everyone. Stoners, jocks, dipshits, loners, brains, music-geeks, it didn't matter to her.

"That's so true!" Molly says smiling.

"Chris introduced me to lots of people, which was really nice of her. She put me in her study group with Tony Field and Chris Peele. There's no way I would have passed world history without their help. I pretty much sucked hind-tit at school. Chris knew I was in deep shit, so she hooked me up with the right group and made sure I did the work. I ended up getting a B+ in that class. It was one of the few good grades I ever got in high school."

"I remember you explaining that grade to your mom," I say.

"Why wasn't Myrna allowed to come today? Brad asks. They're still best friends. It feels weird that I'm here and she's not."

"I know. Who knows why Mare is being so seclusive? I say. "I tracked Myrna down. She lives in San Diego and would have gladly made the trip. Mare's all dazed and confused right now just like the rest of us. She told me we'd see Myrna in a few weeks anyway, so what's the big deal? But honestly, I don't see another wake for Chris in our future. Even if there is one, it's not feasible for Molly to be there and if that's the case, then what's the point? Chris's whole family is here now. This is a rare event."

"Well, she's hurt and overwhelmed right now. She might be thinking she'll feel better in a few weeks and be up for seeing Chris's friends. This has got to be hard on her."

"Oh, I know it is. We all know," I say.

"You got to cut her some slack, Billy," Brad says. He calls me that sometimes. It's from Caddy Shack. I forced all my favorite TV shows and movies on him so we could geek on them together. He did the same to me. He too, has taken the time to transcribe, memorize and perform our favorite funny movie scenes to the dismay of our eye-rolling of friends and strangers alike. We're still huge nerds to this day and proud of it. The world needs nerds. Nerds get things done. Under normal circumstances, Brad and I would be the life the party. But not today. Not now.

"You might find this hard to believe, but Tom and I were the consummate geeks in high school."

"No way," Molly says sarcastically.

"Maybe *you* were a geek in high school but I—"

"Yes, you were, Brossie and you know it." He calls me Brossie too.

"Okay, fine. I admit it."

"But with Chris to vouch for us we made a lot of friends. She got the Emerson clique to jive with the Holmes clique. She was just so *nice* and funny without trying as hard as me and Tom tended to do. It also didn't hurt that she was beautiful. She was as popular as any of the cheerleaders or student body presidents or homecoming queens. She was just so real and so generous, sincere, and kindhearted. Everyone loved her. There's only one Chris Bross. I'm going to miss her a lot. I already do…" Brad's voice gets shaky, and his eyes fill will tears. He has us laughing and crying at the same time. "She's going to be missed by a lot of people."

"She *was* one of a kind," Molly says right before giving Brad a hug. It's nice having Brad here and listening to his perspective of our sister.

"And she could sing everything; from the Jackson 5 to Jackson Brown." Brad says, remembering more.

"You got that right. From the Pointer Sisters to the Doobie Brothers," I add.

"From Stevie Nicks to Stevie Wonder," Molly says. We stand quietly for a few moments picturing Chris in our minds. I see her singing into a hairbrush. I see her singing at the airport. I see her singing in the talent show…

"So, shouldn't we be leaving soon?" Brad asks.

"We're just waiting for Al—Alex, as you know him, to get out of the shower."

We lollygag our way back inside and a few minutes later, Al enters the living room wearing a monochromatic olive-green Army suit and NBA-sized black leather shoes. He looks polished from head to toe and stands in complete and total contrast to Shelley's shabby garbs. Brad hugs my brother, and they quickly catch up. He learns it's 'Al' now not 'Alex'. And Al reeks of aftershave and assumes an imperious posture. We can't take our eyes off him in his uniform. His boots are like twin black mirrors. His whole look commands attention.

Is this really my animal-loving-little-pacifist-baby brother?

"Standard military protocol. Full uniform when flying on civilian aircraft and attending funerals," he explains, sounding very official. Willie, Joey, and Shane are standing behind him saluting like crazy and trying not to laugh.

"It's time to go," I say.

"Almost time to go," Mare says, lighting up one more joint. Most of us pass but some partake and when they're done, we gather keys, sunglasses, purses, baby bags, water bottles, and—in Mare and Journey's case—even more weed and smoking utensils and head out the door. Mare, Journey and Shelley take the Nova. I drive Molly, her kids and Shane and Skyler in the van. Al rides along in Brad's car, and we're off. I've driven over the causeway to Davis a thousand times, but it's never felt like it does today. We park hodgepodge in proximity of our destination and converge on foot to the funeral home that's ominously located at the end of D Street.

When we're a couple of blocks away, I spot John and my father down the street, in the shade of a tree, having a conversation. This is a strange sight indeed. As we continue to stroll in their direction, Journey, Mare and Shelley, who must have freshened up their buzz because they reek of pot, merge into our group. We fall into a line shuffling toward the funeral home. John and my father glide into place and join our procession. As we're crossing the street together, I realize that we're a peculiar sight indeed.

Shelley, who looks hopeless and homeless, is walking behind two old-school hippies followed by Ali who looks like a Nickelodeon TV star. She's being followed by her brothers, Willie, and Joey. They appear to be dressed for picture day at school. Molly is one step behind them, looking good as usual in a simple, summer dress. Then it's me and Brad in casual business attire, looking like a nice gay couple; me with a baby on my hip and Brad holding Shane's hand. My Dad and stepfather, John, are behind us, murmuring back and forth. They're dressed in the kind of formal clothes one might wear to an appointment with an attorney or a claims adjuster. Bringing up the back of our procession is my giant little brother in his warmongering military suit. He appears to be escorting a group of community service criminals to a new clean-up site. We look like we've been torn apart and randomly stitched together from different magazine covers; Military World, Mad, Seventeen, Ranger Rick, Spin, Cosmopolitan, Forbes and High Times. I would have stopped and gawked at our group, too, just like everyone else is doing now.

We congregate in front of the funeral home at the base of the stairs. Brad is great in these situations because he's so personable and good-natured. He's able to smooth out some of the uncomfortable moments like when we're saying 'hi' to John for the first time in years. He creates a bridge for Mare and Journey to talk to my Dad and to my surprise, they exchange kind words. I wasn't expecting Mare to be so civilized after her comment this morning and it makes me feel good.

Mare and Journey are the first to announce that they're going in. The rest of us watch them climb the stairs and go through the door. We really don't know what to do, so we linger a little longer before wandering up the steps in random groups when it feels right. When we get to the top, we're awkwardly greeted by a peculiar man standing in the entry. He's tall, emaciated and resembles a zombie with exceptionally nice hair. He has such a long, skinny neck that it's hard not to stare. There's at least one inch of slack all the way around his collar.

"Welcome friends."

His sharp Adam's apple scrapes the inside of his neck as he speaks. The gaps between his teeth are so pronounced; it would have been pointless to floss with anything less than mountain-climbing rope. Yet, despite these unsightly characteristics, his hair is jet-black, thick, shiny, and flawlessly coiffed to perfection. If you saw nothing but his hair, you'd think it belonged to a handsome leading man. If you saw nothing but his neck, you'd swear it belonged to a tortoise.

With a grand gesture of his sweeping arms, zombie-man welcomes us into the foyer. I notice the props that have been added to the room since my brief visit two days ago. The focal point is a giant Bible on a white, fake-marble pedestal. A fancy gold bookmark attached to a ribbon lies in the seam. There's a crucifix on the wall, and even though Jesus's head hangs down, he seems to be looking up at us through his blood-streaked eyes. I can't help it and roll mine back at him.

The dark set of double doors mysteriously open from the inside and we echo our way into the empty room. Except for the narrow-stained glass windows, the room is void of color. It's big enough to seat a hundred people, making our group of fourteen feel extra small. No one sits near the front. We spread out much more than I would have expected. Now that we're separated into small groups, we seem weaker and more fragmented than ever. But with Chris gone, we'll never be whole again anyway.

So much for reaching out to each other for support.

It's fascinating to be in the same room with Dad, John, Journey, and Mare. Three men, each so different, each connected to the same woman. Of course, my mother was, and is, a totally different person to each of them. Seeing them all together in one place is a little freaky. In their presence, it's explicitly clear how much my mother has changed over the years. This is surely the last time this combination of family members will be together. It's remarkable. We've come together to honor Chris. For our disbanded, dysfunctional and generally fucked-up family, this alone is quite an accomplishment. And yet, we're not united. We're not a single unit. We're scattered about this room just as we are in life.

The man with perfect hair recites a cliché speech, which could have been lifted from a series of sympathy cards. He opens his Bible and reads various passages relating to life and death. *Didn't Mare tell him to lay off the religion?* The Christian spin is driving me nuts. It's nothing I can relate to, and this turtle-man never knew Chris, so how can he pay tribute to her beautiful spirit? He's a perfect stranger speaking perfect nonsense in a perfectly strange place. He asks us to join him in prayer then practically tells us what to think and how to feel. He reassures us that her death is part of a greater plan beyond our mortal comprehension. He moves his arms like the people who help guide pilots to their spot on the tarmac. This charade is just as baffling as the endless party at Blue Moon ranch. For me, watching Shane's birthday video with Molly and Al, was Chris's funeral—not this charade. That's the way I choose to remember my sister: alive, beautiful, compassionate, hilarious, kind, gentle, and loving. Yes. She's gone. But she had a life. I close my eyes waiting for this nonsense to end.

"Family and friends may now view the bodily remains of Christina Marie Bross," he says. I open my eyes. *Finally.* Not a single hair is out of place when the turtle-man leaves the stage and walks away.

Mare and Journey are the first to stand and approach the casket. I can hear my mother crying as she looks down at her daughter. It's too painful to watch. I hope she finds her closure and all that, but all I want to do is get myself and the kids out of the room. Molly knows. She tips her head to the door, stands, and walks towards the exit with her kids. Brad and I, along with Shane and Skyler, are right behind her. I didn't realize how cold it was inside until I feel the sun again.

"Well, that was fun," I say, sarcastically. Molly shakes her head and takes a deep breath. She's rubbing her arms to chase away the same chill I feel.

"Do you want a little break, Tom?" Ali asks. I nod yes. She picks up Skyler and leads Shane over to where Mare and Journey are sitting across the street. I look closer. Of course, they're smoking a joint.

"He never invited anyone to say something about Chris in their own words," Brad says.

"I know!" says Molly.

"That would have been nice," says Shelley.

"I agree. I guess we'll have to save that for another time."

Al comes down the steps and joins our group. "You guys should go see Chris. She looks very peaceful," he says.

"No way," replies Molly.

"Fuck that shit," Shelley says.

"I want to remember Chris in living color, not what's left of her in there," I say.

"This is the last chance you'll ever get to see her. It's no big deal. You need closure."

"Not *that* kind."

"What do you think, Brad?"

"Hell no—I mean it's up to you, but I'm not going back in there. Nope. No way. No thanks."

Al won't let up. He works on Shelley for a while, gives up and then drills me until eventually, against my better judgment, I agree. Brad shakes his head at me, and I almost change my mind. Al and I march up the steps, through the door, back into the hollow room, plodding, step-by-step, to the casket. It's too real and surreal at the same time. I want to be in the moment and also want to be a million miles away. I should turn around and run but for some reason I don't.

I'm over her casket looking down at her. There is nothing to say. She certainly looks dead. Al and I stand perfectly still. Now that I'm here, I hope to find a shred of meaning or resolve in this ritual. All I feel is cold and empty. The message is clear. Life is harsh and death is real. My sister does not look beautiful, rested, or at peace. There's a large bruise and considerable swelling on her neck that no amount of make-up can cover. The thick makeup on her face doesn't entirely conceal other gashes and bruises. I've seen enough. This image has burned its way into my mind, the marks, the swelling, the discoloration, the makeup. I feel sick and walk away. As I pass my brother, I hear him whispering his final-final goodbyes. I can't get to the door fast enough.

I'm a fucking idiot.

"Well, that was a huge mistake," I say to Molly and Brad, catching my breath back outside. I sit down on the steps.

"I told you. Who wants to see anyone dead, let alone someone you love?" Brad says.

Al's still in there. Did Dad look at her?"

"He did."

"What about John?"

"He did too."

"I wish I hadn't."

Brad gives me his, *I-told-you-so look.*

Even though I only glanced at her, the image of her lifeless body is something I can't shake. There is no closure for me. We need to remember Chris for the beautiful person she was, celebrate all her great qualities, and rekindle our memories so it's easier to always keep her in our hearts. We need to play her favorite music, eat her favorite foods, and look at old pictures of her. I want to do all those things as soon as possible so I can get that last image I just saw of her out of my fucking head!

John and Dad wander out side-by-side, still engrossed in conversation.

What on earth are they talking about?

They join us near the steps. I ask John how he's doing. We don't stay in touch anymore, and I can't remember the last time I saw him. He looks like he's aging faster than my Dad. One more reason to quit smoking, I think. He's not quite as big or intimidating as he was when I was little, but he's even stranger and more awkward than ever. He tells us about his apartment in Pacifica and his job editing ophthalmology research papers at the UCSF Medical Center and his black Bombay cat named Bolide. I look at him with a blank expression.

"A bolide is a large meteor that explodes in the atmosphere."

"Of course, it is. Duh."

I'm a man now. John can handle a little sarcasm. He chuckles. Despite his professional accolades, I still can't imagine how he manages to function in society with his oversized brain.

"Moe moved out a long time ago, but we're still friends. She left the cat with me when he was just a kitten. *This man drowns kittens. What the hell?* This personal tidbit is followed by a solid minute of dead air. Even as an adult, I don't understand John at all.

Dad looks at his watch again and announces he has to leave in order to catch his flight out of San Francisco. We begin the process of saying our goodbyes. He gets hugs from all of us except Al and John, with whom solid handshakes are exchanged. Mare and Journey don't even notice him leaving. Molly keeps an eye on the boys while I walk Dad to his car.

"I can't believe I was in the same room with my ex-wife's second and third husband," he says, scratching his head. Journey's an interesting choice."

"What were you talking to John about?"

"All kinds of things and nothing at all. That man is hard to figure out."

"We're a strange family. You really see it when we're all together."

"Like a bag of mixed nuts," he says, laughing a little. "Promise to keep me posted on everything, okay? I love you. Don't make any rash decisions. Not without talking to your old man, okay?"

"Okay."

"Promise?"

"I promise."

"Okay then."

Dad pats me on the shoulder three times like a high school debate coach and is about to leave when I pull him in for a hug that lasts a whopping one point five seconds. He needs lessons. "I love you, Dad."

"Gotcha."

Gotcha?

I feel close to Dad even when he's flying to the other side of the country.

"Hang in there, Billy," Brad says, before we hug goodbye. He wants to leave from Davis because it's closer to home.

"Oh, I will."

"Buddies for life, Brossie."

"Buddies for life, Brad."

He says goodbye to everyone else and lots of hugs are exchanged. He walks across the street and says goodbye to Mare and Journey. Then I see him disappear behind the tinted glass of his car and drive away.

During the drive home, I think about everything that's happened during the last eleven days. The familiar pattern of bumps I feel as we cross the causeway from Davis back to Sacramento lulls me into a daydream. I spend the rest of the ride home inside my head thinking about Chris and some of the silly things we used to do. In San Francisco, she used to sell me mud pies in the backyard. We learned gymnastics at the park and made a life-long game out of saluting the imaginary judges. In Placerville we made ramps on Flying Saucer Hill and took turns jumping over each other on our bikes. In Fair Oaks we put on idiotic plays for our siblings and staged a mock wedding. It was Chris who came out of her bedroom as the smell of burning urine was engulfing our house and tentatively asked our mother what she was cooking for dinner. At the Cincinnati airport, she belted out a song for everyone's entertainment while we waited for our luggage. In Davis, she taught me to dial back my wild dancing and gave me tips on how to treat girls with the respect and dignity they deserve. She lent me money for food when our cupboards were bare. We used to sit together catamaran style and ride our skateboards down the driveway weaving in and out of the trees. Most of the time we spun out and crashed, which was the best part—because it made us laugh. And when mom checked out, Chris stepped in and kept us together. She helped us through all the challenging situations we encountered. That's what really sucks about the situation we're in now. I need her now. Our family needs her now. Her kids really need her now.

And she's gone.

Forever.

Seventeenth

July 13th, 1996

"Come on, everybody," Mare says. "Let's take a shot in honor of Christina!"

"Amen to dat," Journey says.

The moment we get home Mare and Journey break out a bottle of Drambuie liqueur. Everyone, except the youngest three, participate. Mare begins rolling like a freight train and helps Journey finish the bottle. And just like that, another party has begun.

A lot of us want to get out of our dress clothes and relax. A shift in attire commences as we disappear and reappear in regular clothes. Once again, Army-Al's transition is the most dramatic. Now that we have enough joints for a reggae festival, it only seems right to put on the Jimmy Cliff CD, *The Harder They Come*. Ali, who's mature for a thirteen-year-old, but is still just a kid, is the only one who can keep up with Mare and Journey puff for puff. Mare gives Ali a joint-rolling lesson and Ali picks it up really fast, leaving me to wonder if she'd already mastered this skill before. Shelley is immersed in a world of stretching exercises on what little space she can find on the living room floor. Even with upbeat music, drugs and alcohol, our moods are down.

The two elephants in the room commands our thoughts. *One. This is our last day together. Two. What's our plan for Shane and Skyler?* On top of all this I'm still feeling sick to my stomach from seeing my sister in the coffin. It's like the more I try to run from it, the more I end up running directly into it. Just because we don't feel like partying doesn't stop us from trying, which gives the rest of the day an odd feel. We're family. We know everything there is to know about each other and yet we don't know what to say. Maybe it's the impending end of our reunion that's clouding our thoughts. I hate seeing Molly in so much pain. I hate that we live nine hundred miles apart. I'm going to miss Al, and Shelley too. We just don't see each other very much anymore. It took a fucking death in the family to bring us all together.

When I was little, I figured we'd all grow up and live on the same street, babysit each other's kids, help each other out. I pictured us being close our entire life, thumbing through photo albums in rocking chairs on a screened in porch someplace. Then you grow up and you realize how separate our lives have become. And the worst part is, life doesn't bend to give you even the slightest chance of achieving your childhood dreams. You learn to let go, give up, grow up and live with it. You tell yourself it was naïve to harbor such childhood thoughts, that your family bonds were never strong enough to allow for such a closeness later in life. Americans follow job opportunities and money—not family. Why on Earth would our family be any different? And now we're in a unique situation; we've got to figure out a way to keep Shane and Skyler in this very disjointed, dysfunctional, sometimes delusional family of ours.

"Hey guys. Let's meet under the tree again tonight. Final family meeting. Ten o'clock."

Ten? That's a bit late but okay. Whatever.

Mare just gave the inevitable an official start time.

Shane and Skyler appear ready for a nap, so I take them to my room. I close the blinds covering them in a stripped blanket of light like contour lines on a map. I'm so drained from the funeral that I lie down next to them to see if maybe, just maybe I can nap. I didn't realize how tired I was until I stopped moving. It doesn't take long to slip away and while

I'm sleeping, I'm treated to the most lucid dream I've ever experienced in my entire life.

∞   ∞   ∞

It's 1975 and I'm in Cliff's garage packing what little I have into brown paper bags and a medium sized Jolly Green Giant box. Mare called half an hour ago with the news that she had finally rented a 'townhouse' apartment, which sounds perfectly exotic to me. My hands are shaking, not from the cold, but with excitement. Charlie is on his way to pick me up and finally get me out of the cold, dank, not-fit-for-a-dog, garage I've been living in for the last sixty-seven days. Yes, I've been counting. This is where Mare dropped me off after our sudden move back to Davis from San Anselmo—after our brief move to live with our God Family.

The sound of our yellow bus is easy to detect. I hear it pull into the driveway and race outside to greet Charlie. I can feel his beard tickle my cheek and neck. He follows me inside; we grab my meager possessions and carry them onto the bus. I sit where Mare normally sits, on the cushion in the front and we're on our way. I'm so full of anticipation to see my family that I can barely contain my bladder. Charlie parks next to the Alvarado Parkside Apartments carved-wood sign.

Home sweet home. But not for long…

"Alex calls it the Avocado Parkside Apartments, which when you consider the colors inside isn't that far off!"

Charlie laughs at himself and points to our door. The moment the bus doors unfold, I jump down the steps and sprint inside. The green carpet is worn thin, the walls are scuffed, it smells musty, and the space is narrow and small. But as I walk through the door and see my mother along with Shelley, Chris, Molly and Alex, I know this is the nicest home I will ever set foot in. Chris reaches up and hands me the joint that's being passed around.

"You finally made it. Welcome home brother," she says, smiling brilliantly.

I look into my sister's smiling eyes. I study her trademark wavy brown hair flowing over her shoulders and note the dimple that accents her smile. She's in her prime and looks wonderful. This is the sister I know and love. This is the family I've missed so much. Being together again means everything and I become drunk with joy, much too happy to be angry with my mother for what she put us through. This present moment is bright enough to blow out the past. Everyone takes turns hugging me. We're all laughing and giddy and silly. We're completely caught up in the joy of each other's company. I'm overwhelmed and blow a snot bubble. Even more laughter! Just being all together again in the same room, under the same roof is a priceless gift.

This dream is a memory of the actual event that happened years ago. And yet in the dream, it also feels like it's happening for the first time. I certainly feel back in my thirteen-year-old body—occupying that same sliver of time again. After being apart for so long, it's extra exciting to be together again. I feel that same magic, and it's just as strong as it was when it happened so many years ago.

In the next part of the dream, we're upstairs in the bedrooms trying to sleep. Alex and I are in one room, on the floor in our sleeping bags, which is really comfortable compared to the drivetrain disguised as a couch I'd been sleeping on. Shelley, Chris, and Molly are in the other bedroom across the hall. This is our first night back together and it's impossible to settle down. Although their door is closed, Alex and I can hear our sisters perfectly. They're laughing about our latest adventure. Their voices are music to our ears and we're laughing right along with them.

Chris pioneered a linguistic verbal shorthand, then she taught the rest of us how to do it, too. It's essentially a method of compressing every detail, all the drama and emotion from an event, into a simple catchphrase that encompasses the whole thing. This technique cuts directly to the heart of a given situation, so much so that you actually *feel* it again.

Here's how it works: First, we talk and laugh about a particular story, no matter how sad, uncomfortable, or embarrassing, and get the whole thing out in the open. Then, we select or create key words or a phrase that represents the best, and often the worst part of the story. Even long, complicated situations are reduced to their essence this way. This allows us to instantly recall, relive, and re-experience significant events, struggles, and situations. Coming up with the right catchphrase is part of the fun and Chris has a knack for nailing it.

Lying on the floor, inhaling the smell of dusty carpet, Alex and I listen to our sisters jibber-jabber. They cover a lot of ground, racing from one memory to another, quickly jumping forward and backward through time, making incredible connections out of seemingly unrelated events. There's a cycle of tempo and crescendo to their voices. Feeding off each other's energy, they're reliving the past like actors on a stage; only they're playing themselves. We hear them get louder and talk faster until they become a machine gun of rapid-fire dialogue interlaced with bursts of laughter. Eventually, their energy subsides and they quiet down, catch their breath and whisper. Then it starts up again. The next story emerges, and then another. The swell begins to build and the cycle of catch phrases and gut-wrenching laughter repeats itself. It's intoxicating to hear. Sharing our experiences this way has become our primary coping device—followed closely by marijuana, alcohol and other, primarily psychedelic, drugs.

We listen as they test different words and combinations relating to our recent family fiasco, compressing all the craziness from this latest misadventure into a phrase that will trigger a kaleidoscope of feelings for years to come. Our latest adventure to San Anselmo, and our scattered return to Davis becomes known as, *Project Refugee.* Alex and I agree it's a fine phrase indeed. Our sisters continue to laugh and blurt out other catch phrases such as; *So this is the human race, Cuss word Combo, Popsicle Nazi, Urine Burn, XK90-BB, Chris Bross the Great, Matching-Earth-Mama-Hippie-Twins and No Mom— No Marilyn—Just Mare.* Even though Alex and I are in the other room, we're laughing just as hard as they are.

∞   ∞   ∞

The dream must have happened right before I woke up because I remember it with such clarity. I can still hear my sister's voices clear as day when I open my eyes. For a split second, I have no idea what year it is or if I'm waking up in that Davis townhouse apartment, or in my own bed at home in Rancho Cordova. I blink my eyes a few times trying to comprehend what just happened. Shane and Skyler are still sleeping. I can't stop smiling because it feels like Chris deliberately set out to visit me.

I get out of bed feeling energized, excited, and electric— like I was nearly hit by lightning. I'm filled with a strangely familiar sense that everything is going to work out. Life will go on. I lean against the wall, close my eyes, and let the feeling of seeing Chris in her prime and hearing her voice and laughter wash over me. I open the door quietly and run directly into Molly in the hallway. She sees something in my face right away.

"You look happy. Good nap?" she says.

"I am. And I did," I say.

As I describe the dream I just had to my little sister, and how beautiful Chris looked, and how I was able to get close enough to see the freckles in her eyes, a smile grows across her face.

"Oh, that's so special!"

"That was the last time we all lived together under the same roof and—" Molly hugs me before I can finish, as if to feel any residual energy lingering from Christina.

"Amazing," she whispers into my ear.

"I went back in time, Molly. And for a few minutes, I was actually with our sister! She was so full of life and so happy. She was sitting right in front of me… it was the most realistic and incredible dream I've ever experienced…" I have to catch my breath.

"I know how you feel. I've had dreams about Kurt, and it's just amazing. They have the same effect on me," Molly says. "I felt that connection. It was him. He had the same energy. When I have a Kurt dream, he's all healthy and cancer-free. He always looks awesome. They never last long enough but I'm always grateful when they happen."

"If I can have a dream like that every once in a blue moon, then I'll know that Chris isn't completely gone."

Eighteenth
July 13th, 1996

The unexpected, uplifting boost of energy I got from that wonderful dream is still going strong later in the afternoon. It was time travel; I was transported back to a major event from the past. Ninety-nine percent of me was submerged in the experience. I felt the exact same emotions I did when it had happened so long ago. The other one percent of me knew I was being treated to something special. I took the time to linger on Chris a little longer. I made a point to look into her eyes so I could see the freckles in her iris. I told myself to listen to her voice and the sound of her laughter. I sat next to her on the ottoman just so I could lean into her body. This dream was unlike any other I've ever had. I was back in my thirteen-year-old body feeling the relief and joy of having my entire family all together again. That reunion in Davis represents the apex of our family love. We felt whole again. Without having to say it, we knew how much we missed each other; how wrong it was to be separated and how we believed, that no matter what, from that day forward, we'd stick together. The tiny townhouse apartment was our fulcrum, our congregation, our commune. We were all home under the same roof at last. Seeing Chris in her prime again was remarkable. The dark image of her in the coffin that's been polluting my mind has been eclipsed. Now I see her at her radiant best, glowing from the inside out, bursting with energy and full of life.

We're unusually quiet during dinner and into the evening. Everyone occupies themselves independently; Molly does laundry, Ali makes bracelets, Al packs and repacks his duffel bag, Shelley is content thumbing through family photo albums with Shane, and Willie and Joey play Chinese Checkers. Later we turn on the TV and sift through the channels. No one wants to watch *Touched by an Angel* or *Cops*, so I opt for a movie instead. Ali makes some popcorn, and we watch the first good hour of *Stripes* before Skyler falls asleep in my arms. When I get back from putting the boys down for the night in my bed, I pass Mare who's sitting on the floor. She looks up at me from her pot, rolling papers and her growing arsenal of doobies.

"For our meeting tonight, my son."

"Well sure."

We turn off the TV and put on some music but keep it low as to not disturb the kids. We've shared three or four joints before the meeting, but we don't seem to be getting any higher. Willie and Joey head off to bed while I check on the boys. The hallway light illuminates my room enough to see them asleep on top of the covers. Not wanting to wake them, I set a pillow on the floor, lie down on my back, and close the door. I'm not trying to sleep. I just want some quiet time to collect my thoughts. I listen to Shane and Skyler breathing deeply, in unison, fast asleep. I can also hear the hushed voices and soft footsteps in the rest of the house. I lose track of time just thinking about everything that's happened since I got that terrible phone call at work. That call still gives me shivers. It's the proverbial 'one call' that changes everything. While I'm floating through thoughts, recalling our odd reunion, and all the drama and emotions that have hitchhiked along for the ride, I start to hear a familiar song. It's far away at first and then it gets closer and closer until it's on the other side of the door. But it's not a song. It's the sound of my mother's voice.

"Family meeting time… Family meeting time…"

I lift myself up, crack open the door and am greeted with my mother's smiling face. I nod my head and quietly follow her down the hall. She's still so light on her feet after all these years. She rounds up the rest of us with her anthem, hovering from room to room for our final late night pow-wow. We grab our drinks, smokes, weed, matches and whatnot and form the same circle we did eleven days ago beneath the maple tree in the front yard. Only eleven days? It seems like more. Maybe because losing Chris is the biggest crisis we've ever confronted. Maybe because time slows to a crawl during depressing, draining, soul depleting tragedies so you're forced to feel their full wrath. Maybe because our minds work so much harder grappling to understand a world that can be so cruel. The last eleven days have been unlike any other time in my life. On one hand, so much has happened—on the other, it's like absolutely nothing has happened at all. After all, Chris is still dead and we still don't have a plan for Shane and Skyler.

The air is perfectly still and pleasantly warm. The lawn needs mowing, and the long grass is cool without being wet. The matriarch of our circle lights the ceremonial joint, passes it to Journey and waits until it's halfway around before she speaks.

"Today was a heavy day—but also a good day," Mare begins. "We said our goodbyes to Chris. We let her go. I thought she looked beautiful as she begins this new chapter in her journey. I'm going to miss my little girl. And I know we'll be together again one day."

"Most of her ashes will fit in the trippy elephant box Journey and I bought. The rest will go to you—her brothers and sisters. That way, you can keep a little bit of Christina close by. We'll do something special for Chris; a ceremonial wake, a real celebrate-her-life kind of party where we can let it all hang out. I don't know when or where yet, but I do know it will be extra far out and extra special. Doesn't that sound good?"

There are nods of approval, but I know Mare hasn't really thought it through. She didn't mention that Molly won't be there, which will make any kind of celebration for Chris feel incomplete. If it takes place in Davis, she'll have to leave her precious crops unattended, which isn't likely. If she has it in Laytonville, it will be too far away for most of Chris's friends to go. And personally, I have no desire to attend another sleep-in-the-shed-wake-and-bake-numb-and-dumber-endless party with her friends at Blue Moon Ranch.

"The time has come to work out the details of our plan to keep Shane and Skyler in the family."

I feel everyone's eyes on me. I direct my attention downward, to the individual blades of grass that I'm gently pulling from the lawn.

Be patient. See where this goes.

"Mare, since your opinion matters the most, how do you see the plan taking place?" Molly asks wisely, cutting right to the chase.

"We all agree that these kids need to stay in our family. They're a blessing, a gift Christina left for us to share. It's a beautiful thing and we'll each get our equal turn with the boys. Everyone pitches in, everyone gets their fair share of time, everyone is happy, and everything turns out groovy."

"Okay. So, who takes them first?" I ask, wondering if she's reached this point in her plan.

"It doesn't matter who takes them first, or last, because they will be traveling in a circle of family. Look around at our beautiful family. We can do this, right?"

Wrong.

Two joints are now traveling in opposing directions around our group. Al clears his throat and speaks like an Action News TV reporter.

"Well, we better decide something fast or Child Protective Services will step in and put the kids in a foster home. If they end up at the mercy of CPS and we don't get them out quickly, we could end up losing custody. Then the children become wards of the state. They'd probably be separated and moved from home to home until they're eighteen. The sad and unfortunate fact is that many of these kids are physically, mentally, and sexually abused in the foster-care system."

"And, basically fucked up for life," says Shelley.

"Uggghhh, that would suck," says Ali.

"Before they went to a foster home, we'd have both Shane and Skyler adopted into a family," Molly says. "An open adoption is way better than that."

"I don't want the boys put into a foster home! I don't want them to be adopted and raised by some straight, shallow, yuppie, strangers either."

"What's so bad about adoption?" Ali asks. "My friend Aubrey was adopted. Her parents are cool. She's not mental."

"Adoption is a far better scenario than a foster family," Al says. Mare continues to shake her head no.

"What about parents who want kids but can't conceive? Think of the neglected and abused kids who are rescued through adoption," I say, catching my mother's eyes.

Mare is trembling now. "Why are we even talking about this? These boys are already members of *our* family. They are mine and they will remain in *our* family. Got it?" She's on the verge of crying. "We're not here to discuss other options. The plan is for them to stay with us. We just need to hash out the details. Is that clear?"

Journey stops stroking his beard and starts rubbing her shoulders. We cannot stand to see her upset. We never could. There's no need to cause her pain or create unnecessary drama, especially at a time like this; she's been through enough. Now is as good as time as any.

"I'll do it," I say. My three little words hang in the air like two-day-old party balloons. There's a few seconds of silence. "Not take them first but take them for good. They can live with me," I add.

"Shut up, Tom!" Ali shouts in a burst.

"Really?" Molly asks.

"Far-fucking-out Tom!" Shelley says.

"What a relief," Al says, sighing.

"I kind of have to. For a lot of reasons."

No one looks more relieved than Mare. Her big, relaxed smile says it all. This is what she wanted all along. It doesn't matter because I'm not doing it for her. I'm doing it for the boys. They need stability. They need a more permanent solution. They don't need to go from home to home just to keep them in our family. They deserve something better than that. I'm better equipped to give Shane and Skyler the love and security they need. It's that simple.

Yes, my world is spinning out of control. But I also feel grounded and a strong sense of conviction. When did I reach this decision? Was it when I got the news at work—or when Shane said he wanted to live with me? Or was it after hearing Nadine's incredibly generous offer? Was it yesterday afternoon while we were playing with the kids in the yard? All of these things certainly contributed. But more than anything else, it was that wonderful dream I just had that sealed the deal. Once I'd made up my mind, I felt a surprising sense of relief. I must have been subconsciously battling with the decision all along. There are some things you see better by not looking directly at them.

I tried talking myself out of stepping up, but neither my head nor my heart would allow it. I know Mare doesn't want to raise her grandsons. She can't come right out and say it, but it's the truth. Even if we went along with her plan of time-sharing the boys, they would have to start with me. Whoever takes them first will be their primary caregiver, clearly the 'parent' in their young eyes. And then, once they get comfortable, we're supposed to pass them off to the next person? They'll feel abandoned. I know that feeling all too well and it sucks. No way. What these kids need is a healthy routine in a loving and stable environment. I can give them that. I've got to let go of my past and start a new life with them. It is what's best for everyone—the kids, my family—maybe even me.

We all have to grow up sometime, right?

"I can't predict the future or guarantee that everything will work out. But I do promise to try my best. It's obviously a tremendous challenge. There are a million things that need to be done: find a lawyer, register Shane for school, find a daycare provider, locate their doctor, find out if they need shots, buy a highchair, clothes, diapers, wipes, lunchboxes, cook food, buy beds, make a room for them, set up some kind of counseling for Shane… It's a long list and yet at the same time, all they really need right now is love. They had a place in my heart before Chris died. Now it's even bigger."

"Of all people, my psycho ex-girlfriend, Nadine, helped to inspire me to step up. If she's willing to give up her life and start a new one, then so can I. Maybe not with her—but with the kids. I'm a survivor. I've been through a lot and can handle a lot. The goal is to get them settled and into a steady routine. One day at a time. Focus on the present and not the past or too far into the future. I'm sure I'll need to master the art of patience and give them all the love I can."

"I have an opportunity to do something good in a bad situation. I'll be keeping these great kids in the family and maybe giving Chris some peace. I can't comprehend how much life is going to change, but I'd rather dive in and deal with it now, versus kicking myself later for not trying. Reaching a decision was like swimming upstream against the current. But now that my mind is made up, I feel ready for the challenge."

Everyone is smiling at me. Their eyes beg for more.

"This is not a time-sharing plan. This is going to be their one and only home," I say, looking directly at Mare. "There will be plenty of regular visits from us—and you better come visit too, because I can't do this alone. You, you, you, and everyone here in this circle has to help in whatever way you can. I'm not taking on this responsibility unless I can depend on the rest of my family for support."

"I can move in with you for a while!" Shelley offers. "To help while you adjust."

Adjusting to you would be even more of a challenge. Thanks anyway.

"The boys can spend summers with us on the ranch," says Mare.

Not a time-share plan—remember?

"I can send you boxes of clothes they'll grow into," says Molly.

That's more like it!

"I can send money every now and then," offers Al.

Yeah, right! But I love where your heart is at, Bro.

"That's what I'm talking about. Thank you. Thank you. Thank you. We have to stick together—for Chris and for the boys. I have no idea where to start…"

"You already have," Mare says.

"Give yourself time to adjust," Molly says. "It's going to seem impossible at first, but don't give up. That's normal. They say it takes at least three months to get into a rhythm. Check your progress after ninety days. Hopefully, you'll see things are trending for the better. We finally had our first decent day about three months after Kurt died. I'm just saying it takes time."

I take her advice to heart, figuring she should know. "I can't believe I'm going to do this. It's freaky-scary but kind of exciting, too. I can't wait to tell Shane and Skyler…"

"Everyone listen up," commands Mare. "Your brother, your uncle, my son is doing a beautiful thing here. I'm not asking you to help Tom. I am *ordering* you. Is that clear?" The group concurs. "*We* have the power to make this work," she adds dramatically, moving her arms like an arrogant lawyer in court.

"Maybe this will actually bring us closer as a family," Al adds. "We all have a common cause now."

"He's right. From now on, consider us your one and only almighty cause," I say, standing up to stretch and finding myself in the center of a group hug. While we're in the circle, Molly looks up and our eyes meet.

"I'm really proud of you, Tom. This is awesome. Kind of a biggie."

"Yes. Kind of a biggie indeed."

The meeting is over. You can feel a collective sigh of relief. Everyone's much more relaxed. There's laughter. Al blows a smoke ring into the sky. As it dissipates into the night, we go our separate ways, vanishing into different parts of the house to sleep. I experience a sense of pride for bravely accepting the responsibility—for doing what I believe is right, but it doesn't last. As I try to sleep, I feel my body fluctuating between tranquil calmness and holy-fucking-shit waves of anxiety. I tell myself not to freak out, that the waves of fear will pass. But they don't because the fact is, I'm in over my head. I honestly don't know if everything will work out.

Even though the decision was mine, it was forced upon me. Someone has to step up and I'm in the best position to do that. But will this work? Will my family really pitch in? Is this forever? Or will I get them settled and consider my options? We'll be on a 'one-day-at-a-time' routine. Only time will tell.

Nineteenth

July 14th, 1996

There are infinite ways to start the day. Mine begins with a wet pacifier being shoved in and out of my ear. Generally, it's not a pleasant way to wake up, but when I open my eyes and see Skyler's smiling face, I can't help but smile back. He slides off the bed in his heavy damp diaper, looks up at me and says, "Eee—sur-real!"

It's impossible not to smile. It's a one-two-three combination of his wild hair, his gap-toothed grin, and the squeak of his helium-like voice. I have to laugh. Don't get me wrong, this is also extremely annoying, but still too cute for words. My next thought is catapulted into my head; *I'll never get to sleep in again. No more lazy Sundays, coasting through the day, reading the paper in bed.* And while this sucks, I know it's the least of my worries. There are much bigger changes and sacrifices ahead. Right now, I need to stand up and stand firm so that's exactly what I do. In a way, I'm acting like Mare; embracing change, never looking back, and feeling grateful for what the universe has brought me. At least that's what I tell myself as I get out of bed. I'm excited to tell the kids the news. Shane is hovering over a small lake of drool. He rubs his eyes open and looks at me like a crazy old man.

"You drool so much, just to be on the safe side, I'm getting you a life jacket to sleep in."

His expression doesn't change. Skyler, on the other hand, giggles and says with authority what sounds exactly like,

"Monkey queefs!" which makes me shake my head and smile as I lead him into the bathroom. As we're coming out, Shane's coming in.

"Meet us in the kitchen. Okay?"

"Okay," Shane says yawn-talking. Mare and Journey appear to have been up for a while; drinking coffee, social grooming on the floor; a lazy line of smoke rises from their second or third morning joint. "Good morning," they murmur as I walk by.

"I hope you both slept well," I say.

"Oh, we always sleep well. Right Journey?"

"Uh huh."

Shane and Skyler are waiting patiently at the table. I pour two bowls of cereal, hand out spoons, splash on milk and put a bagel in the toaster oven for me. I'm content just watching them eat their Quaker Oh's. Shane is very efficient. He leans over the bowl with his spoon clutched firmly in his hand. It sounds like he's eating fresh walnut shells. It's noticeably quiet between bites. One minute after serving Skyler his breakfast, it looks like a micro-tornado destroyed my dining room.

"Mess Master Skyler, you have three Oh's stuck to your head."

"Four," says Shane. He's right. I didn't see the one on the back of his neck. Major news requires their full attention, so I'll wait until we're done eating before I start talking. I take our plates and bowls to the sink and sit back down with them at the table.

"Hey guys, listen up. Everyone's been trying to figure out where you guys should live," I say to get the ball rolling. Shane temporarily stops reading the cereal box and looks up at me with a furrowed brow. "I know," he says.

"So how would you like to live with me?"

"Okay."

"Isn't this great?"

"Skyler too?"

"Of course. Both you guys."

"Okay." He repositions the cereal box to continue reading.

"In the fall, you can go to the school right behind my house."

"Okay." That's all he says. He's more interested in cereal ingredients than anything I have to say.

"Are you sure?" I ask, expecting this to be a more joyous and boisterous conversation. *Hey man, I'm making the biggest sacrifice of my life here! A little gratitude would be nice!* Just then, I realize how stupid my expectations are. I mean considering his age, his grasp of the situation, and what he's already been through, it's not about me at all. Suddenly, I feel incredibly small and humble and would like to hide behind a giant rock.

"Can I have more cereal, please?" he asks.

"Of course." He's an eating machine. "You're so polite, Shane. I love that."

I get up, grab his bowl, and spoon and bring it back to the table. Then we're intercepted by Molly and her three kids, and the next shift of breakfast begins. Later that morning, while I'm doing the dishes, I find myself still feeling very stupid for expecting some kind of made-for-TV-magical-moment with the kids this morning. Then all of a sudden, I feel the strange sensation of little arms wrapping around my waist. I look down to see Shane and almost cry in a primal surge of pure love that's unlike anything I've ever felt before. I get down to his level and we hug. Then I grab Skyler's arm as he wanders by, pull his hand out of his diaper, and hug him, too. Everything in my little corner of the world has changed. I went to bed as a bachelor and woke up as a parent. This is my family now. Meet the Bross boys. Sounds like *Lost Boys* but don't worry. We'll find our way without biting anyone. Hopefully…

Sitting side-by-side with the kids on the couch, the three of us watch everyone else scurry about, gathering their things, packing, and moving around preparing to leave. It's not easy to say goodbye to Molly and her kids. Just the fact that they're about to go makes me miss them. Idaho is far away. We both know it will be a while before we see each other again and we know 'a while' is a very vague term in our family. It sucks we had to reunite under such drastic circumstances. But it was also wonderful to have her company, her support, and her love during this crisis. Molly and Ali helped me so much with the kids the whole time they were here. Now my sister is focused on getting home and keeping things together for her family. Right before she leaves for the airport with Al, she pulls me into the garage for privacy.

"I just wanted to tell you again how proud I am of you. Remember, the first ninety days will be the hardest. Stay patient. It will get easier. One more thing. Those boys are very lucky to have you, Tom. You're great with kids. My kids adore you and they hardly even know you. So do Shane and Skyler."

Hearing this puts a lump in my throat.

"Don't forget how good you are with kids, she says. "You're a lot like Chris that way. Only more silly."

"And Chris was pretty silly."

"Yes, she was. She certainly was."

We hug a for long time because we know this is the last one for a long time.

Back in the house, Molly and her kids say goodbye to Shelley, Mare and Journey. They get big hugs from me and then Al whisks them away to the airport.

When Al gets back, he follows me in the Z to West Sacramento; first, to drop off the cargo box, then the van. An obese man, drenched in sweat and stuffed into orange U-Haul overalls, immediately notices the dent on the corner of our cargo box. He rolls towards us like a giant peach. The extra meat on his face gives him a fat-blind appearance.

"That thing is toast!" he says, pointing directly at the damage. "It's gonna cost you."

I hear him clearly, but my focus is stuck on the streaks of sweat dripping down his mutton chops.

Before I can mention the insurance, my brother quips, "I hit a tree, but it wasn't my fault because I honked." Al laughs, inviting the man to join him. Mutton Chop Man doesn't laugh—but I do. He examines my brother like something he picked from his teeth. We go inside and watch him turn his body sideways to move behind the counter, which doesn't help because he's a sphere.

"Here's the no-hassle, no questions, full-coverage insurance I bought for the cargo box." I say, placing the papers on the counter. He studies them carefully in search of an error or loophole then shakes his head in disbelief.

"We'll, ain't that a bitch?" He says, louder than intended.

No. Not for me.

"So, are we good to go?"

"Just sign out here," he says.

"Okay."

"You're soooo lucky," he says.

I think about how drastically my life has just changed. *Maybe I am lucky, maybe I'm not.*

Al and I drive to another part of town and return the van. By the time we get home, Mare, Journey, and Shelley have the car loaded and are eager to hit the road.

"We need to water our garden," Mare says with a wink. She's leaning on the kitchen counter smiling. "I left you some 'J's' on top of the fridge. Split 'em with your brother."

"Oh, thanks." I start to hug her goodbye, but she stops me.

"Listen, I did a damn good job raising five kids all by myself," she says. "I know you can raise these two. I'm proud of you. You're doing the right thing. A really good thing. And great things will happen for you. Good karma is on its way—really!"

It's sweet of her to say. Of course, I have mixed feelings about her doing a 'damn good job' raising us, but that's a conversation for another time, or more likely, never.

"This is a big change, but change is good, right?"

"Change is all we have, my good son. It's everything," she says. There's comfort in knowing she still feels this way after all these years. In fact, it might be the one and only thing that hasn't changed.

"Don't call me your good son," I say before we embrace. Journey is standing behind her like a shadow. When Mare and I let go, he steps forward.

"So, you're a Daddy now," he says in a condescending tone, like I'm a sucker in over my head. Then he laughs in that deep tone of his, "Ha, ha, ha." He's rude but I hug him goodbye anyway. His torso is as wide and as pungent as a 55-gallon drum of THC oil. A few minutes later Shelley pulls me aside and tells me she's serious about moving in for a while.

"All you have to say is 'yes' and I'll be here for you and the boys. Maybe I can't do it by myself, but I can sure help you big time. I mean it, Tom."

"Oh Shelley, I love you so much for wanting to help. Let us get settled first. If I need you, I promise you'll be the first person I call. In the meantime, you need to take care of yourself. You've got to grieve and get through this. The stronger you are when I need you, the more you'll be able to help. Okay?"

"Okay."

We hug harder than we've ever hugged before. I've never loved my big sister more in my entire life. I need them all, and in ways I never imagined. I need my family to know how we're doing—good and bad. I need their help. I'm counting on Mare and Journey to come down for at least a week so I can get situated. I need to find a daycare provider within striking distance of work, get Shane registered for school, find out if they need shots, file for guardianship…Plus, I want the boys to feel the kind of love that comes from an entire family. I want everyone to stay and feel connected with Shane and Skyler. I want the kids to know and love their wonderful cousins, aunts and uncles and of course, their hippy-dippy-trippy-grandparents, too.

Once they're sure they have everything, I carry Skyler out front for our final farewell. I can see my reflection in the lenses of my mother's cheap sunglasses as she sits in the car parked in the driveway. That's one of the strange things about a crisis situation; it will force you to see things differently. It will make you reevaluate your priorities. I realize how important it is to have my family, no matter how weird—or as Peggy would say—how different they are. Any family is better than no family. I fully accept each of them for who they are, young and old, enlightened or in the dark, right and wrong, strong and weak, good and bad. You have to if you want to be happy. I've spent too much time; first trying to change them, then trying to run from them. And in the end, they're a part of me, just as I am to them. Sadly, it took losing a sister to open my eyes and realize how awful it would be to lose another. Mare is smiling brightly as Journey backs down the driveway. Skyler and I are waving goodbye. Journey pulls onto the road and they disappear around the bend. *When they're here, they're here. When they're gone, they're gone. Well, sometimes when they're here, they're gone as well.*

Al sticks around for an afternoon snack then hefts his pillar of a duffel bag into the back of his truck. Thud! It lands like a marble column. It stops Shane and Skyler in their tracks. They look up, see us, and go back to playing in the yard.

"Lend me twenty bucks for the road, Bro? Just need enough gas to get home."

I give him forty. "Get yourself some fuel as well."

"I'll pay you back."

A car speeds by dangerously fast. "Slow down!" I shout in vain, knowing he's too far gone—though I can still hear his music blasting. "What an asshole. Not you. Him. I know you'll pay me back. You always do."

Al drops his lower lip like Bill Murray in Stripes. "That's a fact, Jack!"

We hug. He buckles up, adjusts his mirror, and gives me an honorable salute.

"I admire your courage, soldier," he says. He lets the truck warm up a minute before driving away through a cloud of oily white smoke. He doesn't look back.

Suddenly everything is so *silent*, which thanks to Mare's stupid word game, I happen to know the word can be rearranged to spell *listen*. The all-encompassing chaos that comes with my family is gone. The crisis hasn't budged. Once again, my family has vanished, leaving me all alone. But I'm not alone. I have a new family now. I dash into the house and grab some Popsicles.

We sit on the grass, in the broken shadows under the maple tree, with our sticky treats. I can't help looking at them wondering how we'll do. Right now, they look happy enough—messy, but happy. *So far so good,* I think, smiling at the absurdity of it all. One minute you live a carefree existence, the next you're responsible for raising two kids. This is a game changer. But that's life—and life is change. I have no idea what the next ten minutes or the next ten years will bring. How on earth am I going to manage the cooking, the cleaning, the laundry, the diapers, the baths, the bedtime routines; let alone the time, love, and attention they need? I have no idea if I can actually pull this off. Only time will tell.

"Let's play red-light-green-light!" Shane shouts.

Suddenly I'm back where my feet are.

"Okay."

They run barefoot to the far end of the yard. Shane is shirtless in cut-off jeans. Skyler, in nothing but a diaper, is only a few steps behind. I watch them spin to face me and place their foot on an imaginary starting line. Their faces: pure and innocent, so full of life and anticipation—are so eager to start.

I turn around and shout, "green light!"

And the game begins.

Then there were three.

∞   ∞   ∞

There's more to this story. What charges, if any, will Jeff face for his part of Chris's death? How will Tom adapt to this sudden, life-changing event? Can the wild and crazy bachelor become the loving parent Shane and Skyler need? Will Chris's death rip the family apart or bring them closer together? Find out in the final book of the series; *Don't Call Me Jupiter, Book Three, Wheel in the Sky.*

ABOUT THE AUTHOR

Tom Bross looks familiar, doesn't he? Could it be that you recognize the 1968 San Francisco Hula Hoop Champion? Or, do you remember him as 'the mustard stain kid' from a Clorox bleach ad he appeared in back in 1969? Either way, Tom peaked at an early age and it's been downhill ever since.

After his mother's second divorce, things went from strict to strange as his mother fully embraced her inner hippie. Not only did she change her name to Mare, (it wasn't short for Marilyn, it had something to do with her astrological sign and her need to live near the sea), she purchased Birkenstocks from the *Whole Earth Catalog*, quit shaving and no longer owned any clothes Tom deemed appropriate for parent/teacher conferences. For the next several years Tom excelled in school because it was the exact opposite of what his mother wanted. He worked his way through college and earned a Bachelor of Arts degree in Graphic Design from California State University Chico in 1986.

"I was an extremely sensitive kid who always felt the force of emotions growing up. I realized how different my family was at an early age and literally started taking notes, which eventually led to this book series."

Don't Call Me Jupiter — The Complete Series

Book One "Tightrope"

Book Two "Lightning Crashes"

Book Three "Wheel in the Sky"

Evergreen Lodge: A Memoir

Coming in 2024!

Help get the books into the hands of more readers; leave a review on **GoodReads.com** or **Amazon** and tell others about it.

Bonus images and sides stories that didn't make the series are published regularly on social media, be sure to follow Tom J. Bross.

 Facebook | tom.bross.author

 Instagram | tom.bross

Be the first to find out about new book releases, and more by becoming a Jupiter fan, sign up today!

.

Printed in Great Britain
by Amazon

40764318R00179